Power and the People

Power and the People

A GUIDE TO CONSTITUTIONAL REFORM

VERNON BOGDANOR

VICTOR GOLLANCZ

LONDON

First published in Great Britain 1997
by Victor Gollancz
An imprint of the Cassell Group
Wellington House, 125 Strand, London WC2R 0BB

© Vernon Bogdanor 1997

The right of Vernon Bogdanor to be identified as author
of this work has been asserted by him in accordance with
the Copyright, Designs and Patents Act, 1988.

A catalogue record for this book is
available from the British Library.

ISBN 0 575 06491 9

Typeset by Rowland Phototypesetting Ltd,
Bury St Edmunds, Suffolk
Printed in Great Britain by
St Edmundsbury Press Ltd,
Bury St Edmunds, Suffolk

97 98 5 4 3 2 1

For Judy, Paul and Adam
With thanks

Contents

Preface

The purpose of this book is to analyse the main elements of the constitutional reform agenda in the United Kingdom. Constitutional reform is likely to play an increasingly important part in the future of British politics. It is, indeed, already a major area of contention between the parties. Whereas in the 1950s and 1960s the parties argued about economics but agreed about the constitution, today they are much closer in their economic prescriptions, but in fundamental disagreement about the constitution. This book is intended as a contribution to the debate.

Power and the People makes no claim to be comprehensive. It excludes consideration of various legal reforms which would undoubtedly be of constitutional significance, such as the adoption of a Freedom of Information Act or a Bill of Rights. It also excludes consideration of the European dimension, an important aspect of the constitutional reform debate. Yet the future of the British Constitution is for us to determine. If reform is needed, its primary purpose should be not to make our system congruent with those of other member states of the European Union but rather to improve it in accordance with our own particular needs. That, after all, is what subsidiarity means.

I owe thanks to my friends, David Butler, Lord Holme of Cheltenham and Michael Steed, for reading an early draft of the book and for their very helpful comments. In addition, the chapter on the House of Lords has been read by Lord Windlesham, the Principal of my college, and by Andrew Adonis of *The Observer*, and the chapter on the funding of parties by Philip Bassett, Industrial Editor of *The Times* and Paul Blagbrough, the Labour Party's Finance and Commercial Director. I am deeply grateful to them, but they are not to be implicated in my arguments, still less in my errors. I am grateful to Sean Magee of Victor Gollancz for encouraging me to write this book and for his patience in waiting for it.

The chapter on electoral reform is drawn in part from a book I wrote some years ago, which has long been out of print (*What is Proportional Representation?*, published by Martin Robertson in 1984), and on a pamphlet, *Which System?*, which I wrote in 1992 for the Electoral Reform Society. The chapter on the funding of parties draws on an article I wrote for *Parliamentary Affairs* in 1982 entitled 'Reflections on British Political Finance'. I am grateful to the publishers for permission to use this material. I should like to thank Ted Nealon for allowing me to reproduce the table on the Longford-Roscommon constituency, which appears here as Table 3.5. I am grateful also to Pat Spight for her efficient secretarial help.

I owe a great debt to the Principal and Fellows of Brasenose for providing over so long a period a uniquely friendly and stimulating intellectual environment. My greatest debt, however, is to my wife Judy and my sons, Paul and Adam, for suggesting that I undertake this book, for their forbearance while I was writing it, and for encouraging me to complete it.

Vernon Bogdanor
Brasenose College, Oxford
January 1997

1

Introduction

In the years immediately after the Second World War, the British Constitution was widely admired. In the 1950s and 1960s, the Westminster model was exported to the former colonies of Africa and Asia – for whom, indeed, it was the very touchstone of a democratic system. Today, by contrast, what was once an example to be imitated has become a warning of what to avoid. In the 1990s, not one of the new democracies of Central and Eastern Europe contemplated adopting the British system. Not one of them favoured a constitution providing for an omnicompetent government, chosen by the largest minority among the voters. All of the new democracies have codified constitutions with constitutional courts, judicial review of legislation and parliaments elected by proportional representation; none of them has chosen the first past the post electoral system which Britain, alone in Europe, continues to retain.

The defining feature of the British system of government is the concentration of power at the centre and the absence of checks or balances on government. The British Constitution can be defined in eight words: 'What the Queen in Parliament enacts is law.' It is largely for this reason that we have no codified constitution; for there would be no point in having such a constitution if its provisions could be amended through the same procedures as ordinary, non-constitutional legislation. After all, part of the purpose of a constitution is to distinguish certain laws of fundamental importance which are more difficult to change than non-fundamental laws. In France, for example, the constitution can be changed only by referendum or by a three-fifths vote of the two houses of parliament meeting together as a congress. In Ireland, the constitution can be changed only by referendum. In the United States, amendments to the constitution require a two-thirds vote in Congress and ratification by three-quarters of the states. A constitution is thus, as Article VI of the American Constitution puts it, 'the supreme Law of the Land'.

In Britain, by contrast, there is just one single legislative process for all laws. A simple majority in the House of Common is all that is needed. The House of Lords can delay, but it cannot veto. In practice, of course, the House of Commons is almost always controlled by the government of the day, which is generally able to secure passage of its legislation. If 'all power to the Soviets' was the slogan of the Bolsheviks in the former Soviet Union, 'all power to the governing party' is the slogan of those who rule in Britain.

Governments in Britain do, of course, accept limits upon their power. But these derive not from statute, but from convention, from understandings as to how it is appropriate or not appropriate to act. It is, however, becoming increasingly doubtful whether such understandings are any longer sufficient to provide good government. Between 1974 and 1979, the period of the last Labour government, which for much of its term had only minority support in the Commons, there was considerable concern that it was pushing through Parliament measures which had but little support in the country. It was during these years that Lord Hailsham coined the term 'elective dictatorship' to describe the British system of government. 'I have reached the conclusion,' he declared in his 1976 Dimbleby Lecture – itself entitled 'The Elective Dictatorship' – 'that our constitution is wearing out. Its central defects are gradually coming to outweigh its merits, and its central defects consist in the absolute powers we confer on our sovereign body, and the concentration of those powers in an executive government formed out of one party which may not fairly represent the popular will.'

Lord Hailsham's concerns did not prevent him from resuming the Lord Chancellorship in the Conservative administration formed by Margaret Thatcher in 1979. But the criticisms which he had put forward could not be answered by a mere change of government. Indeed, during the long years of Conservative rule from 1979 to 1997, Margaret Thatcher and John Major were frequently accused of straining the limits of the constitution. To this accusation they replied that Britain was a unitary state in which Parliament could legislate as it pleased. This conception of the constitution, however, is tolerable only when there is deference among the people and consensus among the politicians on the conventions which should limit government action. Neither of these conditions obtained any longer in the 1980s, years which saw the end of deference and the death of the idea of the constitutional convention. So it is that constitutional reform has become, for the first time since the First World War, a major issue in British politics, culminating in the 1997 general election.

In a speech in June 1996, John Major declared that he hoped to initiate 'the most thorough debate on the constitution for a generation'. 'Our constitution,' he declared, 'is the lifeblood of the United Kingdom. It upholds our freedom. It binds Parliament and the government to the citizen. It provides the checks and balances that prevent abuse of power. It cements the Union together.' The Conservatives, Major added, while by no means opposed to all constitutional change, favoured 'practical change, not grand plans'.

There have indeed been many changes of constitutional significance during the years of Conservative government. In 1979, for example, departmentally related select committees were established in the House of Commons so that MPs could scrutinise government. In 1985, legislation was passed abolishing the Greater London Council and the metropolitan county councils. The Treaty of Rome, the founding treaty of the European Communities, was amended in 1986, with the passage of the Single European Act, and again in 1993, when Parliament ratified the Maastricht Treaty. In addition, there has been a radical restructuring of the Civil Service together with public service reform involving such innovations as the Citizen's Charter. These reforms were characterised by William Waldegrave, when Minister of Public Service and Science, as 'a revolution in Whitehall'.

Although some of these reforms have been achieved by statute, the emphasis has been very much on non-statutory measures. There has been a particular focus in recent years on codes of conduct for those in government, Parliament and the public services. In this way Britain has been moving gradually from a system based on conventional understandings, not to a formal codified constitution, but to the half-way house of a series of codes. It has been moving, in Peter Hennessy's words, 'from the back of an envelope to the back of a code'. 'The British,' according to a member of the Nolan Committee on Standards of Conduct in Public Life, 'like to live in a series of half-way houses.' And Lord Nolan himself commented of his committee's report: 'The feel of our recommendations tends if anything towards informality. We've tried to avoid anything that requires legislation: partly because we want it to move quickly, but also because legislation produces inflexibility'.[1]

If the Conservatives have been sceptical of legislative reform of the constitution, the opposition parties, by contrast, favour sweeping legislative change which would fundamentally alter the contours of the constitution. The Liberals, predecessors of the Liberal Democrats, long favoured constitutional reform. Indeed, the Liberals first supported proportional representation as long ago as the general election of 1922. They and their successor party also have a long-standing commitment to devolution for Scotland and Wales, to a Bill of Rights and to legislation on freedom of information. The Liberal Democrats now propose a new constitutional settlement. In their Constitutional Declaration, published in 1996, they advocated a codified constitution, whose main features would be proportional representation for elections to the House of Commons, a reformed second chamber, two-thirds of whose members would be elected, a Bill of Rights, a federal United Kingdom and the abolition of the Royal Prerogative. It is proposed that this Declaration be embodied in a Reform Bill, a framework bill, to be passed by Parliament in a single session.

Labour has also become a party of constitutional reform. 'I do not regard changing the way we are governed,' Tony Blair declared in the John Smith Memorial Lecture in February 1996, 'as an afterthought, a detailed fragment of our programme. I regard it as an essential part of the new Britain, of us becoming a young confident country again.' In the 1970s Labour sought to implement devolution for Scotland and Wales, and this remains a priority for a Labour government. 'Scotland,' Blair insisted, 'will have its parliament. Wales shall have an assembly. They will be legislated for in the first year.' Labour also proposes regional government for England, reform of the House of Lords, a transfer of power to local government, a Freedom of Information Act and, perhaps most important of all, a referendum on voting systems – all during the lifetime of the next Labour government.

The battle lines between the parties, then, are clear. Conservative defence of the constitution is based on a defence of the principle of the supremacy of Parliament. 'In Britain,' John Major declared in his June 1996 speech on the constitution, 'it is our Parliament ... that is, and should be, at the centre of that democratic political process. That's why piecemeal reforms that threaten to erode the power and supremacy of

Parliament are so dangerous.' Parliament, Major continued, 'is where things happen. It is the voice of the people of Britain – it is the focus of the nation's unity at times of national grief or outrage. And it is the theatre for the great convulsions of political history.'

For Labour, by contrast, the emphasis on Parliament serves but to legitimise a centralised and remote system of government, in which the people can play only a passive role. 'The reforms I have set out,' Blair declared in February 1996, 'will transform our policies. They will redraw the boundaries between what is done in the name of the people and the people themselves. They will create a new relationship between government and the people based on trust, freedom, choice and responsibility.'

The constitutional reforms proposed by Labour and the Liberal Democrats are of a sweep and scope quite new in British politics. 'If implemented,' the Constitutional Unit has declared, 'the package of reforms proposed by the Labour Party and the Liberal Democrats will represent change at a pace and of a significance unprecedented in British constitutional history.'[2] The aim of *Power and the People* is to evaluate these proposed reforms.

Three of the reforms discussed in this book – devolution, electoral reform and the referendum – would, in practice if not in theory, limit the supremacy of the House of Commons. Devolution would establish alternative centres of power in Scotland and Wales so that Parliament's power to legislate over their domestic affairs would be severely limited. Electoral reform would make government by a single party less likely. The referendum would require the Commons to share power with the people. The first theme, then, of the constitutional reform debate is a limitation on the power of Parliament and hence of government, so that government is required to share power instead of monopolising it. But there is also a second theme. It is to increase the power of the people over government, by giving them a greater say in legislation and, with electoral reform, in their choice of MP. These reforms would introduce an element of direct democracy into our representative system, and their implications could be very radical indeed. For the British Constitution, as it is at present, knows nothing of the people. If Parliament is sovereign, then the people cannot be. If the people are to become sovereign, then Parliament can no longer be sovereign. So it is that constitutional reform would alter, in a quite fundamental way, the relationship between those who hold power and the people.

II

Constitutional reformers, then, seek to end the monopoly of power which
the governing party in Britain enjoys. That is a more feasible aim today
than it would have been in the immediate post-war years when each
of the two major parties had much greater sociological and ideological
coherence, and therefore greater popular support. The last decades of the
twentieth century, however, have seen the death of the grand ideological
struggles which used to breathe life into the political parties. In his John
Smith Memorial Lecture, Tony Blair admitted as much, declaring that
'the clash of the all-encompassing and absolutist ideologies of the first
part of the twentieth century grows muted and distant – the right having
accepted the need for social provision, the left the necessity of a market
economy'. In an interview with *The Economist* in September 1996, Blair
reiterated the point. 'Britain is struggling to find its way after the collapse
of the grand twentieth-century ideologies of left and right.'[3] With the
decline of the ideological and class loyalties which sustained them, the
parties have been losing their function as mass organisations. In earlier
years, the parties were real vehicles of representation, offering as they
did close contact with organised groups and communities. But these
communities are themselves now breaking down under the pressures
of competitive individualism. In the more fragmented world which has
resulted, people find themselves better represented by single-issue groups
and new social movements – Greenpeace, Friends of the Earth, Shelter
– than they do by political parties. Indeed, the Royal Society for the
Protection of Birds has more members than the Conservatives, Labour
and the Liberal Democrats put together. In these conditions, it is hardly
surprising if a political system which depends for its vigour upon strong
governing parties has come under attack.

In the 1980s, Margaret Thatcher fuelled disenchantment with the representative system by mobilising popular support for an assault on what
she saw as archaic institutions – the trade unions, the Civil Service,
the universities and the professions. In achieving, for a while, a direct
relationship with the people, she dramatised what had hitherto been but
dimly perceived: that the era in which the political parties could be
mediators between leaders and voters was rapidly drawing to an end.
Margaret Thatcher appeared for a time as a leader above party. Many
voters, feeling remote from power and from the institutions which gov-

erned them, warmed to a political leader who seemed to be on their side, who seemed to understand their aspirations. With the end of the Thatcher experiment, however, the disenchantment remains, but without any leader who can channel it effectively into populist politics. This disenchantment has acted as a powerful spur to the movement for constitutional reform.

Political parties, then, seem no longer to be effective vehicles of representation. On the great constitutional issues of politics, such as Europe and devolution, they have been divided and irresolute, unable to reflect the real divisions of opinion among voters.

The first departure from the traditional norms of the British Constitution came in Northern Ireland. In 1973, in an effort to reconcile the two communities, Edward Heath's government proposed a directly elected assembly for the province, in which, whatever the outcome of the election, unionists and nationalists would be required to share power. Elections for the assembly, and also local elections in Northern Ireland, were to be held by the single transferable vote method of proportional representation, and this system was shown to be a perfectly feasible one, introduced as it was without administrative or technical difficulty. In 1973, also, a border poll was held in Northern Ireland: Britain's first referendum (see p. 127 below). More recently, the Anglo-Irish Framework Document, published in 1995, proposed a whole host of constitutional devices – proportional representation, devolution, referendums, power-sharing and a Charter of Rights – which the Conservative government had ruled out for any other part of the United Kingdom as destructive of the British Constitution.

For nearly twenty years, the European issue has had a uniquely corrosive impact upon both major parties. In the 1970s, it divided the Labour Party, and in 1981 was a prominent cause of the split when the SDP was formed. In the 1990s, it threatens to wreak comparable havoc on the Conservatives. Yet in the 1970s, all three parties favoured membership of the European Community, while in 1992 all three parties favoured ratification of the Maastricht Treaty. The parties, therefore, have not been very successful in representing the anti-European voter. For the real divisions on Europe lie within the parties, not between them. Indeed, the referendum on membership of the European Community in 1975 was a tacit admission that the European issue could not be resolved by the normal machinery of party politics.

Devolution, too, divided both major parties in the 1970s. The Labour government of 1974–9 was united behind the policy, albeit with considerable misgivings, but many Labour backbenchers from the north and from Wales, including at the time Neil Kinnock, as well as some Scottish MPs such as Robin Cook, were bitterly opposed. Margaret Thatcher, the Conservative leader, was hostile to devolution, but Edward Heath, her predecessor, was sympathetic, as were Conservatives such as Peter Walker and Malcolm Rifkind. Divisions in the House of Commons were such that the Labour government was forced to concede referendums on the devolution proposals, although they had previously insisted that the referendum on membership of the European Community would be a unique departure from normal constitutional practice.

The issue of electoral reform was also raised in the debates on devolution and Europe. Labour refused to consider proportional representation for elections to the proposed assemblies in Scotland and Wales. But this gave rise to fears that the assemblies, elected under the first past the post system, would be dominated by Labour on a minority of the vote. This was a significant factor fuelling opposition to the proposals in the referendums on devolution.

By the time the House of Commons came to legislate for direct elections to the European Parliament, the Labour government had been forced to rely upon the support of the Liberals for its survival. Under the terms of the Lib–Lab pact, Labour proposed a system of proportional representation for European Parliament elections. But the Commons voted it down. In 1979, when the elections took place, Britain found itself the only member state not to use one of the various proportional electoral systems, something which caused resentment among the other member states.

Europe has been of particular importance in the debate on constitutional reform given that the style of politics on the continent is quite different from that prevailing at Westminster. Politics in Europe is corporatist, coalitional and proportional; in Britain, by contrast, it remains adversarial and confrontational. Moreover, constitutionally, the European Community was based on the principle not of sovereignty, but of power-sharing. There is a separation of powers at the centre between the Commission, the Council of Ministers, the Parliament and the Court. There is also a territorial separation of powers between the Community and the member states. The pressures of Community membership, therefore, were bound to weaken the principle of parliamentary sovereignty. For, having transferred power upwards to the Community, sharing it with Brussels, it no longer seemed inconceivable for Westminster to transfer power downwards, to Edinburgh and Cardiff. If the state was too small for the satisfactory exercise of some functions, why should it not be too large for the exercise of others?

Westminster, then, found itself ill-suited to dealing with Northern Ireland, devolution and Europe. On territorial issues, issues involving the sharing of power, the party system seemed inadequate as a vehicle of representation for alternative viewpoints. All of these issues called for referendums to ascertain the will of the people; all of them raised the further question of whether the first past the post system was the best method of ensuring that the popular voice was heard.

The growing gap between the parties and the people was compounded by the rigidity of party lines in post-war Britain. Before 1939, periodic realignments had brought fluidity to the party system as new political issues stimulated new alliances. At the beginning of the century, a group of Conservative MPs, including Winston Churchill, crossed the floor to the Liberals to defend free trade. Between the wars, as the Liberal Party was breaking up, its MPs defected to both left and right. In 1931, in the midst of the depression, Ramsay MacDonald, the Labour Prime Minister, together with three of his Cabinet, formed a coalition with Liberals and Conservatives.

Many of the great party leaders of the past had switched party allegiance. Gladstone had begun his political career as, in Macaulay's famous words, 'the rising hope of the stern unbending Tories'; but he ended it on the radical wing of the Liberal Party. Disraeli took the opposite route, as did Joseph Chamberlain, beginning as a radical and ending as a Tory imperialist. Lloyd George also was to move from radicalism in peacetime to coalition with the Conservatives during the First World War. Churchill switched twice, first in 1904 to the Liberals, and then, in 1924, back to the Conservatives, declaring that 'anyone can rat, but it takes a certain amount of ingenuity to re-rat'. Since 1945, however, the system has become frozen. There has been no fundamental realignment of parties and when, in the 1980s, the Liberal–SDP Alliance threatened to 'break the mould' of British politics, it succeeded only in ending the political careers of nearly all of the MPs who had joined it. With the collapse of the Alliance after the 1987 general election, it seemed that the traditional parties were more entrenched than ever.

The effective working of the British Constitution presupposes a party system which, by clarifying choices, yields genuinely accountable and therefore strong government. The assumption is that voters, like the parties which represent them, are grouped naturally into opposing factions. This picture, however, presupposes both that the main parties are stable and cohesive entities capable of organising the electorate into opposing political camps, and also that the two major viewpoints are represented by the government and opposition front benches respectively. On many issues that is no longer the case.

With the collapse of traditional ideologies has gone the social divisions which underpinned the two major parties. The Conservatives and Labour derived their *raison d'être* from being the representatives of capital and labour. They reflected a society which was polarised by class. Of course, not all voters would support the party which represented their class. The Conservatives could never have won power had they not managed to secure the support of an important minority of the working class. Nevertheless, for the first 30 years after the Second World War, class position remained the most powerful indicator of voting behaviour. With the growth of a meritocratic society and the breaking down of class differences, the traditional foundations of the party system came under strain. In the 1980s, Thatcherism, perhaps as much a consequence as a cause of these changes, relied for its success upon the growth of an upwardly mobile working class hostile to collectivism. Labour, by contrast, broadened its appeal to those middle-class professionals whose perquisites and privileges were being attacked. In the mid-1990s, the two party leaders themselves symbolised the blurring of class and party alignments. Sociologically, John Major could have been expected to be the Labour leader and Tony Blair the Tory.

Today, political divisions on such issues as Europe, family policy and reform of the welfare state lie as much within the major parties as between them. On these issues the party system stifles sensible debate. It locks together incompatibles – Europhiles and Eurosceptics, libertarians and communitarians – in what Roy Jenkins once called loveless marriages, while keeping like-minded politicians apart. The result has been the growth of that most dangerous of all political cleavages: that between the political class and the people. It is because the party system has become frozen, because it no longer seems capable of renewing itself, that parties are no longer seen as effective vehicles of representation.

Constitutional reform is fundamentally an attempt to renew a political system whose conventions seem outworn, an attempt to fashion a new relationship between government and the governed, between power and the people.

2

Devolution

'It is easy to centralise power but impossible to centralise all that knowledge which is distributed over many individual minds, and whose centralisation would be necessary for the wise yielding of centralised power.'

Karl Popper, *The Poverty of Historicism*

I

Devolution is the transfer of powers at present exercised by ministers and Parliament to regional or sub-national bodies which are both subordinate to Parliament and directly elected. Devolution is thus a process by which Parliament transfers its powers without relinquishing its supremacy. For, being subordinate, the regional or sub-national bodies could in the last resort be over-ruled by Westminster; or they could be abolished by a decision of the British government supported by Parliament, as indeed the parliament of Northern Ireland was in 1972. It is this characteristic of being a subordinate body which distinguishes devolution from federalism, for the latter offers a legal guarantee to a sub-national layer of government. It would not, therefore, be possible for the United States government unilaterally to abolish, for example, the legislature of Texas, nor for the German government to abolish the legislature of Bavaria.

Devolution, or home rule as it used to be known, was a key issue of British politics between the years 1886 and 1914. In 1886, the Liberal Party, led by W. E. Gladstone, proposed to establish a parliament in Dublin to conciliate the Irish nationalists. This proposal, however, split the Liberals and the Home Rule Bill was defeated in the House of Commons. In 1893 a second bill passed the Commons but was defeated in the Lords, while a third bill succeeded in reaching the statute book in 1914 only for its operation to be suspended following the outbreak of war. By the time the First World War had ended, however, the Irish national demand had become one for independence and home rule had become irrelevant.

Ironically, however, home rule was bestowed by Westminster in 1920 upon the one part of Ireland which did not want it and which indeed had been the most strenuous in resisting it: the six counties of Northern Ireland. A home rule parliament was established in Belfast in 1921 with power to legislate for the domestic affairs of Northern Ireland, and it lasted until 1972 when it was abolished by the Heath government. Since that time, both Conservative and Labour governments have advocated a form of devolution to Northern Ireland in which both communities, unionist and nationalist, share power. But, apart from a brief experiment in 1974, agreement on power-sharing has not been forthcoming.

By the 1970s, however, devolution had once again become a topic of contention at Westminster, largely as a result of the electoral advance of the Scottish National Party (SNP). In the general election of February 1974, the SNP gained 21 per cent of the Scottish vote, and in the second general election that year, held in October, it gained 30 per cent of the Scottish vote, becoming the second largest party in Scotland in terms of votes and the most successful 'ethnic' party in Western Europe.

The Labour government elected in February 1974 – which was in a minority for much of its ensuing five years in office – sought to meet the challenge of the SNP, and the lesser threat of Plaid Cymru, the Welsh nationalist party, by enacting legislation providing for directly elected assemblies in Scotland and Wales. Labour's attempts to legislate for devolution, however, foundered as badly as the efforts of the Liberals had done before the First World War. Labour's first bill, the Scotland and Wales Bill, became bogged down in committee in the House of Commons and, after an attempt to guillotine it was defeated in March 1977, had to be abandoned. Separate bills for Scotland and Wales were then introduced and enacted in 1978 – incorporating, however, the proviso that 40 per cent of the Scottish and Welsh electorate would have to support the measures in referendums if they were to come into effect.

Accordingly, referendums were held in March 1979 to elicit the response of Scottish and Welsh voters to the legislation. These referendums occurred at a time when Labour, the main sponsor of devolution, was suffering massive unpopularity following severe strikes in the public services during the so-called 'Winter of Discontent'. Partly for this reason, the results proved a setback for devolution. In Wales, it was

Table 2.1   Distribution of seats and votes among main parties at general elections, 1979–1992: UK and Scotland

Year	Party	United Kingdom		Scotland	
		Seats (no.)	Votes (%)	Seats (no.)	Votes (%)
1979	Conservatives	339	43.9	22	31.4
	Labour	269	36.9	44	41.6
	Liberals	11	13.8	3	9.0
	SNP	2	1.6	2	17.3
1983	Conservatives	397	42.4	21	28.4
	Labour	209	27.6	41	35.1
	Alliance	23	25.4	8	24.5
	SNP	2	1.1	2	11.8
1987	Conservatives	376	43.4	10	24.0
	Labour	229	31.7	50	42.4
	Alliance	22	23.2	9	19.2
	SNP	3	1.3	3	14.0
1992	Conservatives	336	42.3	11	25.7
	Labour	271	35.2	49	39.0
	Lib. Dem.	20	18.3	9	13.1
	SNP	3	1.9	3	21.5

defeated by a four to one majority. In Scotland, there was a small majority for devolution, 33 per cent of the electorate voting for it, 31 per cent against. This level of support, however, fell far short of the 40 per cent requirement which Parliament had imposed, and the Scotland Act, together with the Wales Act, was repealed in June 1979 by the new Conservative government under Margaret Thatcher.

While the referendum result in 1979 clearly represented a crushing defeat for Welsh devolution, the outcome in Scotland was far less clear-cut, for Conservative opponents of the Scotland Act, including the former Prime Minister, Lord Home, had argued that a 'No' vote would be interpreted not as a vote against devolution but as a vote against the specific form of devolution which was being proposed. The Scotland Act was widely agreed to be a complex and cumbrous piece of legislation which would cause many practical problems were it to be implemented. Margaret Thatcher's government did not, however, produce any alternative form of devolution and, with the fall in SNP representation after the general election of 1979, the Conservatives felt able to ignore the question. It was not to be expected, however, that devolution in Scotland would disappear as a political issue. Indeed, with a Labour majority in Scotland facing a Conservative government in London for 18 years, the demand for devolution has probably increased.

Since 1979, the divergence in voting habits between Scotland and the United Kingdom as a whole, exacerbated admittedly by the working of the first past the post electoral system, has increased significantly (see Table 2.1). It may be argued that this merely represents the opposite disparity to that which occurred in, for example, 1964 and 1974 when Labour won narrow majorities and English Conservatives found themselves outvoted by Labour MPs from Scotland and Wales. The English did not react to this condition by demanding a separate parliament in York! However, the Scottish situation is somewhat different, for two reasons. The first is the extent of the divergence between Scotland and the rest of the kingdom: since 1987 the Conservative government has been unable to muster more than 11 of the 72 MPs from Scotland, representing just 25 per cent of Scottish voters, in support of its legislation. This meant that legislation affecting Scotland could be passed despite being opposed by the vast majority of Scottish MPs and three-quarters of Scottish voters. The second is the added colour given to the divergence between Scotland and the rest of the kingdom by the sense of separate nationality felt by many in Scotland, even by those who would not contemplate voting for the SNP. A Rowntree Reform Trust survey conducted in Scotland in 1996 found that no fewer than 60 per cent of Scots saw themselves as more Scottish than British, while a further 25 per cent gave equal weight to both identities.[1]

The sense of nationality in Scotland was recognised by the Acts of Union of 1707 which united England and Scotland in the kingdom of Great Britain. The new British parliament was to be a sovereign parliament; nevertheless, it was the outcome not of conquest, subordinating one nation to another, but of a political bargain. Indeed, the Acts of Union imposed an obligation of honour upon the new parliament of Great Britain to preserve the Scottish judicial system, while in a separate act accompanying the Scottish Act of Union provision was made for the reservation of the position of the Church of Scotland. A further factor preserving Scottish distinctiveness has been the retention of its separate education system.

Institutional arrangements since 1707 have continued to give recognition to the sense of nationality in Scotland in such a way as to allow its distinctive voice to be heard in Whitehall and Westminster. The Scottish Office was created in 1885, and since 1892 the Scottish Secretary has normally been a member of the Cabinet. The responsibilities of the Scottish Office have gradually been widened until it is now responsible for administering the bulk of Scotland's domestic affairs. In addition, the Secretary of State is widely regarded as a spokesman for Scottish interests in Cabinet, even in areas for which he does not have statutory responsibility.

These executive arrangements are mirrored in the House of Commons, where there are separate standing committees for Scottish legislation and a Scottish Grand Committee, meeting frequently in Scotland, at which the second and third reading debates and the report stage of non-controversial Scottish bills may be taken. Since 1981 the Scottish Grand Committee has comprised only Scottish MPs, and so, by contrast with other legislative and select committees, the government lacks a majority on it.

The operation of the Scottish Grand Committee, however, as of the other Scottish legislative committees, is conditioned by the fundamental principles on which the House of Commons operates. For committees cannot pass legislation without the approval of the Commons itself; and, while ministers take part in the debates of the Grand Committee and can be questioned there, they cannot be required by the committee to change their policies. When, in November 1995, MPs asked whether the Grand Committee could block the imposition of nursery vouchers in Scotland, Michael Forsyth, the Secretary of State for Scotland, declared that 'the absolute Westminster veto over Scottish business remains,' adding that 'the Scottish Grand Committee is not a Scottish Parliament'.[2]

Thus, although Scotland has long been recognised by Parliament as a separate unit for administrative purposes, it remains in the anomalous position of having a separate judiciary and separate arrangements for handling executive business but no separate legislature to which the Scottish executive is responsible. This might not matter were the party system to transcend the border, as it did between 1945 and 1979 when the party with a majority in the United Kingdom also enjoyed a majority in Scotland (except in 1951 when the two parties were level north of the border, and in 1959 and 1970 when a Conservative majority at Westminster faced a Labour majority in Scotland). But in recent years Labour has been the dominant party in Scotland, and it seems likely to remain so for some

Table 2.2 Distribution of seats and votes among main parties at general elections, 1979–1992: UK and Wales

Year	Party	United Kingdom Seats (no.)	Votes (%)	Wales Seats (no.)	Votes (%)
1979	Conservatives	339	43.9	11	32.7
	Labour	269	36.9	22	48.6
	Liberals	11	13.8	1	12.8
	Plaid Cymru	2	0.4	2	8.1
1983	Conservatives	397	42.4	14	31.0
	Labour	209	27.6	20	37.5
	Alliance	23	25.4	2	23.2
	Plaid Cymru	2	0.4	2	7.8
1987	Conservatives	376	43.4	8	29.6
	Labour	229	31.7	24	45.1
	Alliance	22	23.2	3	17.9
	Plaid Cymru	3	0.3	3	7.3
1992	Conservatives	336	42.3	6	28.6
	Labour	271	35.2	27	49.5
	Lib. Dem.	20	18.3	1	12.4
	Plaid Cymru	4	0.5	4	8.8

time to come. Not since 1955 has the Conservative Party won a majority of the Scottish seats. It should be noted that 1955 was also the last year in which either party won a majority – 50.1 per cent – of the Scottish vote: Labour's dominance since then has been obtained on a minority of the Scottish vote, with the first past the post electoral system exaggerating Labour's strength in terms of seats. Nevertheless, this striking contrast between the relative strength of Labour in Scotland and its weakness at Westminster since 1979 has helped to fuel the demand for devolution in Scotland. In particular, many of the liberalising policies associated with Margaret Thatcher were seen as assaults on the Scottish idea of community – the poll tax being particularly resented – and the Secretary of State for Scotland was unable to defend Scotland against them. The poll tax, in fact, was first introduced north of the border, although hostility to it in Scotland was even greater than in England. Thus the institutions supposedly designed to protect Scotland's autonomy were failing to do so. Only with devolution, it may be argued, will Scotland be able to defend its interests effectively.

From the electoral point of view, there seems at first sight to be some similarity between Wales and Scotland, since in Wales too a Labour majority has since 1979 been consistently outvoted by the Conservatives' overall majority (see Table 2.2). There are, however, important differences between the electoral situation in Wales and in Scotland. Plaid Cymru, the Welsh nationalist party, has attracted far less support than the SNP. Since October 1974, it has secured less than 10 per cent of the total Welsh vote, its share averaging 8 per cent, while the SNP has not fallen below 11 per cent of the total Scottish vote during this period, and its average share has been around 16 per cent. Welsh nationalism, unlike Scottish, has had to confront the language issue, the Welsh language being spoken by only around one-fifth of the Welsh people, congregated primarily in north-west Wales where Plaid Cymru's strength mainly lies. Because its vote is so concentrated, Plaid Cymru returned four MPs in the 1992 general election, as compared with three SNP members from a vote over twice that of Plaid. Conversely, because its vote was so concentrated, Plaid Cymru lost its deposit in 23 of the 38 Welsh seats, while the SNP was the only major party not to lose its deposit in any constituency. The main symbol of Welsh nationhood, the language, is a divisive one, while the main symbols of Scottish nationhood, the judicial system, the Kirk and the educational system, are integrative. It is this factor which largely explains the different responses of Scotland and Wales in the devolution referendums of 1979.

Wales, like Scotland, has a Secretary of State able to press its particular interests in the Cabinet, and there are special arrangements for the passage of Welsh legislation through the Commons. There has been a Welsh Office headed by a Secretary of State since 1964 and, as with Scotland, further responsibilities have been transferred to it until it is now responsible for the bulk of Welsh domestic affairs and for around 70 per cent of total public expenditure in Wales. The Welsh Secretary, like his Scottish counterpart, is widely regarded as being spokesman for Welsh interests in the Cabinet even where he does not possess specific statutory powers. However, all four of the holders of this post between 1987 and 1997 – Peter Walker, David Hunt, John Redwood and William Hague – were Members of Parliament sitting for English constituencies.

As with Scotland, the parliamentary arrangements for Wales mirror the executive structure. In 1960, a Welsh Grand Committee was set up.

Between 1992 and 1995, however, this committee met on only eight occasions. This is partly because there is much less separate Welsh legislation than there is Scottish, for Wales, unlike Scotland, has no separate legal system. For the same reason, the influence of the Welsh Office is rather less than that of its Scottish counterpart. Draft legislation for Wales normally emanates from the London departments and, while it can on occasion be modified by the Welsh Office, it is difficult for the Secretary of State to alter it in any fundamental way. The Welsh Office, therefore, does not really create policy for Wales, but is more often borne along by events; and although the Secretary of State for Wales is formally responsible for Welsh legislation, in practice his contribution tends to be minimal, his main responsibility being for the execution of laws primarily decided elsewhere. The Welsh Office bears more resemblance perhaps to an English regional office than it does to the Scottish Office, which is responsible for the bulk of Scottish domestic law-making.

These differences between the Scottish and Welsh Offices provide a rationale for the different degrees of devolution offered to Scotland and Wales. For Scotland, Labour and the Liberal Democrats propose legislative devolution. For Wales, the Liberal Democrats also propose legislative devolution, but Labour proposes, as it did in the 1970s, executive devolution, that is, devolution of the power to make secondary legislation. The law-making power would remain with the Whitehall departments, as it does today: the power of execution, however, would be transferred from the Secretary of State to a directly elected Welsh assembly. Such executive devolution would also be offered to the English regions should they seek devolution.[3] Thus the debate on devolution in Wales has much less to do with the classical arguments about nationalism and more to do with issues of decentralisation and regionalism. As such, the Welsh debate is highly relevant to England.

II

Britain is generally classed as a unitary state, to mark the contrast with federal states such as the United States and Germany. Yet in Britain, unitary has never meant uniform, for the British administrative system has long been highly asymmetrical in order to accommodate Scottish and Welsh identities within the framework of a multinational state. So it is that the retention of Scottish and Welsh identity has proved perfectly compatible with membership of the United Kingdom.

The symbol of unitary and centralised authority in Britain – the mace – has thus proved to be perfectly compatible with acceptance of the maze – recognition of territorial diversity where that is necessary to administer a multinational state effectively.[4] Britain might perhaps better be classed not as a unitary state but as a union state. The distinction is well drawn by Urwin:

> The unitary state [is] built up around one unambiguous political centre which enjoys economic dominance and pursues a more or less undeviating policy of administrative standardisation. All areas of the state are treated alike, and all institutions are directly under the control of the centre. The union state [is] not the result of straightforward dynastic conquest. Incorporation of at least parts of its territory . . . [is] through personal dynastic union, for example by treaty, marriage or inheritance. Integration is less than perfect. While administrative standardisation prevails over most of the territory, the consequences of personal union entail survival of pre-union rights and institutional infrastructures which preserve some degree of regional autonomy and serve as agencies of indigenous elite recruitment.[5]

The fundamental issue raised by devolution is whether the creation of separate parliaments in one or more parts of the country is merely an extension of this recognition of diversity, or whether, by contrast, it extends the principle too far, so that the tolerance, the 'tacit understandings' on which the United Kingdom rests, will snap in twain.[6]

The distinctiveness of Scotland as a political entity has long been recognised, both at the executive level in the role played by the Scottish Office, and at parliamentary level in the Scottish committees of the Commons. The government in Scotland is unusual if not unique in the modern world, in that the phenomenon of a Scottish administration with an executive and a Scottish legal system but without its own legislature finds no precise parallel elsewhere. No one suggests that these arrangements should be ended. It has thus long been accepted that the union between England and Scotland, although an incorporating one, must accommodate the sense of Scottishness if it is to maintain the spirit of the bargain agreed in 1707. But the conventions of the constitution severely limit the extent to which Scotland can be given separate treatment within the confines even of the union state.

Collective Cabinet responsibility imposes inevitable limitations on the extent to which the Secretary of State for Scotland can act as a genuine Minister for Scotland. This is, of course, particularly the case when the majority at Westminster is a minority in Scotland, as in the years of Conservative government between 1979 and 1997. Similarly, the conventions of parliamentary government, and in particular the unwillingness of the Commons to surrender control of its business to any sub-group within it, restricts Scottish control over Scottish business to relatively uncontroversial matters.

The union between Scotland and England envisaged Scottish identity being preserved by the legal system and the Kirk. These institutions, however, have long been displaced from their centrality as guarantors of Scottish identity. In the modern world, Scottish identity is determined far more by what government does than by the activities of the courts or the church. Today, Scottish distinctiveness is likely to be preserved only if the government of Scotland is reformed so that it can reflect Scottish interests more effectively.

Scottish devolution is often presented as a defensive response to the rise of the SNP. The real case for devolution, however, is rather different. Its mainspring consists of the need to re-establish a relationship which has been seriously undermined, so as to make the governmental arrangements providing for Scottish distinctiveness real rather than merely symbolic. That can be done only through devolution. Without devolution, the arrangements for handling Scottish business, both at executive and at parliamentary level, are likely to remain highly unsatisfactory; for these arrangements are unable any longer to provide effectively for the expression of Scottish nationality. Scottish devolution would involve a renegotiation of the terms of the Union to provide for the establishment of a subordinate parliament in Edinburgh. Such a renegotiation may be the only way to re-establish the kind of relationship between England and Scotland envisaged in 1707, a relationship which has been eroded by developments in government and in electoral behaviour in the latter part of the twentieth century.

In Britain, however, the history of devolution is primarily the history of something that has not happened. Of five devolution bills proposed by governments – those of 1886, 1893, 1914, 1920 and 1978 – only three have reached the statute book: those of 1914, 1920 and 1978. The Act of 1914 was never implemented, however, owing to the outbreak of war, while the Acts of 1978 failed to surmount the hurdle of the referendum. The Act of 1920 is the only one to have been implemented, and that only in part: intended for the whole of Ireland, it came into effect only for the six counties of Northern Ireland, the one part of Ireland which had never sought devolution.

Home rule for Ireland was staunchly resisted by Westminster for many years, even though, from the time of the 1886 general election until that of 1918, a vast preponderance of the 103 Irish seats – never fewer than 85 – were won by Irish nationalists. In the 1970s, however, Westminster decided that if either Scotland or Wales wanted devolution, they could have it. But Wales rejected devolution resoundingly in 1979, while Scotland has twice appeared lukewarm. The first occasion was on 1 March 1979, the day of the referendum, a day which *The Scotsman* dubbed 'Scotland's Day of Destiny' – and a day when only 64 per cent of Scots turned out to vote and only 33 per cent of the Scottish electorate voted 'Yes', an insufficient percentage to secure devolution. The second occasion was the general election of 1992. This was seen by many in Scotland – beforehand at least – as in effect a second referendum on devolution. For, with the Conservatives the only party in Scotland opposed to devolution, an anti-Tory vote could be interpreted as a vote for a Scottish parliament. There was even some possibility, it seemed, of defeating all ten Scottish Conservative MPs, thus rendering Scotland a Tory-free zone. But Scotland's second rendezvous with destiny also failed to yield a mandate for devolution: indeed, Scotland was the only part of the United Kingdom where there was a swing to the Conservatives in 1992 and where, far from being wiped out, they actually gained a seat.

The first precondition of Scottish devolution, then, is that the Scots should genuinely want it. That can be established only by a referendum. In 1996, the Labour Party proposed that a referendum be held on Scottish devolution. This referendum would pose two questions, the first asking whether the Scots wanted a parliament, the second whether a Scottish parliament should have revenue-raising powers. This referendum, how-ever, unlike that of 1979, would occur not after the legislation had been enacted, but before its passage through Parliament, once the terms of the legislation had been announced in a White Paper. A referendum held at this stage of the parliamentary procedure would serve not only to test

Scottish opinion but also to overcome the hostility of English Members of Parliament. In the 1970s, most English MPs, and especially Members from the north of England, were highly sceptical of devolution which, they believed, would lead to a transfer of resources to Scotland and Wales from their own constituencies. These objections were overcome only by the concession of a referendum. It is, therefore, a second vital precondition of Scottish devolution that its terms be acceptable to a Parliament 587 of whose 659 Members will come, not from Scotland, but from England, Wales and Northern Ireland.

What kind of devolution settlement would be acceptable to non-Scottish MPs? Westminster will be very conscious of the danger that devolution to Scotland would accelerate an already existing constitutional imbalance. For Scotland, in addition to having a Secretary of State defending its interests in the Cabinet, is over-represented in the House of Commons compared with England. Scotland has 72 MPs, rather than the 57 to which it would be entitled on the basis of the average population of United Kingdom constituencies. It takes 69,000 votes to elect the average English MP, but only 54,000 to elect the average Scottish MP. Legislative devolution to Scotland would accelerate this constitutional imbalance and perhaps make it intolerable to non-Scottish Members of Parliament. It could create a lop-sided system of government in the United Kingdom in which citizens of England, Wales and Northern Ireland saw themselves as second-class citizens, under-represented at Westminster and without a parliament to fight for their interests.

Proponents of devolution, then, might conclude that the post of Secretary of State for Scotland would no longer be necessary once a parliament had been established in Edinburgh. For the Scottish Office exists primarily to administer policies where a separate Scottish dimension is possible; after devolution, such policy areas will largely be in Scottish hands, and where there is no such Scottish dimension, responsibility would be returned to non-territorial Whitehall departments.

Westminster would be unlikely to countenance the continued over-representation of Scotland in the House of Commons. Scottish over-representation is not, as is sometimes suggested, guaranteed by the Union, Article XXII of which provides only that there should be 45 Scottish MPs in Parliament. Scotland was indeed under-represented at Westminster until 1884, and has been over-represented there only since 1922. In the post-1945 period, over-representation has derived from political vicissitudes, from 'bargained compromises' in the Speaker's Conference of 1944, 'which have been frozen into the legislation governing the allocation of seats'.[7] Over-representation is a contingent arrangement, not something that corresponds with any constitutional obligation.

Northern Ireland, during the years between 1921 and 1972 when it enjoyed devolution, far from being over-represented, was actually under-represented, returning only 12 MPs (13 before the abolition of university seats in 1948) rather than the 17 to which it was entitled on a population basis. A similar policy adopted with respect to Scotland would yield it only around 40 seats instead of the 72 which it has at present. This, however, may be seen as against the spirit of the Acts of Union, which may be interpreted as requiring that Scotland have at least 45 seats in the Commons. The best solution is probably a compromise by which Scotland would be required to reduce its representation from 72 to 57 to bring it into parity with England.

A devolution package of this type could be seen as a renegotiation of the terms of the Union of 1707, a renegotiation of the terms under which Scotland remains part of the United Kingdom. Such a package, unlike that of 1978, which provided both for the retention of the Secretary of State for Scotland and the continued over-representation of Scotland in the Commons, imposes losses upon Scotland as well as gains. It would be for the Scottish people to decide, through referendum, whether they believed that the losses would be outweighed by the gains.

III

Any scheme of devolution proposed for Scotland is likely to owe a great deal to the proposals made by the Scottish Constitutional Convention. This body was set up in March 1989, following the publication of 'A Claim of Right for Scotland' by the Campaign for a Scottish Assembly. The 'Claim of Right' asserted that it was for the Scottish people and not for Westminster to decide how Scotland should be governed. The sovereignty of Parliament was seen as an English doctrine with no roots in Scottish life: in Scotland, it was the people and not Parliament which was sovereign. The Scottish people should duly exercise their sovereignty by coming together, through their representatives, at a Convention, to draw up practical proposals for Scotland's government.

All of the main political parties in Scotland were invited to participate in the Convention, but the Conservatives, opposed to devolution, declined, while the SNP withdrew when it became clear that the Convention could not discuss independence. The Convention was thus dominated by MPs and councillors from the Scottish Labour Party and the Scottish Liberal Democrats. But it also included representatives of other main organisations in Scotland – in particular, the Scottish TUC and CBI and the churches. The Convention published its final report, *Scotland's Parliament, Scotland's Right*, in November 1995.

This report proposed a Scottish parliament to sit for a fixed term of four years, with dissolution possible before the end of its term only with the agreement of two-thirds of its members. The parliament would enjoy legislative powers over all the areas of policy currently within the remit of the Scottish Office. It would also have the power to increase or cut the basic rate of income tax for Scottish taxpayers by a maximum of 3p in the pound. The Scottish parliament would be elected by a system of proportional representation resembling that of Germany. Of its 129 members, 73 would be elected in Westminster constituencies by the first past the post method (the constituency of Orkney and Shetland would be divided, becoming two constituencies); the other 56 members would be elected in groups of seven in the eight Euro-constituencies on a list basis so as to ensure that total representation from each of these Euro-constituencies corresponded as closely as possible with the share of the vote cast for each party in each Euro-constituency.[8] In addition, Labour and the Liberal Democrats signed an agreement accepting the principle 'that there should be an equal number of men and women as members of the first Scottish Parliament'. To achieve this aim, the two parties committed themselves to select and field equal numbers of male and female candidates both for the constituencies and for the list, and to ensure that these candidates were fairly distributed with a view to the winnability of seats. The Convention, however, made no recommendation as to the abolition of the office of Secretary of State or any reduction in the number of Scottish seats at Westminster. Nor did it deal in any detail with the most difficult question facing supporters of Scottish devolution – the so-called West Lothian question.

The West Lothian question is named after Tam Dalyell who, as MP for West Lothian in the 1970s, pursued it with obsessive pertinacity in the debates on the devolution bills of 1977 and 1978. The question asks whether it is possible to devolve powers in just one area of a country which remains a unitary state. After devolution, MPs at Westminster would no longer be able to vote on Scottish domestic affairs, as these would have been devolved to Edinburgh. Westminster MPs would no longer be able to vote, for example, on education in West Lothian, but Scottish MPs would still be able to vote on education in West Bromwich. Thus it would be possible for, say, a Labour government at Westminster, whose majority was dependent on the seats held by Scottish MPs, to take decisions on the education systems of England and Wales, even though Westminster no longer had any role in deciding upon the education system of Scotland.

The same anomaly occurred, of course, in the years when Northern Ireland had legislative devolution between 1921 and 1972. It caused little controversy, however, because Northern Ireland returned so few MPs – 13 until 1950, and 12 thereafter. Even so, Attlee's Labour government, which in 1950 was returned with an overall majority of six, insufficient to sustain it for longer than 19 months, might have been able to survive longer had it not been for the Northern Ireland MPs, without whom its majority would have been 18. In 1964, Labour was again returned with a small overall majority of three. The following year the 12 Ulster Unionists, who sat with the Conservatives, voted against Labour's Manchester Corporation Bill and Rent Bill, the provisions of which did not apply to Northern Ireland. Harold Wilson, as Prime Minister, gave the Unionists a veiled warning: 'I would hope that Northern Ireland Members who are here, and who are welcomed here, for the duties they have to perform on behalf of the United Kingdom in many matters affecting Northern Ireland, would consider their position in matters where we have no equivalent right in Northern Ireland.'[9] He further warned the Unionists, unavailingly, not to vote against the nationalisation of steel: 'I am sure the House will agree that there is an apparent lack of logic, for example, about steel, when Northern Ireland can, and presumably will, swell the Tory ranks tonight, when we have no power to vote on questions about steel in Northern Ireland.'[10]

An earlier version of the West Lothian question had baffled Gladstone as he toiled over the Irish home rule bills in the nineteenth century. He sought, at different times, three different answers to the question, but none of them proved satisfactory.[11] The first was to exclude Irish MPs from Westminster entirely. This, however, was constitutionally impossible so long as Ireland remained part of the United Kingdom and continued to be taxed by Westminster, which would, of course, remain responsible for matters not transferred to the Irish parliament. Taxation without representation would inevitably lead to separation since Ireland could not be expected to tolerate a foreign and defence policy decided in a Westminster chamber where it was no longer represented.

The second possible solution was that Irish MPs should vote only on matters not transferred to the Irish parliament. This is the so-called 'in and out' solution, and Wilson hinted at it in his strictures on the Ulster Unionists in 1965. The 'in and out' solution is, however, unworkable for two reasons. The first is that it puts too much power in the hands of the Speaker, who would have to decide on each bill whether or not it was one on which the Irish could vote. 'I am afraid,' Gladstone told Lord Rosebery, who had suggested the 'in and out' solution, 'that the Speakership would hardly bear the weight of your proposal.'[12]

The second reason why the 'in and out' solution is constitutionally impossible is that it could, with different parties in a majority in Scotland and in the United Kingdom as a whole, bifurcate the executive. There would be one majority for matters transferred to Scotland and a different one for matters not so transferred. This would in fact have occurred after the general elections of 1964 and February 1974 when Labour governments would have been transformed into Conservative governments without the Scottish MPs. In February 1992, Robin Cook, then Shadow Health Secretary, drew the conclusion that 'once we have a Scottish Parliament handling health affairs it is not possible for me to continue as Minister of Health administering health in England'.[13] He was, however, immediately disavowed by Neil Kinnock. The reason for the Labour leader's repudiation is clear: Cook was implying that a Labour majority in the United Kingdom would have no legitimacy in deciding the domestic affairs of England unless there were a Labour majority in England.

It has been suggested that such situations would in fact be highly infrequent, since it has only been in the short parliaments of 1964–6 and February–October 1974 that a non-Conservative government has faced a Conservative majority of English MPs, and 'these short parliaments did not inflict major legislative changes on a bitterly hostile electorate'.[14]

The chances of an outcome such as occurred in 1964–6 and between February and October 1974 are, however, much greater now than they have been in the past, for the gap between the number of seats won by

Labour and by the Conservatives in Scotland has grown considerably. In 1950, the two parties won an equal number of seats in Scotland; but in 1987, Labour won 40 more seats than the Conservatives, and in 1992 39 more. Thus a Labour overall majority in the Commons not dependent upon Scottish MPs is much less likely than it has been in the past.

A third approach to the West Lothian question would be to reduce the number of Scottish MPs. This, while it does not provide a solution, might help to reduce the number of occasions on which a majority from the United Kingdom faced a contrary majority from England, Wales and Northern Ireland.

In terms of strict logic, however, the West Lothian question – described by Michael Forsyth, the Scottish Secretary, in a speech on St. Andrew's Day 1995, as 'the Bermuda triangle of devolution' – is unanswerable without a general devolution to regions and nations within the state. It is an inevitable consequence of devolving legislative powers to only one part of a unitary state. The issue is whether it is an acceptable anomaly or a fatal weakness.

The Conservative Party, which in the 1960s and 1970s supported moderate devolution, now claims that there is no half-way house between the unitary state and separatism. Some believe that it would be better to recreate the pre-1707 state by allowing Scotland to go its own way rather than unacceptably muddying the British Constitution. The great constitutional lawyer, A. V. Dicey, took that view with regard to Ireland in the nineteenth century, and Scottish nationalists today argue in similar vein. Yet in a world dominated by globalisation and multinational corporations, separatism seems very much a doctrine of the past. An independent Scotland, too, would be just as much affected by economic and diplomatic trends in the rest of Britain as Scotland is today within the UK; but it would have no MPs at Westminster able to present its views. It would have to argue its case outside rather than inside the House of Commons, just as Ireland after independence, deprived of MPs at Westminster, found itself dependent on British goodwill to secure tariff concessions.

Experience on the continent, where anomalies of the type represented by the West Lothian question seem to be accommodated without difficulty, shows that there is an alternative to the defeatism of the Conservatives and the nationalists. In Denmark, the Faeroe Islands and Greenland both have their own parliaments and both remain outside the European Union, of which Denmark of course is a member state. These divergences have not threatened the integrity of the Danish state. In France, Italy and Spain there has, admittedly, been devolution to all parts of the country, but this has been asymmetric, with some regions enjoying greater powers than others. In France, Corsica and the overseas territories have special status. In Italy, there are 15 ordinary regions with no exclusive legislative powers, but five special regions with exclusive legislative powers in economic, social and cultural matters. In Spain, seven out of the 17 'autonomous communities' enjoy a high degree of autonomy and run their own health and education services; some of them also run their own police forces. Yet there is no 'West Sardinian question' or 'West Catalonian question' in these countries. Part of the reason for this in Spain is that the regions enjoying a lesser degree of autonomy can move, if they so wish, to high autonomy status. Thus the removal of the legislative anomaly is within the power of those suffering from it. A parallel in Britain would be to allow Wales and the English regions to enjoy similar powers to those enjoyed by the Scottish parliament.

Continental experience, however, has a deeper lesson to offer: namely, that where the will to conciliate is present, special treatment for parts of a country, far from stimulating separatism, can actually help contain it. In France, Italy and Spain, devolution has led not to the disintegration but to the strengthening of the state. It is thus not the existence of a West Lothian question that leads to the break-up of the state, but rather, as the experience of Ireland in the nineteenth century shows, the denial of the legitimate claims of nations and regions with strong identities of their own.

Disraeli once said that England – he perhaps meant Britain – was governed not by logic but by Parliament. The question of whether the recognition of Scottish nationality through the establishment of a separate parliament is compatible with the maintenance of the United Kingdom is one to be decided not by a priori reasoning but by practical judgement. The Union with Scotland, after all, is not an end in itself but a means to the effective government of different parts of the country. If it becomes evident that the Union is caught in a logical straitjacket such that it is no longer possible to improve Scottish government within the framework of the United Kingdom, then the framework itself will come under threat. In the late nineteenth century, Conservatives, together with the Liberal splinter group which opposed Gladstone's Irish home rule proposals, also called themselves Unionists. They too argued that there was no half-way house between the unitary state and separation. Yet, by defeating home rule, they eventually brought about the very consequence which they most abhorred – the collapse of the Union. In other words, if there was one objective which the Unionists failed to achieve, it was preservation of the Union with Ireland. Thus, those who argue that devolution to Scotland alone is impossible, and that the only choice is between the unitary state and separation, ignore the lessons of practical experience. Moreover, they endanger the very kingdom whose unity they seek to preserve.

In 1887, after his Irish home rule proposals had been defeated for the first time, Gladstone argued that the way to hold a multinational state together was not by concentrating responsibility and power in an undivided central parliament, but through 'recognition of the distinctive qualities of the separate parts of great countries'.[15] If that assessment is correct, the setting-up of a Scottish parliament would strengthen the unity of the United Kingdom, not weaken it.

IV

Devolution, moreover, has a dual dynamic. Not only could it re-establish the terms of the Union with Scotland; it could also, by dispersing power from Westminster and Whitehall, help to improve the effectiveness of government. While the former aim is specific to Scotland, the latter is applicable to the United Kingdom as a whole. Thus Scottish devolution could provide an example to be followed by other parts of the United Kingdom – by Wales and the English regions.

Britain is by far the most centralised member state of the European Union and one of the most centralised states in the world. It is noticeable that the other member states of the European Union of a similar size to Britain – France, Germany, Italy and Spain – are either federal states or possess a regional layer of government. Britain, by contrast, is characterised by the absence of a regional layer of government, and by local government units which are far larger than those of its continental counterparts. The average ratio of councillors to inhabitants in the member states of the Council of Europe is one to 305; in Britain, one councillor represents on average 2,605 inhabitants. It has been calculated that for Britain to equal the average ratio of local representatives to people in the developed world, it would need a further 120,000 councillors.[16]

The difficulty with any reorganisation of government along regional lines, however, is that in Britain the regions seem to be mere ghosts, lacking any concrete reality either in public administration or in popular feeling. If that were truly the case, then there would be neither an administrative argument for the creation of regional units in England, nor any democratic case for doing so. Yet there is already a 'hidden' layer of regional government in Britain. It consists, first, of ad hoc appointed bodies at regional level, and second, of government offices in the regions.

Many of the functions of central government are conducted at regional level. The National Health Service, the Housing Corporation and the Arts Council are examples of services which are organised in the regions. Some of these functions – for example, those exercised by the Housing Corporation, Housing Action Trusts, Training and Enterprise Councils and the Further Education Funding Council – have been taken away from local government, to be carried out by 'quangos' at regional level staffed by government appointees. In the words of Professor John Stewart of Birmingham University, a 'new magistracy' has been created. The Labour Party has estimated that total public spending by what it calls the unelected state in 1993–4 was around 54 billion pounds, made up as shown in Table 2.3.[17]

It would be unrealistic to suppose that all of these functions could simply be taken over by regional authorities. For, just because an activity may be located in the regions, it does not follow that the activity itself is inherently regional. The National Health Service is of course a national

Table 2.3   Composition of public expenditure by 'quangos', 1993–4

	£m
Non-departmental public bodies	15,410
Training and Enterprise Councils	2,200
Higher Education Funding Council	2,800
Further Education Funding Council	2,700
Grant-maintained schools	912
NHS public bodies	30,400
TOTAL	54,422

Source: House of Commons Library, *Public Bodies*, 1993.

service and it must remain a matter for debate to what extent regional variations in standards should be allowed. The existence of grant-maintained schools follows from policy decisions of the Conservative government, and a Conservative government would not allow a regional authority to subvert the basic principle, while a Labour government might be unwilling to allow regions, for example, to charge for hospital beds. Were there to be devolution to the regions, moreover, the role of White-hall departments would have to change. Whitehall would have to be content with framework legislation, leaving the regions to fill out the details. That would of course amount to a revolution in British administrative procedure; but it would provide one method of making the new magistracy more accountable.

The second element of this layer of 'hidden' regional government consists of the regional offices of the major domestic departments of state. In April 1994, the regional offices of the Departments of the Environment, Transport, and Trade and Industry, and the Training, Enterprise and Education Directorate of the Department of Employment, were brought together in Integrated Regional Offices. The press release accompanying this change declared that its purpose was 'to shift power from Whitehall to local communities and make the government more responsible to local priorities'. The Environment Secretary, John Gummer, declared that in future, 'local needs, rather than departmental interests, will be the prime consideration' and that 'we are devolving responsibility from Whitehall'.

The Integrated Regional Offices administer or advise on programmes such as housing, urban regeneration projects, and training and education budgets; their total annual budgets equal around £6 billion, and their running costs around £90 million. They provide a single point of contact with central government for local businesses and councils whose bids for money for economic development and urban regeneration are submitted via the Regional Offices, as are bids for industrial aid and monies from the European Union regional aid funds.

The establishment of the Integrated Regional Offices involved a further change of great importance for the debate on devolution, in that it marked a step towards the establishment of common regional boundaries in place of the previous unsystematic arrangements. Indeed, when John Gummer commended the Integrated Regional Offices to the Commons, he declared: 'For the first time, there will be coterminous regions for the

Departments, and that is the vital change. It has always seemed ridiculous to me that different departments had different regions. That made any sort of planning almost impossible.'[18] The Housing Corporation has since reorganised its regional structure to match the Regional Offices' boundaries. There is, however, still considerable variation between the boundaries applying to the Regional Offices and the boundaries observed by other government agencies and quangos – even those which are run by the four departments brought together in the Integrated Regional Offices. Major executive agencies within departments participating in the Integrated Regional Offices, for example, the Highways Agency and the Benefits Agency, have established regional structures with boundaries differing markedly from those of the Regional Offices. These anomalies notwithstanding, Jack Straw, the Shadow Home Secretary, has claimed that regional government is 'a Conservative policy which dare not speak its name. The official line remains one of continued opposition to regional government. The practice is, however, very different. The government has been driven by business pressure and economic logic to do what it claims to oppose – to strengthen England's regional tier of administration.'[19]

Howard Davies, speaking as Director-General of the CBI, welcomed the development of regionalism in a speech to regional newspaper editors on 6 February 1995, at which he declared that

> regional businesses have definitely welcomed having a single point of call for government in their region. But curiously, rather than appease the enthusiasm for regional autonomy, and make them think the government really does care about the world beyond the M25, the Integrated Regional Offices seem to have had the opposite effect. It has woken them up to what they have been missing. This is perhaps not surprising. . . . There is a growing consensus that a regional focus for decision-making across the public sector needs to be created, and one with business input.

Local government has followed the logic of regionalism, coming together in regional associations so as to secure a regional input into their deliberations. Indeed, the whole country is now covered by such regional associations, which may be regarded almost as regional authorities in embryo. These regional associations, however, are accountable only at one remove to electors in the regions, and they can act only with the assent of all of their component bodies. Thus the English regions, in the Labour Party's view, 'have administration without representation'.[20]

The issue, then, is not whether there should be regional administration in England, for a regional layer already exists; the question is whether this layer exists in an acceptable form and whether it is democratically accountable. In some cases, the regional layer of administration has involved the bypassing of local government and the transfer of services away from elected members into the hands of unelected officials. The regional layer as a whole is highly fragmented, with services being delivered by a medley of appointed bodies, government agencies and local authorities. The regional directors of the Integrated Regional Offices have little power over these various bodies, lacking both constitutional authority and financial leverage. Moreover, the regional layer of government is run by officials at a distance from ministers, so that democratic accountability to Parliament is in danger of becoming tenuous and merely formal. A similar trend may have occurred in Wales as the functions of the Secretary of State have grown. In such circumstances, as Sir Goronwy Daniel, the then Permanent Under-Secretary at the Welsh Office, told the Royal Commission on the Constitution as long ago as 1969, 'it becomes necessary for him [the Secretary of State] to delegate more and more work to officials'.[21] This raises the danger of a Civil Service elite controlling the affairs of Wales. An elected regional structure of government might produce a framework of government which is both more comprehensible and more rational. Instead of continuing to transfer functions from local to central government and establishing new quangos, it might be more sensible to create democratically elected regional authorities. These authorities would be responsible for the strategic services of government – health, environmental services, transport, regional planning and some economic development services – while the personal services – education and social services – would remain with local government.

While it is true that there is little genuine regional feeling in some areas of the country, such feeling probably does exist at least in the north of England and also in London. It is highly significant that the Labour Party has decided to give priority to London among the regions of England in its devolution plans, proposing what it calls a 'strategic authority' for London following a referendum. In London, regular opinion polls by the polling organisation MORI have shown that between 70 and 80 per cent of the population favour a London-wide system of government. London is indeed almost unique among capital cities of the democratic world in having neither an elected authority nor an elected mayor. Its system of government is highly fragmented. The abolition of the GLC in 1986 did not create a unitary system of local government in London, for many of the functions of the GLC went not to the boroughs but to government departments, appointed bodies and joint boards, most of which are not accountable to a London-wide electorate. The complexity of these administrative arrangements inhibits popular understanding of them and thus constitutes an extra obstacle to accountability. If there is, as opinion poll evidence suggests, a genuine feeling of common identity across London, then there would be a strong case for a new London-wide authority. This would not be a revived GLC, which, enjoying only a few functional responsibilities, sought to encroach on the powers of the London boroughs; rather, it would be a body with powers devolved from central government and elected by proportional representation so as to protect it from the fate to which the GLC was alleged to have succumbed, namely, takeover by unrepresentative extremists.

The basic case for regional devolution, however, must rest not upon administrative arguments, but upon the argument from diversity and the dispersal of power. The fundamental purpose of elected regional authorities would be to allow for divergences of policy. There would be no point in creating regional assemblies simply to replicate national policies at regional level. There would have to be a genuine devolution of power from Whitehall, with less policy control from central government. To what extent, however, would such diversity be acceptable in England? The Conservatives, despite an ethos which has emphasised the dispersal of power, did not on the whole encourage regional diversity during their 18 years of government, while Labour adopted a highly centralist approach towards local authorities during its periods of office in the 1960s and 1970s. Until a government has decided that diversity is to be encouraged rather than regarded as anomalous, it would be pointless to proceed with regional devolution in England.

The dual dynamic of devolution, nevertheless, could serve both to contain nationalism in Scotland by regenerating the Union between Scotland and the rest of the United Kingdom, and also to improve the effectiveness of government in England by allowing for greater regional diversity where that corresponded with popular wishes. The devolution debate, then, is not one just between nationalists and defenders of the unitary state. For there are three positions in the debate – the nationalist, the regionalist and the defence of the unitary state. In the 1970s, the last two combined against the first to defeat devolution, regionalists in the north of England being more concerned to prevent Scotland from gaining a dominant role in the constitution than to pursue their own claims. Devolution is only likely to succeed if the regionalists can ally with the nationalists – a conjunction that is by no means impossible, for, although regionalism and nationalism are different phenomena, they have enough in common, in a shared dislike of over-centralisation and alienation from Whitehall and Westminster, to justify combining in pursuit of a shared objective.

In the last resort, a policy of devolution applied to the whole of the United Kingdom would imply the creation of a quasi-federal state, such as the Spanish state which comprises communities with varying degrees of autonomy. Clearly, most parts of Britain are not ready for so radical a constitutional overhaul. Perhaps they will never be ready for it. 'As to home rule in your sense – which is Federation,' Lord Salisbury wrote to a correspondent in April 1889, 'I do not see in it any elements of practicability. Nations do not change their political nature like that except through blood.'[22] The post-1945 history of Belgium and Spain, however, both of which have peacefully transformed themselves into quasi-federal states, serves to refute Lord Salisbury's dictum.

The different degrees of urgency attached to the question in different parts of the United Kingdom pose a problem for the implementation of devolution. To introduce devolution at the same time across the country as a whole would mean either requiring Scotland to wait until every part of England wanted devolution – which might mean a very long wait indeed – or imposing devolution on the regions of England so as to meet the needs of Scotland. Either solution would be highly impracticable. Labour and the Liberal Democrats have decided to resolve this dilemma by adopting the principle of rolling devolution on the Spanish model. In Spain, following the death of Franco in 1975 and the return to democratic government, a distinction was made between the so-called historic communities – Catalonia and the Basque country, where the demand for devolution was very strong, as it is today in Scotland – and the other provinces, where the demand for devolution seemed less pressing. The new democratic government of Spain therefore legislated immediately for devolution to Catalonia and the Basque country, and established two different routes towards devolution.

The route intended for the historic communities was laid down in Article 151 of the Spanish Constitution. First, all the provinces in a region, together with three-quarters of the municipalities and an absolute majority of electors in each of the provinces in the region, had to support devolution. A scheme would then be prepared and presented to the Cortes, the Spanish parliament. Following endorsement, a second referendum would be held in the region concerned, at which a simple majority of those voting would be sufficient for ratification. Seven regions, rather than just Catalonia and the Basque country (Euskadi), eventually took advantage of this route. They were given a greater degree of autonomy than the regions taking the easier route laid down in Article 143 of the Constitution. The Article 143 route required either all of the provincial councils or three-quarters of the municipalities to propose devolution. Statutes of autonomy would then be submitted by assemblies of regional representatives – members of the Cortes from that region and councillors – to the Cortes for approval. No referendum was required.

Three inter-related features of the Spanish reform are worthy of note. The first is that it was a bottom-up procedure. Devolution was to be triggered not by the government of the day but by local authorities and, in the case of the Article 151 procedure, also by the voters themselves. No region would have devolution unless it actively sought it. Secondly, and consequently, there would be rolling devolution. It would not be introduced at the same time for all regions of the country, but established only if and when the demand was there. The hope was that the success of devolution in the historic communities would lead to a demand for devolution elsewhere; and that, indeed, was what occurred. Finally, devolution has been asymmetrical. The Article 151 procedure and the Article 143 procedure distinguish between the historic communities and other regions which sought a high degree of autonomy, corresponding perhaps in the British context to Scotland, and the other regions, where there was no history of independent statehood or urgent demand for devolution, corresponding perhaps to many of the English regions. All of these three features, obviously, hold lessons for Britain. In particular, the principle of rolling devolution offers the best hope of constructing a practical devolution policy for Britain, one which addresses the fact that the different nations and regions of the country want devolution, if at all, with different degrees of intensity. For the principle of rolling devolution entails both that no nation or region of the United Kingdom should be required to accept devolution unless and until it actively seeks it; and that a nation or region which does not seek devolution should not be able to prevent any other nation or region which does seek it from enjoying it.

Jack Straw, in putting forward Labour's policy proposals as Shadow Home Secretary in July 1995, explicitly accepted the principle of rolling devolution. He promised devolution for Scotland, Wales and London, and also for any other region of England that sought it, following a test of public opinion such as a referendum. Straw envisaged three regional assemblies in England – in the north, the north-west and the south-west – in addition to a London authority, in existence by the end of a full term of Labour government. 'We want to process this swiftly,' Straw declared; 'over a period of five years they would get them.'[23]

Rolling devolution would be achieved by transforming the regional associations of local authorities into directly elected bodies as and when demand for them was sufficient. The first precondition for regionalism must surely be a unitary tier of local government, as currently exists in Scotland, Wales and London. The imposition of regions upon a two-tier system of local government would yield an unacceptable degree of over-government. At present, however, two-tier local government covers part at least of 34 of the 39 English shire counties, and there is two-tier local government in all of the standard regions except for Greater London. Left to themselves, existing local authorities would hardly be likely to produce a consensus on a unitary system. Therefore, it seems, if Labour wishes to implement regional devolution, it will have to require local authorities to produce proposals within a set timescale. Once unitary local government has been accepted, the regional association – i.e. most of the local authorities comprising it – will have to favour regional government; Parliament must agree to it; and it must be ratified in a referendum. This is the so-called triple lock, preventing devolution being introduced without a wide public consensus in favour of it.

The problem with rolling devolution, however, is that it if it were to require separate legislation for each part of the country, it would be enormously time-consuming and allow many opportunities for parliamentary filibustering and time-wasting. Therefore, if rolling devolution is sought, it would be best to legislate for it through a single act with a model regional assembly in it. This could be brought into play for any region which met the requirements and triggered by an affirmative resolution in the House of Commons.

The West Lothian question is symbol and shorthand for the general problem facing lop-sided devolution. Combining a framework act with rolling devolution would by no means resolve the problem constitutionally. For, unless there were to be legislative devolution for Wales and the English regions, there would still be an asymmetry, with legislative powers remaining with Westminster for domestic affairs except in Scotland. Regionalism, however, might help to reduce the political salience of the West Lothian question. If Scottish MPs were to continue to legislate in detail on the domestic affairs of, for example, the north of England, that would be because the north of England had chosen not to take advantage of an offer of devolution, less than that granted to Scotland, but substantial nevertheless.

V

Scottish devolution would create a new locus of political power in Scotland. The Scottish parliament would be the only elected body to represent the people of Scotland, and it would claim to represent Scottish opinion at least as well as Scottish MPs or government ministers. In theory, Westminster would remain sovereign, and would no doubt seek to buttress its supremacy in various ways. But what would this supremacy amount to in practice? Political authority depends upon its regular and continuous exercise, not upon its incursion in pathological circumstances. The experience of devolution in Northern Ireland showed how difficult it was for Westminster actually to exert its theoretical supremacy. Westminster would be able to exercise its supremacy over the Scottish parliament only at the risk of considerable disaffection among the people of Scotland. It would be difficult, indeed, to imagine an issue more likely to galvanise the Scottish people than a conflict between their own parliament and a London-based government. Being applied so very rarely as a result, the exercise of power by Westminster over the Scottish parliament would come to appear very like a revolutionary act. In practice, therefore, devolution to Scotland would effectively limit the power of Westminster to legislate for Scotland.

Thus the position of Scotland under devolution would come to bear considerable resemblance to that of a province in a federal state, with legislative powers in practice divided between London and Edinburgh. This division of powers would be guaranteed, not by the constitution as in a federal state, but by the force of Scottish opinion. The only circumstances in which Westminster would be able to intervene with impunity would be pathological ones of the kind that occurred in Northern Ireland after the troubles erupted in 1969. Thus devolution would lead to federal government in Scotland in normal times, but a return to unitary government in periods of emergency or crisis.

Devolution has been opposed from the right on the grounds that any departure from the unitary state would lead to separation, and from the left on the grounds that it would deprive the central government of control of the economy and distort the allocation of resources. Neither of these criticisms, however, can be justified.

Perhaps the main political objection to devolution has been that it would encourage separatism and endanger the Union with Scotland. This is highly unlikely. Were Scotland genuinely to seek independence, Westminster no doubt would grant it. Governments would not make the same mistake as they did with Ireland, fighting, for 36 years between 1885 and 1921, against the clear demand of the Irish people to be allowed to run their own affairs. That was a fight which the British government could never win; and in 1921, it had to yield to force what it had refused to reason. Scottish independence, however, would be unlikely to come about solely because a Scottish parliament had been established; indeed, the continental experience has been that the satisfaction of national claims – whether in Catalonia, the Basque country, Corsica or Brittany – serves to contain nationalism rather than encourage it. Nor are there wanting Conservatives in Britain, such as Sir Edward Heath and Lord Hailsham, who take the view that devolution, far from threatening national unity, would actually strengthen it.

Nevertheless, opposition to devolution from the right can be taken for granted. But, both in 1886 and in 1979, it was opposition from the left which, added to that of the Conservatives, killed devolution. In 1886, Joseph Chamberlain argued that the problems of the Irish peasant were no different from those of the Scottish crofter or the English agricultural labourer, and the cure likewise was the same: not home rule for Ireland but the coming to power of a radical government at Westminster, which could cure all these grievances together. In the 1970s, Eric Heffer and Neil Kinnock argued that the problems of the Scottish and Welsh working class were no different from those of the English working class and were to be resolved by the coming to power of a socialist government at Westminster. (Kinnock, however, later recanted to become, as party leader from 1983 to 1992, an enthusiastic supporter of devolution.) Both in the 1880s and in the 1970s, leaders of the left were guilty of chronically under-estimating the force and power of nationalist sentiment.

In the 1990s, government control of the economy seems less important than it once did. It is certainly far more difficult to achieve in a world of multinational corporations and global finance. Accordingly, parties of the left now find themselves more concerned with controlling centralised power and bureaucracy than with controlling the economy. Parties of the left no longer believe (if they ever did) that the man in Whitehall knows best. Governments, whether Conservative or Labour, have been unable to find a way to make centralised government accountable through the conventional forms of parliamentary control and ministerial accountability. Perhaps the span of control in a centralised state is simply too great for power to be made properly accountable; perhaps, indeed, power can only be made more accountable if it is dispersed. Perhaps centralised government can only be controlled by the creation of countervailing centres of power. Parties of the left are now coming to appreciate the force of Montesquieu's dictum that only power can check power. That is an alternative path to the traditional British conception of seeking to control power by trying to make centralised government accountable in one supreme parliament – a traditional conception of control that now seems manifestly to have failed.

Devolution, then, is unlikely to encourage separatism or prevent a government of the left from carrying out its economic policies. The real problems of devolution are in fact rather different. They are, first, whether Britain is really prepared to accommodate the degree of diversity in administering the public services which devolution makes possible; and, second, whether devolution can operate successfully in a state whose fundamental constitutional concept is the sovereignty of Parliament.

The sovereignty of Parliament which in practice legitimises the omnicompetence of government has been underpinned since 1945 by the two-party system. Devolution, however, would lead to a more decentralised politics, a politics of territory. The politics of territory would cut across the politics of the two-party system, as attachment to place came to compete with party allegiance. Whether an MP were Conservative or Labour might come to appear less important than what part of the country he or she came from, whether he or she was a Conservative or Labour MP from London, for example, or from the north of England.

The two-party system could be further undermined by electoral reform. Under proportional representation, Britain would be less likely to see a plethora of new parties than an alteration in the relative strengths of existing parties, together perhaps with some party realignment. With the growth of a multi-party system and the decline of adversarial politics, the West Lothian question would come to lose its importance; for major reversals of policy following general elections would become far less likely.

It may be, indeed, that the successful working of devolution depends in the last resort upon a change in the style of party politics in Britain. A symbol of such a change, and a sign that it had occurred, would be the reform of the electoral system. For electoral reform is the key that turns the lock, a precondition for the success of devolution and perhaps of other constitutional reforms as well.

3

Electoral Reform

An electoral system in a democracy is required to perform two functions: first, to ensure that the majority rules, and second, to ensure that all significant minorities are represented. The British electoral system – the first past the post system – achieves neither of these aims.

The last government to achieve over half of the vote took office in 1935. Between 1945 and 1959, the average electoral support for the governing party was 48.2 per cent – very near to the 50 per cent mark; but it fell to only 46.1 per cent between 1964 and 1970. In the general election after 1970, however, held in February 1974, the Liberal Party, which since 1945 had not succeeded in gaining more than 11.2 per cent of the vote in any general election, won 19.3 per cent. In no election since has it gained less than 13.8 per cent of the vote. The average share of the vote gained by the Liberals, Liberal–SDP Alliance and Liberal Democrats in the six general elections from February 1974 was 19.7 per cent. As a result, the average percentage of votes gained by the winning party in the general elections between February 1974 and 1992 has fallen to 41.2 per cent. Harold Wilson's Labour government, elected with a majority of three in October 1974, was supported by only 39.2 per cent of the voters. Margaret Thatcher's two landslides – in 1983 and 1987, when she won overall majorities of 144 and 102 respectively – were won on 42.4 per cent and 43.4 per cent of the popular vote. Whatever the ideological significance of Thatcherism, it is clear that it never succeeded in winning the allegiance of much more than two-fifths of the British people. Three-fifths of those voting remained resolutely opposed to it.

It is sometimes suggested that the debate between supporters and opponents of the first past the post system is one about the fundamental purpose of elections. Supporters of proportional representation, it is argued, believe that the purpose of an election is to choose a representative parliament. Supporters of first past the post, by contrast, believe that the purpose of an election is to choose a government. Thus, while proportional representation might be justifiable for a primarily deliberative assembly, it is difficult to justify it for an executive-producing one such as the House of Commons, where the aim is to produce 'strong government'. This was, in fact, the view taken by the working party on electoral reform (the Plant Commission) in chapter 3 of its 1991 report, commissioned by the Labour Party.[1]

In 1923, in an endeavour to secure a single-party majority, Mussolini amended the Italian electoral law so that the winning party would automatically receive two-thirds of the seats. In 1983, the British electoral system yielded a similar result without gerrymandering, giving Margaret Thatcher's Conservatives 61 per cent of the seats for 42 per cent of the vote. Her government enjoyed a massive parliamentary majority, although in a minority of the popular vote to the tune of over four and a half million. In no other European democracy could such a distortion of the popular will occur. How, in a democracy, can a government be 'strong' when nearly 60 per cent of the voters are against it? The British electoral system does not yield majority rule, but rule by the strongest minority. That minority may come fairly near to 50 per cent, as it did in the years immediately after 1945, or it may fall some way short of it, as it has done in more recent years, when the system has manifestly failed to achieve at least one of its two crucial aims.

Giving power to the strongest minority is more worrying in Britain than it would be in most other democracies since we are one of only three democracies in the world – the other two being New Zealand and Israel – without a codified constitution. We are also now almost the only democracy in the world which offers no constitutional check or balance to the power of government – no constitutional court, no federal system, no powerful second chamber and a weak system of local government, hardly capable of resisting the depredations of the centre. It is the absence of constitutional checks which makes British government omnicompetent. But it is the first past the post system which allows an omnicompetent government to assume power even though a majority of the voters may be opposed to it. An omnicompetent government supported by a minority of the voters is difficult to reconcile with the canons of either democratic or constitutional government.

Nor is the British electoral system more successful in ensuring the representation of all significant minorities. It has, in particular, penalised the Liberal Democrats, and their predecessors, the Liberal–SDP Alliance and the Liberal Party. Table 3.1 compares their share of the vote with seats won in the general elections since February 1974. The Liberals and their successors, despite gaining an average of nearly one-fifth of the vote over six consecutive general elections, have at none of them been able to secure more than a bare handful of MPs, hardly sufficient to carry out the duties of a national party in Parliament.

The fundamental reason why the electoral system treats the Liberal Democrats so brutally is that electoral support for the Liberal Democrats is geographically fairly evenly spread, rather than being concentrated in particular areas as is the case with the Labour and Conservative parties. This tendency was at its most marked in the 1983 general election, when the Liberal–SDP Alliance vote was within 2 per cent of its average value in every region of the country. Labour's overall vote in the 1983 election was, at 27.6 per cent, only 2.2 per cent higher than the Liberal–SDP Alliance vote; yet Labour won 209 seats as compared with the 23 gained by the Alliance. It is clear, then, that the electoral system discriminates not so much against third parties or minority parties as against parties whose vote is evenly spread rather than concentrated. It is difficult to justify such a discrimination on the basis of any of the tenets of democratic theory.

Table 3.1   Liberal, Liberal–SDP Alliance and
Liberal Democrat votes and seats, 1974–1992

Election	Vote %	Seats No.	%
February 1974	19.3	14	2.2
October 1974	18.3	13	2.0
1979	13.8	11	1.7
1983	25.4	23	3.5
1987	23.2	22	3.5
1992	18.3	20	3.1

The effect of geographical concentration – or lack of it – means that
the electoral system does not discriminate equally against all minor parties. Table 3.2 shows the percentage of votes and seats gained by the
main parties other than Labour and the Conservatives in the 1992 general
election. It will be seen that the Liberal Democrats and the SNP have
suffered the most from the electoral system, while Plaid Cymru and the
Ulster Unionists benefit from it and the SDLP is represented exactly in
proportion to the votes which it receives. These differences relate to the
relative degree of concentration of the vote of the different parties. The
SNP vote is fairly evenly distributed across Scotland – in 1992, indeed,
it did not lose a single deposit, and the standard deviation of the SNP
vote share (8.3 per cent) was lower than that of the Liberal Democrats
(10.2 per cent). Plaid Cymru, by contrast, is concentrated in Welsh-
speaking north-west Wales. In the five seats in Wales with the most
Welsh speakers, it gained an average of 40 per cent of the vote. Its highest
vote elsewhere was 15.6 per cent.[2]

Thus the British electoral system favours two kinds of parties: first,
the Conservative and Labour parties, whose support has in the past been
largely based upon social class – for social classes have been distributed
not randomly but in concentrated pockets, the working classes in the
inner cities and conurbations, the wealthier classes in the countryside –
and second, Plaid Cymru and the main parties of Northern Ireland,
parties representing geographically concentrated cultural and religious

*Table 3.2 Votes and seats gained by minor parties in the
1992 general election*

Party	% votes	% seats
Liberal Democrats	18.3	3.1
SNP	1.9	0.5
SNP in Scotland	21.5	4.2
Plaid Cymru	0.3	0.6
Plaid Cymru in Wales	8.8	10.5
Ulster Unionists	1.2	2.0
Ulster Unionists in Northern Ireland	34.5	52.9
SDLP	0.6	0.6
SDLP in Northern Ireland	23.5	23.5

minorities. A class basis of support or a concentrated cultural or religious basis offers advantages to parties under the first past the post system, while parties with different sorts of appeal are likely to be discriminated against.

II

The first past the post system, then, fails to perform either of the two functions required of an effective electoral system. It gives power not to the majority but to the strongest minority; and it fails to ensure that all significant minorities are properly represented. It represents minorities not according to their electoral strength, but according to the geographical structure of the vote of minority parties, favouring those whose support is concentrated at the expense of those whose vote is more evenly spread.

Many supporters of the first past the post system acknowledge these weaknesses, but dismiss them as entirely theoretical. Whatever its weaknesses from the point of view of the democratic ideal, they argue, the first past the post system has the practical virtue that it generates a clear outcome, enabling voters to choose between two alternative parties and producing a majority government. In doing this, the first past the post system ensures accountable government.

Processes of electoral change, however, have seriously weakened this practical defence of the first past the post system. In 1992, John Major won, in terms of votes, a more sweeping victory over Labour than any Conservative leader since 1945, except for Margaret Thatcher in the elections of 1983 and 1987. The gap between the Conservative and Labour parties was 7.6 per cent of the vote, far larger than the margin of Edward Heath's victory in 1970, when the Conservative lead was just 3.4 per cent, or Harold Macmillan's triumph in 1959 (5.6 per cent) or Anthony Eden's victory in 1955 (3.3 per cent). Yet Major won a majority of only 21 as compared with Heath's majority of 30, Macmillan's of 100 and Eden's of 58. Why was this?

The first reason is that, partly through tactical voting, the Labour vote in 1992 was more efficiently distributed in marginal seats than the Conservative vote. Thus, the swing to Labour in Conservative/Labour marginals was higher than it was in the country as a whole. In seats where the Conservatives were first in 1987 and less than 16 per cent ahead of a second-placed Labour candidate (excluding two Labour by-election gains), the average swing to Labour was 4.7 per cent, compared with the nationwide swing of 2.5 per cent. This may have cost the Conservatives up to 10 seats.[3]

Two further reasons why the large Conservative lead in votes did not lead to a large majority of seats have been adduced by Curtice and Steed in their analysis of the 1992 election.[4] The first is that turnout rose by far less in Labour constituencies than in Conservative ones, average turn-out in Labour constituencies being 73.5 per cent compared with 80.2 per cent in Conservative constituencies, 'a gap of 6.7 per cent, twice that in 1987'. The second is that 'the electorates in Labour constituencies continued to decline while those in Conservative ones increased. This is a long-standing trend which has repeated itself at every post-war British election. It reflects the gradual and continuing shift of the population out of the (mainly Labour) conurbations into the (more Conservative) countryside. It is the reason why each boundary review necessarily takes seats away from Labour and gives them to the Conservatives.' By 1992, 'the gap in the size of the average Labour and the average Conservative constituency rose to just two short of 10,000 votes'. Part of the reason for this, of course, is the over-representation of Scotland and Wales in the House of Commons. Because the 1992 general election yielded an overall majority, this iniquity of the electoral system was not noticed. Had there been a further 0.5 per cent swing away from the Conservatives, they would have lost their overall majority, even though they would still have been over 6.5 percentage points ahead of Labour. Paradoxically, the Conservatives would have been defeated by the very electoral system which they alone, among the major parties, continue to support.

One estimate of the effects of the boundary review is that it gives the Conservatives 11 extra seats, so that, had it been effected before 1992, their majority in that election would have been 32 rather than 21. But if, at the 1997 general election, both parties had won the same proportion of the national vote, and Labour had maintained the relative efficiency of its distribution of the vote while turnout remained depressed in Labour areas, the Conservatives would have won seven fewer seats than Labour. The Conservatives needed around a 4.8 per cent lead for an overall majority while Labour required only around a 2.1 per cent lead.[5]

Thus the first past the post system is now much less able than it was to secure an overall majority for one party. Any outcome between a 2.1

per cent Labour lead and a 4.8 per cent Conservative lead would have yielded a hung parliament. With such an electoral distribution, the general elections of 1950, 1951, 1955, 1964, 1970 and October 1974, as well as the general election of February 1974, would have led to hung parliaments. Of the 14 post-war parliaments, seven would have been hung.

Since the mid-1950s, moreover, patterns of electoral change have led to an increasingly marked division of the nation along geographical lines. There has been a cumulative process whereby the two major parties have gained support in their respective areas of strength: the Conservatives in the south, Labour in the industrial conurbations and Scotland. In 1951, when the Conservatives were returned with an overall majority of 17 – roughly similar to their 1992 majority of 21 – 119 of the 321 Conservative MPs came from north-west of the Severn–Wash line, compared with only 70 out of 336 in 1992. Moreover, Conservative representation in the industrial conurbations has been almost annihilated. Of the 54 constituencies in Birmingham, Bradford, Glasgow, Hull, Leeds, Liverpool, Manchester, Newcastle and Sheffield, the Conservatives held, after the 1992 election, just five. Conversely, despite securing around 20 per cent of the votes in the south, Labour held, after the 1992 election, just 10 seats outside Greater London.

The division between the Britain south-east of the Severn–Wash line and the Britain north-west of it corresponds very broadly with the division between the more advantaged and the less advantaged part of the country. It is hardly surprising if Conservative governments have failed to comprehend the problems of the inner cities when so few of their parliamentary representatives sit for inner-city constituencies. It is hardly surprising if Labour has found it difficult to come to terms with the problems of the more prosperous parts of the country when so few of its MPs sat for seats in the south of England. Even though this pattern was somewhat reversed in the 1992 election, and could be further reversed in the 1997 election, it remains a highly disturbing and divisive tendency.

The electoral system, then, discriminates not only against certain kinds of minority parties, but also against the second party in areas where that party is weak – against Labour in the south of England and against the Conservatives in the conurbations and in Scotland. The resulting geographical polarisation of politics exacerbates Britain's social divisions to an extent unmatched in any other democracy in Western Europe. In the years of Conservative dominance between 1979 and 1997, it became almost impossible for those living in the less advantaged part of the country to acquire the political leverage to enable their voices to be heard. In no other West European democracy could a government be elected on so narrow an electoral or geographical base.

The electoral system has made it appear as if all of the south-east of England outside London were Conservative, while all of the large industrial conurbations were solidly Labour. In exaggerating the electoral disparity between north and south, the electoral system served to emphasise the geographically uneven spread of social and economic advantage in Britain. The situation has been exacerbated by the growing and excessive centralisation of government in recent years, which has meant that those excluded from power at national level have also lost access to other, alternative, centres of power.

III

The first past the post system is often defended, not on the grounds that it produces fair representation, but that it is a guarantor of moderate government, while proportional representation would encourage extremist parties such as the National Front. 'Proportional representation,' Home Secretary Kenneth Baker declared three days before the 1992 general election, when it seemed the Conservatives might lose, 'would be a pact with the devil. PR has helped the fascists to march again in Europe.'[6]

However, as we have seen, the first past the post system artificially strengthens some parties while weakening others. It will not necessarily benefit moderate parties. That was clear in Northern Ireland, where in 1981 an H-block prisoner and a member of Sinn Fein were returned to Westminster in by-elections, while in the general elections of 1983 and 1987 Gerry Adams, vice-president of Sinn Fein, was returned for West Belfast. Nor has the first past the post system prevented the election of Protestant extremist candidates such as the Reverend Ian Paisley in Northern Ireland.

Indeed, it was precisely because first past the post was likely to perpetuate sectarianism that the Government of Ireland Act 1920 provided that both local elections in Northern Ireland and elections to the Northern Ireland parliament – Stormont – should be by proportional representation. The unionists, however, abolished proportional representation as soon as they could. This had the effect of polarising opinion between unionists and nationalists at the expense of less sectarian parties. Following the return to first past the post at Stormont in 1929, four independent centrist members, elected under PR in 1925, lost their seats, while Labour, Liberals and Independents were permanently under-represented at Stormont. From 1929, the border became the sole issue in Northern Ireland's politics. It is just possible that if proportional representation had been maintained, tribal allegiances would not have congealed during Northern Ireland's formative years.

By the 1970s, however, when Westminster re-introduced proportional representation for local and assembly elections in Northern Ireland, it was too late. Sectarianism was too deeply rooted in the province for a biconfessional party to be able to break the mould. Even so, the non-sectarian Alliance Party has always gained greater representation than the non-sectarian parties were able to achieve in Stormont, although its support in the electorate has been no greater.

First past the post and proportional representation favour different kinds of minorities, but neither necessarily favours the extreme or the moderate. The geographically concentrated minorities which first past the post favours may be (as with Ian Paisley's Democratic Unionists) extremist or (as with Plaid Cymru) moderate. Proportional representation, by contrast, will give a minority party, whether its support is evenly spread or not, representation roughly in proportion to its electoral support. An evenly spread minority party might be either moderate (as with the Liberal Democrats) or extremist (as with the Nazis in pre-war Germany).

In the 1930 German election, when the Nazis secured 18 per cent of the vote, they would probably have been under-represented had the elections been held by the first past the post system. It is possible, therefore, that proportional representation helped Hitler achieve momentum, although, in the midst of the depression, it is unlikely that a movement of the force and sweep of Nazism would have suffered much from being under-represented in parliament. In July 1932, however, when the Nazis gained 37 per cent of the vote, they might well have gained an overall majority of the seats in the German parliament under the first past the post system, for by that time the Nazis were very definitely a major and not a minor party. Indeed, Goering told the judges at Nuremberg after the war that, under first past the post, the Nazis would have won every single seat in this election!

It could be argued, therefore, that proportional representation prevented Hitler from gaining an overall majority in the German parliament and delayed his accession to power by six months. When Hitler did finally become Chancellor, this was due to intrigue on the part of those surrounding the president of Germany rather than the electoral system. Indeed, Hitler was losing support electorally before January 1933. He found himself unable to gain power through the electoral process since no other large party would support him as Chancellor; nor was he able to secure an overall majority of seats under Germany's proportional representation system. He became Chancellor only because the president of Germany was deceived into appointing him after being assured that he would respect the constitution and seek to govern through parliament.[7]

The German electoral system between the world wars, moreover, had no threshold, whereas today, almost all democracies have a threshold which prevents very small parties from gaining parliamentary seats. Were Britain to adopt proportional representation, it would almost certainly choose a system which incorporated this element. This would exclude parties which failed to gain 5 per cent of the vote in a region, or which failed to secure around 17 per cent in a five-member constituency, from any parliamentary representation. The National Front, even in its best years electorally, in the 1970s, fell far short of these thresholds. Its highest vote in any constituency has been 9.5 per cent, in October 1974; this would have not have won it a seat in a multi-member constituency system. Also, in that same election, its 90 candidates received an average of 3.1 per cent of the vote, and so it would have been unlikely to gain 5 per cent of the vote in any region.

In 1977, however, its very best year, the National Front won just over 5 per cent of the vote in elections for the now defunct Greater London Council. Had there been a general election in 1977, and had national voting patterns followed local ones, the Front might well have gained representation in the House of Commons. But it is by no means clear that this would have endangered the political system. In 1935, at the height of Stalin's terror, a Communist MP was elected in Britain, and in 1945 two were returned. They made little political impact. Moreover, this possibility must be balanced against the advantages which proportional representation holds for ethnic minority candidates. For proportional representation would be likely to lead to a greater number of such candidates being elected, and this could more than outweigh the rather remote danger of the election of extremist candidates to Westminster.

The first past the post system has an important effect on the selection of candidates. There is good evidence that, in single-member constituencies, where only one candidate can be elected, selection committees hesitate to choose either female candidates or candidates from ethnic minorities. They will tend to choose a 'safe' candidate who will be as near to an identikit model of an MP as it is possible to find. The candidate will be white, middle-aged and male. The 1992 general election saw 60 female MPs returned, roughly 10 per cent of the total number. That is by far the largest percentage of women that has ever been returned to Westminster. Indeed, 1987 is the only other general election in which more than 5 per cent of the MPs returned have been female. A similar pattern of under-representation of women can be found in other countries using single-member constituencies, such as the United States – despite its powerful women's movement – and France. The 1992 general election also returned just six MPs from the ethnic minorities, although these minorities comprise nearly 10 per cent of the population. There were no Muslim Members of Parliament to represent the one million Muslims in Britain.

Under proportional representation, however, whether under a list system or a multi-member constituency system, a party will be concerned to secure a 'balanced ticket'. Since the list will contain a large number of names, the absence of a due proportion of women will cause offence and narrow the appeal of the party. For whereas under a single-member constituency system it is the presence of a candidate who deviates from the identikit norm, whether female or black, that is noticed, in a party list system it is the absence of a female or minority candidate, the failure to present a balanced ticket, that will be commented upon and resented.

Fortunately, there is a simple way of testing the argument that a list system is more likely than a single-member constituency system to encourage female representation. It is to compare over a period of time the percentage of women who have achieved election to the German Bundestag. This is possible because the German electoral system comprises two elements: a single-member constituency element, as in Britain, and a party list element; 50 per cent of the candidates are elected in the single-member constituencies and 50 per cent from the list. Between 1949 and 1994, 790 women were elected to the Bundestag. Of these, 185 were elected in the constituencies and 605 from the list.

The first past the post system stands condemned as inequitable, inefficient and socially divisive. Its continuation is harmful both to the democratic process and to the social cohesion of the country. What are the main alternatives?

IV

There are a very large number of alternative electoral systems. As long ago as 1910, a Royal Commission appointed to inquire into electoral systems – the only Royal Commission ever to have been set up in Britain with such a remit – claimed that there were over 300 different such systems. Human ingenuity being what it is, there are probably many more than 300 today. Fortunately, there is no need to analyse all of them. Many are in fact variations on a smaller number of basic types, combining and recombining the same elements in different ways, while others are, for various reasons, quite unsuitable for Britain and have never been advocated for Britain by electoral reformers.

There are just four alternative systems which have been advocated by electoral reformers for Westminster elections, and which are therefore considered in this chapter. They are:

1 the *alternative vote*, an electoral system used for the election of the Australian lower house, the House of Representatives;
2 the *supplementary vote*, a variant of the alternative vote, recommended in 1993 by the Plant Commission, established by the Labour Party to inquire into electoral reform;
3 the *additional member system* of proportional representation, modelled on the electoral system used in the Federal Republic of Germany;
4 the *single transferable vote*, used in the Republic of Ireland, and for local government and European Parliament elections in Northern Ireland.

The latter two of these systems are methods of proportional representation, but the first two, the alternative vote and the supplementary vote, are not.

V

The alternative vote is a system of preferential voting in single-member constituencies. The voter marks his or her ballot paper not with an 'X' but with a '1' by the most favoured candidate, a '2' by the one next favoured, and so on. A valid vote requires that a '1' be unambiguously marked next to the name of a single candidate. If a candidate has an overall majority of first preferences, that candidate is declared elected. If no candidate enjoys an absolute majority, however, the candidate at the bottom of the poll is eliminated and second preferences distributed. This process continues until one candidate has an absolute majority of the votes.

Table 3.3   Distribution of votes among parties, Inverness, 1992

Party	Votes	
	No.	%
Liberal Democrat	13,258	26.0
Labour	12,800	25.1
SNP	12,562	24.7
Conservative	11,517	22.6
Green	766	1.5

The alternative vote is a system designed to avoid the anomaly by which a candidate can win a constituency even though he or she does not enjoy the support of the majority of voters in the constituency. The most extreme example of such a minority victory in 1992 occurred in Inverness, where the result was as shown in Table 3.3. The winner, the Liberal Democrat Sir Russell Johnston, was supported by just over one-quarter of the electorate, and only 1,741 votes separated the four leading candidates. Although Inverness is an extreme and untypical example, minority victories have become more frequent in Britain in recent years with the growth of parties competing with the Conservatives and Labour. In 1951, when the two-party system was at its zenith, the Conservatives and Labour between them won nearly 97 per cent of the popular vote and only 39 seats were won on a minority vote. Since 1974, however, the number of seats won on a minority vote has been as follows:[8]

February 1974	408
October 1974	380
1979	207
1983	334
1987	283
1992	259

The alternative vote has been recommended by Peter Mandelson and Roger Liddle, both of whom are policy advisers to Tony Blair, and it is also the system of election that the Labour Party itself uses in its selection procedures for parliamentary candidates.[9]

The trouble is, however, that although the alternative vote ensures that every MP enjoys the support of the majority of his or her constituents, it does not ensure that the outcome of a general election reflects the number of votes cast for each party across the country. Contrary to what is sometimes suggested, it is not a system of proportional representation. Indeed, it can, under certain circumstances, yield a greater dispro-portionality than the first past the post system.

Consider, for example, two elections for the Australian House of Representatives, in 1990 and 1993, as set out in Table 3.4. In 1990, Labor won an overall majority of the seats on less than two-fifths of the vote, defeating the Liberal–National coalition even though the coalition gained 3.8 per cent more of the vote than Labor. The Democrats, with the support of over one in ten of the voters, failed to achieve any representation at all. In 1993, Labor achieved a comfort-able overall majority on less than 45 per cent of the vote, and with just 0.6 per cent of the vote more than that secured by the Liberal–National coalition.

On these occasions, the system worked to the advantage of Labor; but between 1949 and 1983, it worked against Labor, which received fewer seats than it would have done under first past the post at every general election except four. In 1954 and 1961, the alternative vote kept Labor out of office, although the party secured a higher percentage of the vote than the Liberal–National coalition; in 1977, Labor won more votes than any other party but the Liberals, with 38 per cent of the vote, won an overall majority of the seats. The Liberal–National coalition won over two-thirds of the seats on just 48 per cent of the vote.

The alternative vote does not secure proportional representation

Table 3.4   Election results for the Australian House of Representatives, 1990 and 1993

Party	Votes (%)	Seats (%)
(a) 1990		
Labor Party	39.4	52.7
Liberal Party	34.8	37.2
National Party	8.4	9.4
Liberal–National coalition	43.2	46.6
Democrats	11.3	0.0
Others	6.1	0.7
(b) 1993		
Labor Party	44.9	54.4
Liberal Party	37.1	33.3
National Party	7.2	10.9
Liberal–National coalition	44.3	44.2
Democrats	3.8	0.0
Others	7.1	1.4

because the anomalies in representation under first past the post are due hardly at all to the fact that some MPs are elected on a minority vote. It would be perfectly possible for every constituency to be won on a majority vote and yet for the outcome to fail to reflect the majority view of the voters. This would occur if one party were to pile up large majorities in safe seats, while the second party won a larger number of seats by much smaller majorities. The first party would suffer from having accumulated a large number of wasted votes – votes which do not contribute to the election of an MP. That, in fact, was what occurred in the whites-only first past the post election in South Africa in 1948, when no seat was won on a minority vote, yet the United Party and its Labour Party allies gained 52 per cent of the vote and 71 seats while their opponents, the National Party, won 79 seats on only 42 per cent of the vote. Although there was some weighting in the size of constituencies, with the National Party gaining an advantage from winning in constituencies with smaller electorates, this difference was far too small to explain so glaring an anomaly. The main reason for the outcome was that the United Party piled up large majorities in rural marginals. There were no fewer than

17 United or Labour Party majorities above the largest National majority of 4,025, and the National Party had 28 majorities below 1,000 while the United Party had only 12.[10] Since the 1948 election put South Africa's government in the hands of the National Party, committed to a system of apartheid, the anomalies of the first past the post system had considerable historical significance. These anomalies would in no way have been modified by the alternative vote, since not a single seat was won on a minority vote.

In Britain, the Conservatives have won more seats on a minority vote than Labour at every general election since 1918, but they have been over-represented only in general elections that they have won, for example in 1983 and 1987. In elections such as 1945 and 1966, won by Labour, the Conservatives were under-represented even though they won more seats on a minority vote than Labour. So, in elections such as 1945 and 1966, the elimination of the minority vote would have made the outcome even more unfair, since the Conservatives would probably have been even more under-represented.

The Conservatives have won more seats on a minority vote than Labour, not because the electoral system is biased in their favour but because of the geographical distribution of their electoral support and because the main third force in British politics – the Liberal Democrats – happens to be strong in Conservative seats rather than Labour ones. After the general election of 1987, the Liberal Democrats were second in 261 constituencies, of which 223 were Conservative-held. After the 1992 election, they were second in 154 seats, of which 145 were Conservative-held. It is the geographical distribution of support which determines the proportionality of party representation, and the alternative vote does nothing to take the geography out of elections.

VI

A system closely allied to the alternative vote is the supplementary vote, advocated in 1993 in the third report of the working party on electoral systems set up by the Labour Party and chaired by Lord Plant. This system, which as Lord Plant admits 'is a majoritarian and not a proportional system', allows electors, instead of voting 'X' as at present, to vote for two candidates in order of preference.[11] If no candidate secures 50 per cent of the vote, the second preferences cast for all but the top two candidates are redistributed between the two leading candidates and the winner is then declared elected.

The Plant Commission's report suggests that the supplementary vote is an economical variant of the two-ballot system used for elections to the National Assembly in France. That system, however, produced a result in the 1993 elections to the legislature by which the parties of the right gained 78 per cent of the seats for 39 per cent of the vote. Still, under the two-ballot system, voters at least know who the top two candidates actually are, and there is time between the two ballots for the parties to negotiate. With the supplementary vote, by contrast, the voters and the political parties have no such advantage. Voters have to guess who the top two candidates are likely to be if they are to use their preferences effectively.

Apart from this, the supplementary vote is in fact closer to the alternative vote than it is to the two-ballot system. It would work similarly to the alternative vote where there are only three candidates. Where there are four parties in contention, however, as in Scotland, the system would work capriciously, precisely because voters have to guess who the top two candidates will be. Its capriciousness can be neatly illustrated by considering how it would have affected the result in Inverness in 1992 (see Table 3.3 above). Second-preference votes would only have counted if they had been given for one of the top two parties, the Liberal Democrats or Labour. Thus, a Conservative voter who preferred the Liberal Democrats to Labour but wished at all costs to avoid an SNP victory might have given his or her second preference to Labour, believing that only Labour could defeat the SNP. The consequence, however, might have been that Labour defeated the Liberal Democrats.

The supplementary vote is in fact a crude variant of the alternative vote. By introducing yet another electoral system into the debate, the Plant inquiry has served only to confuse the issue. It could, indeed, discredit the case for electoral reform by proposing a system which, like the alternative vote, would add a further arbitrary distortion to the first past the post system; for the supplementary vote shares with the alternative vote and the first past the post system one crucial weakness. Under all these electoral systems, the number of seats which each party wins in a general election depends not only upon how many votes that party receives, but also upon where those votes are cast. That is the Achilles heel of both first past the post and the two majoritarian systems, the alternative vote and the supplementary vote. They bring to elections a form of distortion which cannot be rationally defended. This distortion can be cured only by proportional representation.

VII

Although proportional representation has been a major topic of political debate in Britain for over two decades, there are probably more misconceptions about it than about any other political issue. The most important misconception, perhaps, is that which treats 'proportional representation' as the name of a single electoral system. It is not. 'Proportional representation' refers not to a specific electoral system but to an ideal or principle to which different electoral systems may seek to conform. There are in fact a large number of proportional systems which work in very different ways to achieve the common goal of proportionality, and which have very diverse political consequences.

In fact, only two proportional representation systems have been seriously recommended for Britain: the additional member system and the single transferable vote. Until the 1970s, indeed, the single transferable vote was the only system advocated by supporters of proportional representation. During that decade, however, many observers came to be favourably impressed by West Germany's economic success and political stability, which they contrasted with Britain's economic difficulties and its adversarial political system. Those who thought in this way attributed West Germany's stability in part to its system of proportional representation, which combines single-member constituencies with what is, in effect, a national list of party candidates, though compiled regionally. It was felt that the single-member constituency element would render such a system more acceptable to British MPs since it was more congruent with the culture of Westminster than a multi-member system such as the single transferable vote.

While the German system has not been advocated as it stands for Westminster elections, it has been recommended by the Scottish Constitutional Convention for elections to the proposed Scottish parliament (see p. 35 above). Under these proposals, each elector would have two votes: the first for a constituency member, elected by first past the post; the second for a list of additional members, seven of whom would be elected from each of the eight Euro-constituencies in Scotland. These seven seats would be allocated so that the total number of seats – first past the post plus list – for each area would correspond as closely as possible with the share of the vote cast for each party in the area, as measured by the list vote. The list, however, would be a closed one in that voters would have no control over the order of candidates on it.

There are two main difficulties with this system. The first is that, as revealed by various surveys of opinion in Germany, by no means all of the electors understand it. A survey undertaken by political scientist Eckhard Jesse and reported in *Der Spiegel* on 18 August 1980 is typical. It showed that only around half of the electorate were aware of the different functions of the constituency and the list votes. Only one-quarter of the electorate were aware that it was the party list vote which determined the level of party representation in the legislature. Many thought that the second vote was a second preference – indeed, it was for this reason that the Free Democrats, the German equivalent of the Liberal Democrats, performed so well on the list vote.[12] It would be better, in fact, under this particular system, for the list vote to appear on the ballot paper as the first vote rather than the second, with the constituency vote appearing in second place. This would help to dispel ignorance about the system by allowing its conceptual basis to be more precisely displayed. Nevertheless, the widespread ignorance concerning the attributes of the German system contrasts remarkably with the speed with which the single transferable vote came to be understood by and to gain the confidence of the electorate in Northern Ireland following its introduction there for local elections in 1973. It contrasts, also, with the sophistication with which the single transferable vote is employed in the Irish Republic.

A further possible problem with this system in the Scottish context concerns its creation of two different kinds of MPs – constituency members and list members. In Germany, there is no difference in status between the two kinds; once in the Bundestag, they perform similar functions. But that is in large part due to the special circumstances of German federalism. For in Germany, constituency work is the responsibility not of members of the Bundestag but of local councillors and members of the Landtage (provincial assemblies). Members of the Bundestag, unlike MPs, are not expected to involve themselves in constituency work. In Scotland, on the other hand, the constituency representatives will presumably be expected to have a constituency function.

Therefore, a difference in status between the two kinds of member would probably arise. Further, at current levels of voting, most of the additional seats would probably go to the SNP and perhaps also to the Liberal Democrats, the two parties most disadvantaged by the first past the post system, and therefore the two parties with the most to gain from proportional representation. If that happened, Labour and Conservative members of the Scottish parliament would bear a disproportionate burden of constituency work, while Liberal Democrats and SNP members of the parliament would be able to devote all their time to legislative activity. The difference in function between the two types of member might soon become very marked.

The fundamental difficulty with the German system, however, is that it gives too much power to the party machine. The elector has no choice over the candidates imposed on him or her through the party list. Party nomination will often be sufficient to secure election. Even if primary elections were instituted, these would, presumably, be confined to party members, a comparatively small proportion of the electorate. In Scotland, as in the rest of Britain, it might be felt that, rather than increasing the power of the party machines, it would be better to open up the political system so as to secure greater voter participation in the choice of candidates. It was for reasons of this kind that in 1976 a Commission on Electoral Reform, established by the Hansard Society and chaired by the eminent Conservative historian Lord Blake, came to the conclusion that the German system 'as it stands' was not 'suitable for adoption in Britain'.[13] The Commission took the view that it would be unacceptable for candidates who had not presented themselves directly to the electorate to be imposed upon voters through a party list. This could lead, so the Commission believed, to central domination of the nominating process. MPs, rather than being chosen by the electorate, would owe their election to nomination by party headquarters. Therefore the Commission recommended that the supplementary seats be filled not by a party list but by the voters themselves.

The Commission advocated the system of election used in Germany for Land elections in Baden-Württemberg. Under an additional member system of this type, all candidates for election would have to present themselves to the electorate as constituency candidates. The method of voting would be with an 'X', as in the first past the post system. The Commons would contain 640 MPs, but only three-quarters of them –

480 (although the percentage could be varied) – would be elected in single-member constituencies. This would, of course, mean that the size of constituencies would have to be enlarged by one-third. The remaining seats – 160, one-quarter of the Commons – would be allocated to the 'best losers' among defeated candidates. That is, the defeated candidates with the highest percentage of the vote would become MPs – as additional members – so as to secure overall proportionality in the relationship between seats and votes. There would be a 5 per cent regional threshold to exclude very small parties.

In order to see how such a system might work in practice, let us consider a simplified version of the outcome of the 1992 general election, in terms of the percentage of the vote gained:

Conservatives	42%
Labour	35%
Liberal Democrats	18%
Others	5%

Let us assume that the election had been held under the additional member system and that, out of the 480 constituency seats, each grouping had won the following number:

Conservatives	250
Labour	180
Liberal Democrats	40
Others	10

The proportional share of the total of 640 seats which each grouping ought to secure, based on its percentage of the vote, would be:

Conservatives	269
Labour	224
Liberal Democrats	115
Others	32

This means that each grouping would be entitled to the following number of additional members:

Conservatives	19
Labour	44
Liberal Democrats	75
Others	22

The additional Conservative members would be selected by placing in order, according to their percentage share of the vote, all those Conservative candidates who had failed to secure election as constituency MPs. The top 19 Conservative candidates would then become MPs as additional members. A similar procedure would be followed to select the 'best losers' from the other parties.

The additional member system has the virtue of preserving the single-member constituency system and also that of doing away with the need for a list of candidates chosen by party headquarters. Under this system, no one could be elected to the House of Commons without directly facing the voters. Moreover, the system spares the voter the need to learn the details of a new and unfamiliar electoral system. 'X' voting remains.

Unfortunately, however, the additional member system also has serious defects. It seems to give the voter some influence over which candidates enter the Commons as 'best losers'. But this appearance is deceptive, for a candidate's vote in a single-member constituency is less a measure of his or her personal popularity, or the popularity of the policies he or she supports, than of the popularity of the party to which he or she belongs. An unpopular Conservative will still poll better in Oxford East than in Ogmore and better in Edinburgh South than in Edinburgh East. Additional members, therefore, enter the Commons less because the voters want them there than because they have had the good fortune to be selected for a constituency in which their party polls well and in which there are not too many candidates competing for election. For, other things being equal, it is obviously easier to secure a high share of the vote in a constituency where there are only three candidates than one in which there are four or five. Thus, the 'best losers' are, in reality, selected not by the voters but by their constituency parties. The additional member system is in fact very much like a closed list system in which the voter lacks any choice over the candidate chosen by his or her party. The only difference is that the list is drawn up, not by national party headquarters, but by the local constituency party.

Thus the additional member system only apparently does away with the need for a party list; in reality there is a hidden list, which is formed by the 'best losers'. But the composition of this hidden list cannot, by definition, be inspected by the voter before the election. This contrasts markedly with the two-vote system used in elections to the Bundestag, which at least allows the voter to see the names of the candidates on the list. Under the additional member system, by contrast, the list is formed capriciously through the very operation of the first past the post electoral system which advocates of proportional representation criticise.

Further, the additional member system would encourage candidates with no chance of election as constituency members to stand so as to boost their party's share of the vote. The National Front, for example, might put up a candidate in every constituency in an attempt to surmount the 5 per cent threshold. One consequence of such a proliferation of candidates would be the election of more constituency MPs by a minority vote. These constituency MPs would then be even less representative of their constituents than they are at present.

One likely consequence of proportional representation would be coalition government. Tony Blair has criticised proportional representation on these grounds, because it gives small parties excessive leverage in the formation of coalitions. 'I have never been convinced,' he has declared, 'that small parties do not then get disproportionate power'.[14] In Germany, proportional representation seems to allow the Free Democrat tail to wag the Christian Democrat dog. In Britain, the Liberal Democrats would decide which of the two larger parties they would condescend to join in a coalition government. Blair's fears were realised in New Zealand when, following the first general election held under a proportional system of the German type in 1996, the small New Zealand First party decided, after eight weeks of negotiations and against the wishes of its supporters, to ally itself with the National Party, which it had campaigned against, rather than Labour, which seemed its natural ally.

Blair's criticism, however, applies to some but not all proportional systems. It would certainly apply to the additional member system, which does not allow the individual voter to signal which coalition he or she favours. But the German electoral system and the single transferable vote, to be considered shortly, both have the advantage that they allow the voter to signal coalition. The single transferable vote does this through the opportunity which it offers to the voter to distribute his or her preferences among candidates from different parties. The German system does it by allowing the voter to use his or her first vote, the constituency vote, for e.g. the Christian Democrats, and the second vote, the party list vote, for e.g. the Free Democrats, thus indicating that he or she is in favour of a Christian Democrat–Free Democrat coalition. It is for this reason that the Free Democrats have in the past used the slogan: 'a FIRST class decision; your SECOND vote for a THIRD force'. The additional member system, by contrast, does not allow the voter to indicate his or her choice of coalition, since there is only one vote and it cannot be transferred. Were Britain to adopt proportional representation, therefore, it would be important to meet Blair's criticism by adopting a system which allows voters to signal which coalitions they want. Then conventions might develop so that smaller parties indicate their coalition preferences before elections rather than afterwards. That, in fact, is normally the case in Germany. No German voter can have been in any doubt since 1983 that the Free Democrats would join in coalition with the Christian Democrats; nor, in the 1970s, that they would join in coalition with the Social Democrats. Where, under proportional representation, a party supports the government in contravention of its pledges, it can expect to lose electoral support later on. A small party, therefore, will be strongly accountable to those who have voted for it, and that accountability will be manifested at the next general election.

Under the additional member system, some constituencies will return two or even three MPs, and others only one, according to no rational criterion. This could affect the relative political weight of different parts of the country. If, for example, most of the additional members in Scotland came from the rural areas rather than from the cities, then the rural areas would gain extra political leverage. Moreover, the additional member system is likely to be unfair as between defeated candidates. In Scotland, if it were the Liberal Democrats and the SNP who gained the most additional seats, Liberal Democrat or SNP candidates who came third in a particular constituency would be elected as 'best losers' while second-placed Conservative and Labour candidates, with higher percentages of the vote in the same constituencies, would not become additional members and would not secure election.

These objections are not merely theoretical. The additional member system has in fact been discussed in the House of Commons. In January 1977, it was proposed in an all-party amendment for use in the Scottish and Welsh assemblies.[15] If, however, one considers who might have been chosen as additional members in Scotland and Wales, on the basis of the results of the most recent general election, in October 1974, one finds some striking anomalies. In Wales there would have been 14 additional members. Defeated candidates from Cardiff North and Cardiff North West, with electorates of 44,000, would have gained additional members, while Newport, Barry and Pontypridd, each with an electorate of 75,000, would not have gained any additional members at all. Clwyd would have gained four additional members, while Gwynedd would have gained none. Cardiff as a whole would have gained four additional members, while Gwent, Mid-Glamorgan and West Glamorgan would have gained only four additional members between them. This would clearly have altered the geographical balance of the proposed Welsh assembly. A similar anomaly would have occurred in Scotland, where all seven of the Conservative additional members would have come from the rural periphery and none from Clydeside.

The system would also, as suggested above, have operated unfairly as between defeated candidates. In Cardiff South East, a Labour seat, the Liberal candidate in October 1974 secured over 2,000 fewer votes than the second-placed Conservative, and yet the Liberal would have become an additional member while the Conservative would not. The Labour candidate in Carmarthen, with over 38 per cent of the vote, and the Conservative in Newport, with nearly 29 per cent of the vote, would not have become additional members, but three Liberals in Cardiff would have become additional members with less than 20 per cent of the vote, and a Plaid Cymru candidate in Aberdare would have become an additional member with 21.2 per cent. A total of nine defeated Labour candidates who would not have become additional members would each have had a higher percentage of the vote than the most successful defeated Liberal who would have become an additional member. Moreover, of the six Liberal additional members, three would have been from Cardiff constituencies where they had come third, while the Liberal who had come second in Llanelli would not have qualified.

These distortions and anomalies, pointed out in the parliamentary debate and in an article in *The Economist* which appeared shortly beforehand, tended to discredit the whole idea of proportional representation. Certainly, they point to an important weakness in this particular variant of the additional member system; but this particular variant is not the only one. It would be perfectly possible to accept the principle behind the Bundestag system or the additional member system while avoiding their respective defects. In the Bundestag system, the crucial weakness is the rigidity of the party list, which denies the voter any choice of candidate. In the additional member system, it is the anomalous manner in which the list is constructed. What is needed is a list system which is not totally rigid but which allows the voter some choice of candidate. That aim is achieved under the Bavarian electoral system, where the party presents a list, but the voter has the power, acting as a kind of appeal court, to alter the order if he or she wishes to do so. A system combining single-member constituencies with a non-rigid list might succeed both in accommodating itself to the cultural preferences of MPs, most of whom would be uncomfortable with multi-member constituencies, while also allowing the voter to use his or her preferences in the selection of candidates. A proportional system of this mixed kind offers perhaps the best hope of securing that wider support for electoral reform without which it is unlikely ever to come about.

VIII

The principle behind the single transferable vote (STV) was probably discovered by Thomas Wright Hill (1763–1851), father of Sir Rowland Hill, inventor of the modern postal system. It was elaborated by Thomas Hare (1806–91), an English lawyer who in 1859 wrote a *Treatise on the Election of Representatives, Parliamentary and Municipal* which is still worth reading as an exposition of the defects of the first past the post system and the way in which Hare proposed to remedy them. Hare succeeded in convincing the political philosopher John Stuart Mill of the merits of his system, and Mill gave it powerful advocacy in chapter 7 of his *Considerations on Representative Government*, published in 1861. From that time until the mid-1970s, STV was the favoured system of almost all advocates of proportional representation in Britain.

Indeed, Britain came very near to adopting it after the First World War. In 1917, a Speaker's Conference, set up to consider the shape of the post-war electoral system, unanimously recommended that STV be adopted for urban constituencies. But this proposal was defeated, ironically as a result of the opposition of the Liberal Prime Minister, Lloyd George – opposition which Lloyd George came to regret when the Liberals were reduced to the status of a minor party in the 1920s. Since

1922, STV has been part of the official programme of the Liberal Party.

STV is sometimes dismissed as being too complicated for electors to understand, and there are still some politicians prepared to use that claim as an argument against it. The system, however, is actually in operation in one part of Britain, Northern Ireland, where it has been used since 1973 for local elections and for elections to the European Parliament. (It was also used for the multi-member university constituencies between 1918 and 1950.) When it was introduced for local elections in Northern Ireland, this had to be done quite hurriedly. There was a short educational campaign of instruction in the new method of voting, with the aid of a cartoon character called 'PR Pete' who told the electors, 'PR is as easy as 1, 2, 3'. In the first local authority elections in Northern Ireland under this system, only 1.5 per cent of the ballot papers were invalid, and in more recent elections the figure has been lower. There can be no doubt therefore that STV is a perfectly feasible system to adopt for elections to the House of Commons. STV is in fact the only proportional system to have been used for public elections in Britain; and it is also regularly employed in various trade union elections, such as those of the National Union of Teachers, and for elections to other bodies such as the General Dental Council. It is used to elect the lower houses in the Irish Republic, Malta and Tasmania, and the upper house, the Senate, in Australia.

STV is essentially a product of mid-Victorian liberalism, whose fundamental aim was to extend the boundaries of individual choice. Accordingly, the system seeks not only to secure proportional representation between parties but also to widen the choice open to the individual elector. If the voter is to have a free choice, he or she must be able to choose not only between parties, but also between candidates representing different shades of opinion. STV offers the elector a method of expressing that choice.

Any party which seeks to govern in a democracy must be a broad-based coalition of opinion. MPs belonging to the same party will legitimately differ in their views on, for example, the European Union or Scottish devolution. Yet under the first past the post system, the voter is presented with one candidate from his or her favoured party whose views he or she may not share. An anti-European Conservative voter in Old Bexley and Sidcup who regards a Labour government as a national disaster has no option but to vote for Edward Heath. A Labour voter in Hamilton South, bitterly opposed to devolution, has nevertheless no option but to vote for George Robertson, one of the leading supporters of devolution in the Labour Party. There is at present much speculation on the precise division of opinion between Europhiles and Eurosceptics in the Conservative Party. The pattern of opinion will be determined, however, not by the voter, but by the decisions of Conservative selection committees, a small proportion of the electorate, in safe Conservative seats. It is here that the pattern of Conservative representation is decided. STV, however, combines a general election with a primary election, so that the Labour voter is able to choose between candidates representing the opinions of Tony Blair and Tony Benn, while the Conservative voter is able to choose between candidates representing the opinions of Kenneth Clarke and John Redwood.

Thomas Wright Hill, the inventor of STV, was a schoolmaster in the Midlands. He used to ask his pupils to elect a committee by standing closest to the boys they liked best. It would take time for the result to be secured. Some extremely popular boys would have so many other boys standing next to them that they had more support than they needed to secure election, while some less popular boys had so little support that it was clear they could not secure election and that support for them was wasted. The 'voters' would soon appreciate this, of course, and they would move around the playground so as to ensure that their 'vote' exerted the maximum effect. It is this principle which STV seeks to put into practice in elections.

To understand the working of the system it is best to consider an actual example of its use. The example chosen is taken from the Irish general election of 1992. Until 1987, only three main parties competed in Irish elections – Fianna Fail, Fine Gael and Labour. The Irish Labour Party is roughly equivalent to its British counterpart, although, operating within a more conservative political culture, it has in the past been somewhat to the right of the Labour Party in Britain, and, far from being a major party, has always been the weakest of the three Irish parties. Indeed, its total vote in 1992 – 19.3 per cent – was the party's highest vote ever in an Irish parliamentary election.

Fianna Fail and Fine Gael have been divided from each other less by the socio-economic issues such as divide the Conservatives and Labour than by historical memories. The parties originate from the two factions in the Irish nationalist movement which split in the 1920s over whether to accept the treaty with Britain, a split which led to civil war. Fianna

Fail was the party of the Irish nationalist leader, Eamon de Valera, and it is the more republican of the two parties. Since 1932 it has been the largest party in Ireland, and it has been in power either alone or in coalition for over three-quarters of the period since Ireland became independent. Fine Gael, by contrast, developed from the grouping which accepted the treaty with Britain and rejected de Valera's uncompromising claims.

In 1987, a new party appeared on the scene: the Progressive Democrats, led by an ex-minister of Fianna Fail, Desmond O'Malley, who had been expelled from the party in 1985 because of his liberal views on Northern Ireland and church–state issues. In 1989, the Progressive Democrats entered into coalition with Fianna Fail and it was this coalition government that went to the polls in 1992. The Progressive Democrats did not, however, field a candidate in the illustrative constituency of Longford-Roscommon which is considered below.

STV requires multi-member constituencies – constituencies each returning more than one member to parliament. The 1992 election was fought in 41 multi-member constituencies, 14 returning five members, 15 returning four members and 12 returning three members. The example below used to illustrate the working of the system, Longford-Roscommon, was a four-member constituency. The voting procedure is quite straightforward. Instead of marking an 'X' for one candidate as in Britain, the vote is cast preferentially, as with the alternative vote method discussed above. A vote in the Irish Republic is valid so long as there is a '1' placed unambiguously beside the name of a single candidate. There is no requirement to list further preferences. If, however, a voter's first preference vote cannot be used to help elect a candidate, either because the candidate for whom the first preference vote is cast has no chance of election or because the candidate has more votes than he or she needs, then instead of the vote being wasted, it is transferred to a second-choice candidate whose election it may help to secure. Under STV, then, the vote may be conceived of as a direction to the returning officer, asking him or her to transfer it if necessary, in accordance with the preferences of the voter, so that it can be of maximum use in helping to elect a candidate.

The first step in counting the votes is to work out the minimum number of votes which a candidate needs to be sure of election. This is called the 'electoral quota'. What would the quota be in a four-member constituency such as Longford-Roscommon? At first sight, it might seem as if the quota would be one-quarter of the total vote, but in fact a candidate can win fewer

Table 3.5 The results of the ballot at Longford-Roscommon, 1992 (seats: 4; quota: 9,062)

	1st Count	2nd Count Transfer of Reynolds' Surplus	3rd Count Transfer of O'Leary's and Sweetman's Votes	4th Count Transfer of Hogan's and Nolan's Votes	5th Count Transfer of Sexton's Votes	6th Count Transfer of Finneran's Votes	7th Count Transfer of Naughten's Votes	8th Count Transfer of Belton's Votes	9th Count Transfer of Connor's Surplus
Belton, Louis J. (FG)	4,769	+205 4,974	+18 4,992	+99 5,091	+576 5,667	+24 5,691	+705 6,396	-6,396 —	
Connor, John (FG)	5,154	+6 5,160	+13 5,173	+143 5,316	+27 5,343	+40 5,383	+1,612 6,995	+3,814 10,809	-1,747 9,062
Doherty, Sean (FF)	5,788	+336 6,124	+23 6,147	+100 6,247	+88 6,335	+795 7,130	+380 7,510	+289 7,799	+195 7,994
Finneran, Michael (FF)	3,261	+117 3,378	+7 3,385	+36 3,421	+43 3,464	-3,464 —			
Foxe, Tom (Ind)	5,585	+36 5,621	+36 5,657	+294 5,951	+414 6,365	+400 6,765	+1,104 7,869	+740 8,609	+1,121 9,730
Hogan, Martin (Ind)	459	+3 462	+11 473	-473 —					

Leyden, Terry (FF)	4,331	*+401* 4,732	*+20* 4,752	*+86* 4,838	*+124* 4,962	*+1,054* 6,016	*+562* 6,578	*+353* 6,931 · *+201* 7,132
Naughten, Liam (FG)	3,633	*+9* 3,642	*+9* 3,651	*+108* 3,759	*+25* 3,784	*+1,031* 4,815	*−4,815* —		
Nolan, Jim (Lab)	595	*+5* 600	*+55* 655	*−655* —					
O'Leary, Tena (SF)	160	*+5* 165	*−165* —						
Reynolds, Albert (FF)	10,307	*−1,245* 9,062							
Sexton, Mae (Ind)	1,160	*+119* 1,279	*+46* 1,325	*+175* 1,500	*−1,500* —				
Sweetman, Peter (GP)	103	*+3* 106	*−106* —						
Non-transferable		—	33	87	203	120	452	1,200	230

Source: Nealon's Guide to the 27th Dáil and Seanad, 1992 (Gill and Macmillan, 1993), p. 125.

votes than that and still be sure of election. Even if a candidate were to gain only 24 per cent of the vote, for example, he or she would still be sure of election, since it would be quite impossible for four other candidates to secure 24 per cent of the vote. A candidate would in fact be sure of election if he or she could secure just over one-fifth of the vote, for only when his or her vote fell to one-fifth would it be possible for four other candidates to secure the same vote. By the same process of reasoning, the quota in a five-member seat will be just over one-sixth of the vote, and in a three-member seat just over one-quarter. In general the quota will be:

$$\frac{V}{S+1} + 1$$

where V is the total number of valid votes cast in the election, and S the total number of seats.

In Longford-Roscommon, the total number of valid votes cast, which can be calculated by adding up the votes in the column of Table 3.5 headed '1st Count', was 45,305. If we divide this sum by five, we obtain the figure 9,061. Adding one gives the quota which is 9,062. Any candidate, therefore, who has succeeded in reaching 9,062 votes is declared elected, since it is impossible for more than four candidates to reach this figure. In fact, one candidate, Albert Reynolds, the Fianna Fail leader and Taoiseach – Prime Minister of the Republic – achieved 1,245 more votes than this. This surplus of 1,245 votes is now transferred to other candidates.

In the Irish Republic, the surplus is transferred by sorting all of Reynolds's 10,307 votes into sub-parcels, according to the next available preferences recorded on them for other candidates. A separate sub-parcel is made of the non-transferable votes, i.e. votes on which no effective subsequent preference is recorded. The proportion of transferable papers in each sub-parcel which is to be transferred is determined by the following formula:

$$\text{Number of votes in sub-parcel} \times \frac{\text{surplus}}{\text{total transferable papers.}}$$

Thus, let us suppose that 2,781 of Reynolds's votes were marked with a second preference for Doherty. Then the actual number of votes to be transferred to Doherty would be not 2,781, but 2,781 multiplied by the surplus, which is 1,245, and divided by the total number of Reynolds's transferable votes, which is in fact equal to his total vote, i.e 10,307. The result,

$$2{,}781 \times \frac{1{,}245}{10{,}307} = 336$$

is the number of votes which is transferred to Doherty. A similar procedure is carried out with other preference votes.

It might be objected that it could make a difference to the result of the election precisely *which* 336 votes are transferred from Reynolds to Doherty, since the pattern of later preferences in the 336 votes will depend upon which votes are chosen. In an election with a total poll of over 45,000 votes, the chance that the result will be affected by such a procedure is quite remote. Nevertheless, there is a more accurate procedure for transferring surpluses which is used in STV elections in Northern Ireland. This method is sometimes known as the 'senatorial rules'. Instead of transferring just the top votes in each sub-parcel, as was done in this election, each transferable vote is given a fractional value, and all of the papers in each sub-parcel are transferred to each of the remaining candidates at their reduced, fractional value. Such a method leads to the elimination of the very slight element of chance which exists in the method used to transfer a surplus for elections to the Irish lower house.

We may now resume our analysis of the count in Longford-Roscommon. After the transfer of Reynolds's surplus, since no other candidate has reached the quota, the votes of O'Leary and Sweetman, the candidates with the fewest votes, are transferred. Then, since there is still no candidate who has reached the quota, the votes of Hogan and Nolan, Sexton, Finneran, Naughten and Belton are transferred in turn. By that stage, Connor has achieved the quota and his surplus votes are transferred. This is sufficient to bring Foxe over the quota.

There are now only two candidates left in the count, Doherty and Leyden, competing for the one remaining seat. Neither of these candidates has reached the quota, but clearly further transfers would be pointless. Doherty is therefore declared elected, with Leyden the runner-up. At this final stage of the count it is possible to win election without reaching the quota. This is because the 7,132 votes of the runner-up, Leyden, and the total number of non-transferable votes, 2,325, which do not help to elect any candidate, themselves total more than a quota.

The count is now complete and Reynolds, Connor, Foxe and Doherty

are the elected members for Longford-Roscommon. The result is as
shown in Table 3.6. Two of the candidates are from Fianna Fail and one
from Fine Gael, and there is one Independent. There has in fact never
been an instance in the Irish Republic, even in the smallest, three-member
constituencies, of an election giving all of the seats in a constituency to
one party.

In the country as a whole, the election yielded a result which was very
close to proportionality, although not as proportional as the result which

*Table 3.6   Election results in Longford-Roscommon,
1992*

(a) Members elected	
Albert Reynolds (Fianna Fail)	1st count
John Connor (Fine Gael)	8th count
Tom Foxe (Independent)	9th count
Sean Doherty (Fianna Fail)	9th count

(b) Voting by party		
1st preference	Votes (no.)	Votes (%)
Fianna Fail	23,687	52.28
Fine Gael	13,556	29.92
Labour	595	1.31
Others	7,467	16.48

(c) Statistics	
Population	82,193
Electorate	60,709
Total poll	45,806 (75.45%)
Spoiled votes	501 (1.09%)
Valid poll	45,305 (74.63%)
Seats	4
Quota	9,062
Candidates	13

(d) Seats	
Fianna Fail	2
Fine Gael	1
Independent	1

Table 3.7   Distribution of votes and seats in Irish election of 1992

Party	%1st preference votes	% seats
Fianna Fail	39.11	40.96
Fine Gael	24.47	27.11
Labour	19.31	19.88
Progressive Democrats	4.68	6.02
Others	12.43	6.02

might be obtained by a national list system of the German type (Table 3.7).

STV seems complicated to explain. The task for the voter, however, is simple. All that he or she has to do is to mark his or her preferences on the ballot paper – an operation only a little more complicated than filling in a lottery ticket. Voters do not have to master the precise details behind the transfer of surplus votes, the most difficult part of the operation of the system to comprehend, provided that they understand the basic principle of the electoral system. In fact, as we shall see, Irish voters display a highly sophisticated grasp of the working of the system and are able to use their votes to ensure that they secure the kind of representation they want.

It takes rather longer in the Irish Republic to complete the count than it does in Britain – usually a couple of days. However, the process could be speeded up by the use of a computer.[16]

IX

The first point to be noted concerning the political aspects of STV is that a far larger percentage of the votes have contributed to the election of a candidate than is possible under first past the post. Of the 45,305 valid votes, all but those cast for the runner-up, Leyden (7,132), and the non-transferable votes (2,325) have been used to elect a candidate. Of those votes which did not help to elect a candidate, the 2,325 non-transferable votes could not be effective because voters chose not to indicate any further preferences; while those who voted for Leyden at least had the satisfaction of knowing that two other members of their preferred party, Fianna Fail – Reynolds and Doherty – were elected. This may be contrasted with the situation in the average British constituency where the votes of all of those who did not vote for the winning candidate are wasted. In a very extreme case such as Inverness in the 1992 general election (Table 3.3 above), nearly three-quarters of the votes were wasted.

Moreover, the two main parties – Fianna Fail and Fine Gael – are each represented by the candidate whom the voters most favour. STV has given the voters a choice between candidates, a primary election as well as a general election; and STV is superior to a separate primary election for two reasons. The first is that where a separate primary is held, as in the United States, the winner of the primary becomes the party's sole nominee. Supporters of other candidates, therefore, have to vote for a candidate who is not their first preference. Under STV, by contrast, the minority is not disenfranchised. In a multi-member constituency, voters can still support a candidate who may not be the first choice of their party and can hope that he or she may win with the aid of transfers from other candidates. Secondly, a primary election is open only to dues-paying or registered party members: enthusiasts, rather than the electorate as a whole. Under STV, on the other hand, the primary election is open to every elector who chooses to vote. It is this primary element which constitutes the distinctive feature of STV. It gives the elector a wider choice than is available under either first past the post or other proportional systems.

Let us turn again to the Longford-Roscommon constituency to see how the voters used the power which STV gives them of choosing between candidates of the same party. Let us look first at the 6th count, the transfer of Finneran's votes. It is noticeable that only 1,054 + 795 i.e. 1,849 of his 3,464 votes, around 53.4 per cent, were transferred to the other Fianna Fail candidates, Doherty and Leyden; 1,031 of Finneran's votes, around 29.8 per cent, went to a candidate of the opposing party, Naughten of Fine Gael. The reason for this was that Finneran and Naughten came from adjoining towns. Similarly, on the 7th count, of the 4,815 of Naughten's votes, only 48.1 per cent – 2,317 – went to the other Fine Gael candidates, Connor and Belton. More of his votes were transferred to the Independent, Foxe, than to Naughten's Fine Gael colleague, Belton. The reason is again to be found in the territorial allegiance of the candidates: Foxe, like Naughten and Connor, was from Roscommon, while Belton was from Longford. Reynolds also came from Longford, and one-sixth of his surplus went to a Longford candidate from another party, Belton, rather than to Roscommon candidates from Reynolds's own Fianna Fail party.

Thus, voters in Longford-Roscommon were using STV to ensure that they would elect a member from their own county even if he were from another party. This is particularly likely to happen in two-county constituencies, especially where, as in Longford-Roscommon, the constituency is a new one whose creation was much resented by voters in both counties who felt that they had little in common with each other.[17]

STV, unlike first past the post, ensures that the main political groupings are represented in every constituency. In Britain, it would ensure that the Conservative minority in Liverpool and Glasgow and the Labour minority in the south of England secured representation in the Commons. That would have beneficial effects on Parliament, since it would make the Conservatives more sensitive to the problems of the inner cities and Labour more aware of issues affecting voters in the more prosperous parts of the country. There would also be an incentive for candidates to stand for the Commons in the area in which they lived and which they knew best. At present, a Labour candidate living in Hampshire has to migrate to inner London or the north of England to find a safe seat. Similarly, a Conservative in Liverpool must migrate to the south if he or she seriously wants to win. In the Irish Republic, by contrast, local ties are vital, and almost every member of the Dail is a long-standing resident of his or her constituency and well known personally to many constituents.

Under first past the post or list systems, there are safe seats for certain favoured candidates, those who have been able to cultivate the support of candidate selectors, local activists and the like. Under STV, by contrast, candidates have to cultivate the favours of voters as well. STV is the only proportional system under which the voters themselves decide which candidates should receive the seats which a party wins. There are safe seats under STV for particular parties but not for particular candidates. A candidate can always be defeated by another candidate from the same party. Indeed, in 1992, 12 of the 32 members of the Dail who lost their seats were defeated by members of their own party.

Thus, contrary to an argument often used against proportional representation, STV would provide an incentive for an MP to be a good constituency member. Irish voters do not complain that the link between member and constituent has been broken by proportional representation.

The complaint is, in fact, precisely the opposite: it is often suggested that the relationship is far too close, and that members of the Dail have become little more than glorified constituency welfare officers – that they have to spend so much time looking after their constituents that they are unable to devote sufficient attention to the issues of the day or the scrutiny of legislation. Under first past the post, by contrast, there is no similar incentive for an MP from a safe seat. He or she may be a poor constituency representative and also inadequate at Westminster, but this would be unlikely to cost him or her more than 2,000 votes at the very outside. No doubt the majority of MPs are thoroughly conscientious; but nevertheless, first past the post does serve to protect the lazy MP. STV, therefore, would almost certainly yield much more effective constituency representation.

The primary mechanism which is part of STV can also be used for other purposes. In the Irish election of November 1982, Fianna Fail was split between supporters of Charles Haughey, the party leader, and his opponents. Fianna Fail voters were able to indicate their opinion of Haughey's leadership by their use of transfers. They could, as it were, 'send a message' to the party and, if they wished, indicate their disapproval of Haughey without voting against their party, something that is not possible under first past the post. It was in Fianna Fail's interest to put up both pro- and anti-Haughey candidates in a multi-member constituency. To put up just pro-Haughey candidates would alienate Fianna Fail voters who disliked Haughey. Similarly, in Britain, it would be in the interest of the Conservative Party to put up, in multi-member constituencies, both Europhile and Eurosceptic candidates, so as to maximise the Conservative vote.

In general, a party maximises its vote under STV by putting together a balanced list of candidates. This would help secure the election of female candidates, for a party which puts up five male candidates in a five-member constituency is immediately exposed to criticism for being male chauvinist. Thus, in the 1992 Irish election, 36 of the 41 multi-member constituencies contained at least one female candidate, and 20 women candidates were in fact elected, nearly one-eighth of the total membership of the Dail (166). That is a higher percentage of women than was ever returned to the House of Commons before 1997, despite the fact that the women's movement is far stronger in Britain than it is in the Irish Republic, which has a far more conservative political culture.

STV can be expected to favour candidates from ethnic minorities on similar grounds.

STV, however, can lead to intra-party competition, not only on the basis of locality or gender, but on a policy basis. In the Conservative Party, for example, the competition could be between Europhiles and Eurosceptics, and in Labour, between New Labour and traditional socialists. The outcome of such contests would provide a clear indication of the direction which voters believed their favoured party should take. While the mechanics of STV foster intra-party competition, it is the particular cultural configuration of the society in which it operates that determines the form of that competition. In Ireland, the competition is expressed in localist terms. In a different sort of society, such as Britain, it could be expressed in quite different terms.

Proportional representation can normally be expected to lead to coalition government unless a party wins over 50 per cent of the vote, something that has occurred in Ireland on only two occasions. STV, however, enables voters, through the pattern of inter-party transfers, to endorse or reject a coalition arrangement proposed by party leaders. In 1973 Fine Gael and Labour formed a 'National Coalition' shortly before the general election, each party recommending its supporters to give their later preferences to the other. In November 1982, although there was no explicit coalition agreement, Fine Gael and Labour voters indicated through the pattern of their transfers that they favoured a coalition between their two parties. By contrast, under first past the post, if two parties wish to combine, they have to agree upon a reciprocal withdrawal of candidates to avoid splitting the vote. But to reach agreement over which candidates should withdraw in which constituencies can be a time-consuming and contentious business, as the Liberals and SDP found out in the general elections of 1983 and 1987 which they fought together as an Alliance. Thus STV offers the possibility of a more cohesive coalition government than one that is formed under first past the post because it can be based on proven support in the constituencies. Under first past the post, parties allying together in government, as Labour and the Liberal Democrats hope to do, can find themselves enemies in the constituencies. Under STV, on the other hand, allies in government can also become allies in the constituencies.

In 1992 in Ireland, however, STV did not secure a coalition favoured by the voters. The politicians ignored their signals. The election resulted, after six weeks of closed negotiations between the party leaders, in the formation of a coalition between Fianna Fail and Labour. Yet, in the 24 constituencies where transfers from Labour would have to be to either Fianna Fail or Fine Gael, there being no further Labour candidates to receive transfers, only 19.2 per cent of transfers went to Fianna Fail as compared with 39.5 per cent to Fine Gael.[18] Moreover, opinion surveys held before the election showed that a Fianna Fail–Labour coalition was favoured by only 20 per cent of the voters. Among Labour voters, support for a coalition with Fianna Fail came fourth in their order of preferred governments.[19] The coalition government thus began without popular endorsement. It also ended without popular endorsement when, in 1994, Albert Reynolds resigned as Taoiseach and was succeeded by John Bruton, leading a Fine Gael–Labour coalition, without a general election.

This was the first occasion on which, after an Irish general election, a major party had continued in power but with a new coalition partner. The Irish system worked better during the years from 1927 to 1987 when Labour, together with the two large parties – Fianna Fail and Fine Gael – were the only parties to retain continuous parliamentary representation. During this period, elections generally produced clear-cut results. Since then, however, a political system broadly characterised by the existence of two large parties – Fianna Fail and Fine Gael – and one smaller party – Labour – has become transformed into a genuinely multi-party system with five effective parties represented in the Dail. Thus, a bipolar choice of government between Fianna Fail and a Fine Gael–Labour coalition has been replaced by a wider number of alternative possible governments. This has made the system much less predictable, and it is now less responsive to the signals of the voters.

Perhaps the greatest difficulty facing advocates of STV in Britain, however, is that the system has been used only in small societies dominated by localism, where party divisions are as much 'tribal' as socio-economic in nature. The experience of countries such as Ireland and Malta is not necessarily a good guide as to how STV might work in a large industrial society. To adopt STV in Britain, therefore, might be thought to be something of a leap in the dark. But it would be a leap many would believe worth taking in order to secure the undoubted benefits of the system in terms of the widening of electoral choice. For the greatest strength of STV is that it provides the kind of representation that voters want – whether good constituency representatives or efficient legislators.

It is in this sense a transparent electoral system, one in which the elected representatives will reflect the qualities of those who elect them. STV is a system which holds up a mirror to society. For that reason it has good claim to be the most open of all of the various forms of proportional representation. It is also the only form of proportional representation that has ever been used in Britain.

Yet the chances of STV being adopted in Britain for elections to the House of Commons are rather slight. That is because almost all MPs, even those sympathetic to proportional representation, are wedded to the single-member constituency which has become deeply embedded in the political culture of Westminster. Moreover, party leaders and the political professionals also dislike the system because the mechanism for a choice of candidates within parties serves to set one member of the party against another, so highlighting party divisions. STV, then, even though it may serve the interests of the voter, threatens those of MPs and of the political professionals. Yet this, for those who support STV, constitutes the strongest argument in its favour. For, were Britain ever to adopt STV, that would be the clearest indication possible that power had finally been transferred from the political professionals to the voters, from the politicians to the people.

4

Reform of the House of Lords

'The history of all former attempts at coming to close quarters
with the House of Lords question, shows a record of disorder,
dissipation of energy, of words and solemn exhortation, of individual rhetoric and impressive *ipse dixits* without any definite
scheme of action, nothing more substantial than dark hints of
preconceived plans.'

Edwin Montagu to Asquith, 9 November 1909

I

Most democracies have two chambers of parliament. Of 29 long-
established democracies, only ten are unicameral and most of these –
countries such as Denmark, Sweden and New Zealand – are small, homo-
geneous and tightly knit countries with a long history of consensus.[1]

The problem, however, is to discover how the second chamber should
be chosen. In a federal state, such as Australia, Germany, Switzerland or
the United States, it is not too difficult to find an answer. The lower
house represents individuals, while the upper house represents geographical units – the provinces or regions. In a unitary state such as Britain,
however, it is much harder to find a solution which can be logically
defended.

Britain's second chamber, the House of Lords, is the product not of
logic but of history. Its composition makes it quite unique among modern
democracies and one of only a very small number of parliamentary chambers which is not elected, either directly or indirectly. The composition
of the House of Lords in October 1996 was as follows.

Hereditary peers	767
Life peers	382
Law lords[2]	24
Archbishops and bishops	26

The total membership of the Lords was 1,199. Of this total, in October 1996, 80 peers, of whom three were minors, had not claimed the writ of summons entitling them to sit in the House of Lords, while a further 66 peers had taken leave of absence. Thus, the total potential attendance of the Lords was 1,199 minus 80 minus 66, i.e. 1,053. Of these 1,053 peers, approximately 870 attend at least once each session. The working House, usually defined as those who attend at least one-third of the sittings in a sessions, comprises around 460 peers.

Until 1958, all of the members of the House of Lords, except for the 26 archbishops and bishops and the law lords, were hereditary peers. In 1958, however, the Life Peerages Act enabled the Queen, on the advice of the Prime Minister, to create peerages for life. Today, as can be seen from the figures listed above, around two-thirds of the members of the House of Lords are hereditary peers by succession and just under one-third life peers.

The Life Peerages Act 1958 made two innovations: first, the creation of peerages for life, and second, the admission of women to membership of the House. This was followed by three very important non-legislative changes. The first was the virtual abolition of the creation of hereditary peerages. Only four hereditary peers have been created since 1965, one of them a royal peer, the Duke of York. Thus, since the 1958 act provided an alternative method by which peers may be created, one which has now become the norm, the hereditary peerage is becoming a closed and declining class. Consequently, whereas before 1958 membership of the Lords was the result of acquiring or inheriting a peerage, since 1965 the situation has been reversed. Acquiring a title has become the result of being nominated as a peer. Until 1958, membership of the Lords meant belonging to the hereditary aristocracy. Since then it has become primarily the outcome of political patronage.

Second, it became the convention for the Prime Minister to consult with the main opposition parties before creating peerages. Before 1958, it was customary for peers to be created mainly from the government party, except in the case of coronation honours. There was, in general, no consultation with opposition party leaders. Third, as a result the Liberals became entitled to peerages, although they had not been in government since 1922, except for brief periods in 1931–2 and 1940–5. Neither Harold Macmillan nor Sir Alec Douglas-Home created any Liberal peers, however, and it was left to Harold Wilson to nominate the first Liberal life peers. Since then, Liberal life peers have been regularly nominated, and so also, on occasion, have life peers from the other minority parties.

The 1958 Life Peerages Act and the new practices which followed have led to profound changes in the House of Lords. By October 1996 the party composition of the Lords was as shown in Table 4.1.

The intention behind the Life Peerages Act was to invigorate the House of Lords by enabling more Labour peers to be created so as to redress the party imbalance in the upper house – an imbalance which was threatening the credibility of the Lords as a legislative chamber. In 1955, there were only 55 Labour peers as compared with 507 Conservatives, 238 Independents and 42 Liberals. Because the main opposition party, Labour, had so few peers and the party imbalance in the Lords was so gross, few were willing to take the upper house seriously. Largely for this reason, the House of Lords was coming perilously close to fulfilling Bagehot's prediction that its end would come not through abolition but through atrophy.[3]

In consequence of the Life Peerages Act and the innovations which followed, the Conservatives no longer have an overall majority over all other groups in the Lords. They do, however, enjoy a large overall majority over the other parties in the Lords, and a large plurality over all other groups. For the Conservatives to be beaten, there must usually be a full turnout of the opposition parties, as well as a sizeable majority of the cross-benchers voting against them and, usually, a number of Tory

Table 4.1   Composition of the House of Lords by party, October 1996

Party	Life peers	Hereditary peers	Total
Conservative	143	319	462
Labour	96	15	111
Liberal Democrat	32	24	56
Cross-bench[a]	112	191	303
Other	18	77	121[b]
TOTALS	401	626	1,053[b]

[a] Cross-bench peers are those who do not take a party whip.
[b] Including 26 bishops.

rebels prepared to abstain or vote with the opposition. This does not happen very often. Thus, because of the relatively high number of Conservative life peers created, the 1958 Act and other changes have not ended, although they have abated, the Conservative dominance which has been a feature of the House of Lords since the latter part of the nineteenth century.

It is difficult to offer any logical justification of a second chamber so peculiarly composed. Indeed, no other democracy today has a large hereditary element in its legislature, while there are only two long-established democracies – Canada and Ireland – whose upper houses have a large nominated element. The best defence perhaps is that of prescription. The House of Lords is defended because it is there and perhaps also because it works, after a fashion. It is the product of evolution and not of deliberate choice. No one would dream of proposing a second chamber composed in this way for any of the new democracies in, for example, the ex-Communist countries of Central or Eastern Europe. It is, nevertheless, peculiarly difficult to devise a plausible alternative.

The illogical composition of the House of Lords does, however, have one crucial political consequence. Since the Lords lacks democratic legitimacy and therefore political authority it can never mount a determined challenge against an elected government with a majority in the House of Commons. It is, perhaps, largely for this reason that governments of the left have not hitherto been eager to reform the composition of the House of Lords so as to create a more rationally defensible upper house.

For it is the composition of the House of Lords that determines the way in which it uses its powers. Until 1911, its powers were in theory unlimited. It was subject to no statutory restrictions, although by convention it did not reject bills dealing with finance. The House of Commons had, from the end of the seventeenth century, insisted upon its exclusive privilege in this sphere, and the Lords had seemed to acquiesce in this claim, taxation being the prerogative of the elected chamber in accordance with the precept 'no taxation without representation'. In 1909, however, the House of Lords, with its large Conservative majority, threw out Lloyd George's 'People's Budget', objecting to the radical proposals for redistributive taxation contained in it. Two general elections later, the Liberal government had gained a mandate to reform the Lords and passed the Parliament Act 1911, providing for statutory limitations upon the power of the Lords.

Under the Parliament Act, the House of Lords entirely lost its power to reject bills certified by the Speaker as money bills as defined in section 1 of the Act. The definition is in fact so narrow that it would almost certainly not have included Lloyd George's 'People's Budget', which contained many provisions connected with social policy in addition to the strictly financial clauses. Once a bill is certified as a money bill, however, it can be presented for Royal Assent one month after having been passed by the Commons, whether or not the Lords has consented to it. The House of Lords retained the power, under the Parliament Act, to reject non-money bills, but only for two parliamentary sessions. If the same non-money bill was passed by the House of Commons in three successive sessions, then, after the third session, such a bill too would become law over the veto of the Lords. In 1949, the period of delay for non-money bills was, under the Parliament Act of that year, reduced to two successive sessions, whether of the same Parliament or not.

There is, however, one major issue on which the Parliament Act does not apply, and that is a bill to lengthen the life of Parliament. The Lords retain an absolute veto over such a bill, and the Parliament Act provisions cannot be used to overcome its opposition. In addition, the consent of the Lords is required for the dismissal of a High Court judge or law lord. The House of Lords thus offers some protection against a government seeking to subvert either the electoral or the judicial process. It thus performs the function of constitutional protection, albeit over a very limited area.

The common perception of the House of Lords is that it has few powers. In fact, its powers are greater than is usually thought, but its peculiar composition means that it is rarely able to use these powers to threaten government legislation. The Lords, admittedly, have no power to amend or reject money bills. But, as we have seen, the term 'money bill' is so narrowly defined that by no means every financial bill is certified by the Speaker as a money bill. Indeed, of the Finance Bills since 1911, slightly more (51) have not been certified than have (47). It would, nevertheless, be unthinkable for the Lords not to pass a Finance Bill. Non-money bills can be delayed for up to 13 months and one day after the second reading in the House of Commons. That would be sufficient to cause considerable nuisance to any government, since its last year of office would be wasted from the point of view of legislative achievement. But, since the 1949 Parliament Act, the Lords have rejected only one government bill on second reading, and that bill – the War Crimes Bill of 1990 – had not been in the government's election manifesto and had been subject, as a matter of conscience, to a free vote in the Commons. The Lords rejected the bill twice, but it nevertheless became law in 1991 under the Parliament Act procedure.[4] Only two other bills since 1949 have had to be reintroduced under the Parliament Acts: the Trade Union and Labour relations (Amendment) Bill 1975–6, and the Aircraft and Shipbuilding Industries Bill 1976–7. These bills passed their second reading in the Lords but were then made subject to wrecking amendments. However, both bills were manifesto commitments of the Labour government and were eventually enacted without further recourse to the Parliament Acts.

Two further bills of a constitutional kind met with opposition in the Lords. The first, the Redistribution of Seats (No. 2) Bill 1968–9, was seen by many as a gerrymander, an attempt to prevent a redistribution of seats that would disadvantage the Labour government. It was delayed by wrecking amendments, which were rejected in the Commons. The government, however, succeeded in circumventing opposition in the Lords and had its way in the end. The second, the Local Government (Interim Provisions) Bill 1984, abolishing the 1985 elections to the GLC, was amended in the Lords so as to negate its effect and the government responded by conceding the main point at issue (see p. 114 below). Thus, in the case of these two bills, the Lords showed that it still retained some role as a constitutional check and could act in a limited way as a chamber of constitutional protection.

The Parliament Acts apply only to primary legislation. They do not apply to subordinate or secondary legislation – orders, statutory instruments and the like – which governments need in order to make primary legislation effective. A number of such instruments are of a financial character and as such are the concern of the House of Commons alone. There are others which are not subject to any parliamentary proceedings at all. The remaining instruments, however – the vast majority – fall into two categories: those which require the approval of both Houses of Parliament before they can come into or remain in force (affirmative instruments), and those which may be annulled by resolution of either house (negative instruments). With regard to each of these last two categories, the House of Lords retains an absolute veto. Lord Cranborne, the Leader of the Lords, declared in 1994 that the upper house 'has a constitutional right to vote on any subordinate legislation. I do not believe there is any doubt about that fact.'[5]

The Lords could, in theory, by using their power over subordinate legislation, cause chaos to any administration. Yet this power has only once been employed since 1945, when the Lords rejected the Southern Rhodesia (UN Sanctions) Order 1968 – and that was for the purposes of political demonstration rather than to defeat the policy. On that occasion, Lord Carrington, the Conservative leader in the Lords, declared that 'it would be unusual – more, it would be unprecedented, I believe, for your lordships to reject this Order – Yet it is equally clear that this House would be within its constitutional rights in so doing.'[6] This action, however, a product of Conservative frustration with Harold Wilson's government, had no permanent effect since the Lords passed a virtually identical order shortly afterwards.

It is indeed precisely because the Parliament Acts do not limit the power of the Lords over subordinate legislation that the Lords cannot use their power. To do so could easily give rise to a constitutional crisis. The two houses enjoy identical powers in respect of most subordinate legislation, with the Lords having an absolute veto; moreover, the Parliament Acts provide no procedure for dealing with a conflict between the two houses. For this reason the power to reject subordinate legislation is, in Lord Cranborne's words, 'a crude, inflexible power, at odds with our role as a revising chamber . . . the exercise of this crude power could result in stalemate between the two Houses with little scope for resolution'.[7] Accordingly, the House of Lords has voluntarily abstained from using what still amount to very considerable powers. For, as a Labour peer, Lord Stonham, put it in July 1968, the government owes its majority in the Commons to the will of the electorate, but the permanent Conservative majority in the Lords is a result of biological accident and the use of patronage.[8]

The Lords has avoided conflict with the will of the electorate by observing in regard to primary legislation the so-called 'Salisbury convention', laid down by the fifth Marquess of Salisbury, Conservative leader in the Lords during the period of the 1945–51 Labour government, the first majority government of the left since the pre-1914 Liberal administration which had passed the 1911 Parliament Act. Reminiscing in 1970, Lord Salisbury declared: 'In 1945 we had to evolve a method of procedure. We had no previous experience and we had to make up our minds. The

Conservative peers came to the conclusion that where something was in the Labour Party manifesto we would regard it as approved by the country and we'd have Second Reading and amend it in Committee stage.... We passed on Second Reading nearly all the nationalization bills.'[9] The Conservatives in the Lords still regard themselves as generally bound by the convention not to divide on the second reading of any bill prefigured in a government's election manifesto and for which it might legitimately claim a mandate. Were this principle to be disregarded, the Lords could easily find themselves in conflict with the elected government of the day, a conflict which the Lords could not win, and which might invite abolition. The Lords could indeed be abolished at the government's wish, by the House of Commons alone. The Parliament Act of 1949, the last reform of the powers of the Lords, was passed in this way, under the 1911 Parliament Act procedure and against the opposition of the upper house.

Thus the House of Lords, because of its peculiar composition, is unable to make much use of the still extensive powers which it retains. There is some parallel with the wholly nominated Canadian Senate, which has very wide powers indeed, but powers which, lacking democratic legitimacy, it can use only very rarely. In Canada, as in Britain, it is the rise of democratic sentiment rather than statutory limitations on its powers which has restricted the role of the second chamber.

II

The peculiar composition of the House of Lords condemns it, inevitably, to a very limited role. In 1918, the report of the Bryce Conference on Reform of the Second Chamber declared that two of the functions of the Lords were to examine and revise bills brought from the Commons and to ensure 'the interposition of so much delay (and no more) in the passing of a Bill into law as may be needed to enable the opinion of the nation to be adequately expressed upon it'.[10] The first of these two functions is that of legislative revision; the second, that of constitutional protection. Yet the Lords, composed as it is at present, is ill-equipped to carry out either of them very effectively.

For a revising chamber to be effective, it must be able to ensure that the government of the day takes notice of its proposed revisions. The power of revision needs to be accompanied by real political power. But this is what the House of Lords conspicuously lacks. In a study of peers' legislative activity in the 1988–9 session, it was shown that this comprised one Act of their own initiation allowing patrons of members' clubs the right to drink between 2 p.m. and 3 p.m. on Sundays, and a few minor amendments typified by one to the bill privatising water which extended a prohibition on charging for water for fire-fighting to include the effluent used in fire-fighting training. In the 1988–9 session, the government lost 12 out of the 189 votes in the Lords. However, all defeats of consequence were reversed in the Commons.[11] While there are examples of government concessions to feeling in the Lords, and many lobbyists – especially perhaps charities, the local government world and university vice-chancellors – look to the Lords to present their case, conclusions reached by the Lords can be ignored by government even in areas where the Lords does enjoy special expertise. In March 1996, the Lords carried a motion hostile to the privatisation of the Recruitment and Assessment Service. The debate on the motion had been dominated by former permanent secretaries and ministers, almost all of whom were hostile to privatisation. Following the vote, a select committee of the House of Lords was set up to consider the issue. However, the Deputy Prime Minister, Michael Heseltine, told the select committee that the government intended to proceed and that the Lords' motion would make no difference.

The Lords' lack of political power also explains why they are capable of acting as a constitutional check only on very rare occasions. The Lords have exerted hardly any effect on the major constitutional issues of recent years – the reorganisation of local government, entry into the European Community, devolution or the Maastricht Treaty. In the case of the European Communities Act 1972, the government 'in their anxiety to pass the Bill into law ... had allowed no time for Amendments, even on a drafting point. To yield to a single Lords' Amendment, however reasonable, would mean that the Bill would have to return to the Commons and this would delay its enactment.'[12] Thus the Conservative Leader of the Lords and the Chief Whip in the Lords had to persuade Conservative peers not to propose or support amendments. The Maastricht Treaty led to the highest turnout of Conservative peers in living memory in 1993 to defeat an amendment providing for a referendum on the treaty by 445 votes to 176. It is in fact extraordinarily difficult to discover any major item of legislation, whether constitutional or not, since the Irish Home Rule Bill of 1914 on which the House of Lords has made a fundamental difference. Perhaps the one exception is electoral reform. For the House of Lords in 1917 rejected the alternative vote in favour of the single transferable vote; while in 1931 it rejected the alternative vote in favour of retention of first past the post. Apart from this, however, had the Lords been abolished in 1914, it is doubtful if twentieth-century British history would need to be rewritten.

With its present composition, then, it is difficult for the House of Lords to act as an effective revising chamber, or as a chamber offering constitutional protection. Perhaps the most effective work of the Lords lies in a quite different area, that of scrutiny by select committee. There are two permanent select committees in the Lords, on the European Communities and on science and technology. The former committee is widely regarded as providing the most effective scrutiny of European legislation in any country in the European Union. In addition, there are various ad hoc select committees. These have included committees on a Bill of Rights, on unemployment, on sustainable development and on relations between central and local government.

In fact, it can be argued that the main function of the House of Lords today is not legislative at all. Over 20 years ago, a former Leader of the Lords, Lord Windlesham, argued that 'the House of Lords should not attempt to rival the Commons. Whenever it has done so in the past it has failed, and usually made itself look ridiculous in the process.' Lord Windlesham believed that the role of the Lords was quite different. 'In any well-tuned parliamentary system there is a need and a place for a third element besides efficient government and the operation of representative democracy. This third element is the bringing to bear of informed or expert public opinion. . . . It is now one of the principal roles of the Lords to provide a forum in which informed public opinion can take shape and be made known.' 'In assessing the influence of the House of Lords it is worth distinguishing the influence that comes from the ability to delay legislation from the influence that comes from special knowledge or the representation of interests.'[13]

III

The valuable work of the House of Lords in scrutinising European legislation and producing reports on science and technology and on other subjects is not, however, sufficient to protect it from criticism nor to safeguard it against proposals for reform. For, in a world in which legitimacy is obtained by popular election, the House of Lords stands out as containing not a single elected member. The House of Lords, it has been said, represents nobody but itself, but it enjoys the full confidence of its constituents.

Today, the two methods by which peers are created – through hereditary succession and through nomination – are widely regarded as having little legitimacy. In the past, the House of Lords enjoyed legitimacy through the estates system. The Lords represented the land and the church, while the Commons represented the lower orders. Until the end of the nineteenth century, the hereditary element was perhaps accepted as providing a form of legitimacy different from that of the elected chamber – the legitimacy of the past, of tradition. For better or worse, however, the twentieth century has seen the rapid erosion of tradition as a form of legitimacy, and the continued existence of a hereditary peerage with legislative powers is now widely seen as indefensible.

Yet the introduction of life peers has hardly helped to confer that missing legitimacy on the Lords. Instead, it has had an important unforeseen consequence in that it has given Prime Ministers a vast extra seam of patronage to mine through their power of nominating life peers. It is often alleged that this power of patronage is abused to provide rewards for contributors to party funds. Certainly the proportion of those nominated to peerages whose companies have donated money to the Conservative Party is too large to be the result of mere coincidence. (This evidence is considered in detail in Chapter 6 below.) Even were this abuse to be corrected, however, it is not clear why Prime Ministers should enjoy an unlimited right to nominate as many peers as they like.

The fundamental purpose of the 1958 Life Peerages Act was to create extra Labour peers in order to correct the party imbalance in the Lords. Lord Home, Leader of the Lords at the time, declared that it would 'enable the socialist point of view to be put more effectively from the other side of the House'.[14] The Labour Party, and, to a lesser extent, the Liberal Democrats, are now highly dependent on the creation of new life peers for their continued representation in the upper house. Life peers of distinction, however, are unlikely to be in the first flush of youth, and in fact the average age of the life peers in September 1996 was 71. This means that the Labour and Liberal Democrat benches need to be continually replenished by the creation of new life peers, while, in the case of the Conservatives, the death of a hereditary peer is automatically followed by the succession of his son, thus contributing to the comparative youth of the Conservative benches.

There is no mechanism, however, by which Prime Ministers can be required to replenish the Labour and Liberal Democrat benches. Politically, indeed, the pressures are for them to reward members of their own party. For much of the time since the passage of the Life Peerages Act, Prime Ministers, whether Conservative or Labour, have nominated more peers from their own party than from the opposition – indeed, Margaret Thatcher and John Major have put forward almost twice as many Conservative as Labour and Liberal nominees – and, since Conservative governments have been in office for 28 out of the 39 years since 1958, the Conservatives have not been in danger of losing their comfortable majority over the other parties. Margaret Thatcher maintained that her lists of working life peers, rather than bolstering Labour in the upper house, should reflect the existing party balance in the House of Commons, the elected chamber. She was perfectly happy to use the argument from proportionality when it suited her party's interests. Her long tenure of the premiership enabled her to nominate 212 life peers – over one-quarter of the total number of 762 life peers created up to the end of August 1996 – and three hereditary peers. Of these, 95 (45 per cent) were Conservative, 57 (27 per cent) were Labour, and 10 (5 per cent) were Liberal, SDP or Liberal Democrat, the remainder being cross-benchers. There were actually fewer Labour life peers in 1996 (96) than there were in 1979 (180) when the Conservative government came to office. The party balance in the Lords is determined not by considerations of balance or fairness, but by the executive, by the government of the day. That is difficult to reconcile with democratic principle. Clearly, despite the Life Peerages Act 1958, the House of Lords remains an assembly permanently dominated by one party. Such a condition is almost as offensive as a state permanently dominated by one party.

For all these reasons, then – the hereditary element, the lack of any elected element, the power of patronage which the Prime Minister enjoys, and the permanent domination of the chamber by one party – the House of Lords is difficult if not impossible to justify. It survives in its present form primarily because there is no agreement on what should replace it, each of the possible alternatives being open to serious political objections.

IV

It is hardly surprising that there has been no shortage of proposals to reform so illogically constituted a body as the House of Lords. Reform projects have been numerous since passage of the Parliament Act in 1911. Indeed, one paragraph in the preamble to the 1911 act implied that it was but an interim measure and that the Liberals would reconstruct the House of Lords on a more democratic basis, declaring: 'And whereas it is intended to substitute for the House of Lords as it at present exists a Second Chamber constituted on a popular instead of hereditary basis, but such substitution cannot be immediately brought into operation'. This preamble, however, was put in primarily to placate Sir Edward Grey, the Foreign Secretary, who was somewhat obsessive on the need for an elected second chamber.[15] It has no effect in law and is the statement of an aspiration, not a commitment to action.

It is significant that neither the Liberal administration of the time nor succeeding Labour governments sought to give effect to that preamble. They appreciated, no doubt, that a 'Second Chamber constituted on a popular instead of hereditary basis' would prove far more threatening to the legislative programme of a government of the left than the House of Lords as currently constituted. Indeed, it has always been a fundamental problem for parties of the left that while they would prefer to retain the Lords' present very limited powers or even to reduce them, any rationalisation of the composition of the Lords would, by making it more defensible, encourage it to use its powers, or even perhaps lead to a demand for an extension of these powers. For this reason, reform of the Lords has never been a particularly high priority for governments of the left. It is partly because the left has never succeeded in resolving this fundamental dilemma that the only reforms of the Lords which have succeeded since 1911 have been of an evolutionary type – further restrictions on powers in 1949, the creation of life peerages in 1958 and the right to disclaim in 1963. All of the major attempts to reform the Lords have failed.

In 1948, there was a conference, followed by seven meetings of the party leaders, on the reform of the Lords. In an agreed statement, it was accepted that no political party ought to have a permanent majority in a reformed upper house. The party leaders, including the Conservatives, also agreed that 'the present right to attend and vote solely on heredity should not by itself constitute a qualification for admission to a reformed Second Chamber'.[16] The talks, however, broke down on the powers which a reformed House of Lords should enjoy, the Conservatives opposing the Labour government's proposal to reduce further the Lords' delaying power, a proposal given legislative effect in the 1949 Parliament Act.

In 1968–9, Harold Wilson's Labour government produced a complex scheme of reform, supported by the Conservative front bench, which would have greatly increased the Prime Minister's power of patronage. Partly for this reason, the bill met with considerable hostility from both government and opposition backbenchers. An unlikely alliance between Enoch Powell, who was against any reform, and Michael Foot, who favoured abolition, held up the bill in committee and it eventually had to be withdrawn.[17]

During the 1970s, it was the Conservatives, rather than Labour, who seemed most interested in reform. Following the advent of Harold Wilson's minority government in March 1974, and his narrow election victory in October 1974, many Conservatives were anxious lest a government of the left, resting on no more than 39 per cent of the vote, pass radical and irreversible measures opposed by the majority of the electorate. Britain, Lord Hailsham complained in his Dimbleby Lecture in 1976, and in his book *The Dilemma of Democracy*, was in danger of becoming an elective dictatorship.[18] It was the only democracy in the world with an unprotected constitution and a total absence of constitutional checks or balances capable of restraining the government of the day. The House of Lords, because of the way in which it was composed, was, Lord Hailsham believed, unable to stop a determined government of the left. A body composed of hereditary and nominated peers could not hope to stand up to the House of Commons; were it to make the attempt, the Prime Minister of the day had the power to swamp or even abolish a recalcitrant upper house.

The only force capable of curbing an elective dictatorship, Lord Hailsham believed, was an elected second chamber. Lord Carrington, Conservative Leader of the Lords between 1974 and 1979, was also in favour of a directly elected second chamber. In 1977, Margaret Thatcher set up a 'Conservative Review Committee', chaired by Lord Home, to consider the future of the House of Lords. In its report in 1978, this committee declared that it did '*not believe that leaving things just as they are should be considered a viable option*', and that the composition of the Lords was 'virtually impossible to defend'.[19] The committee went on to propose two alternative reforms: first, a wholly elected second chamber, and second – its preferred option – a mixed second chamber, combining elected and appointed members. This second option, however, gives rise to the difficulty that any vote in the Lords which was carried by the non-elected members would seem to lack democratic legitimacy. It would be easier for the government to ignore such a result than one in which the vote was carried solely by the elected members. It may be, then, that there is no half-way house between a totally non-elected chamber and a totally elected chamber.

However, so far as the Conservatives were concerned, these arguments became of merely academic interest when they were returned to office in 1979. The Conservatives in office did not present any proposals for reforming the Lords. For the danger of socialism being imposed by a minority Labour government had now receded, and any reform of the Lords which had the effect of strengthening it would merely make Margaret Thatcher's task more difficult.

The history of past attempts at reform shows that it is only likely to succeed when it is championed by a determined government enjoying full support from its backbenchers. It is sometimes suggested that all-party agreement is, or ought to be, a precondition for reform. But history offers no warrant for this verdict. The 1911 and 1949 Parliament Acts were passed by governments of the left after all-party attempts at reform had broken down. The 1958 Life Peerages Act and the 1963 Peerage Act followed abortive attempts at wider reforms which foundered on the rock of party disagreement. The 1968–9 attempt at reform, by contrast, failed despite cross-party frontbench agreement because of the opposition of backbenchers from each of the major parties.

Since 1979, the Conservative approach to reform of the Lords has been cautious and evolutionary. The party has been sympathetic to proposals to strengthen the legislative role of the Lords by, for example, establishing a committee system for legislation and even perhaps providing for pre-legislative scrutiny of government legislation. In 1992, the Lords established a Delegated Powers Scrutiny Committee to scrutinise the conferring of powers to make subordinate legislation. But the Conservatives have set their face against any wider reforms, either of composition or of powers.

Some Conservatives propose that the hereditary system can be reconciled with modern conditions by providing for the hereditary peers to elect just some of their number who would be entitled to vote, as with the Scottish representative peers elected, between 1707 and 1963, by the Scottish hereditary peers for the duration of each parliament.[20] A reduction in the number of hereditary peers would reduce, although not abolish, the Conservative majority in the Lords. It would also weaken the charge that hereditary peers sat in the Lords solely through the accident of birth. The argument, however, is self-defeating. If the hereditary principle is sound, it should be retained. If it is not, then there is no reason why hereditary peers should become an electoral college able to choose members of the second chamber. Such a change would reaffirm, rather than undermine, the right of hereditary peers to be able to decide who should sit in the legislature. In the words of the Carnarvon committee in 1995, if the hereditary principle is discredited, 'there is no reason why the hereditary peers should be treated as a separate order for the purpose of electing some of their number to Parliament'. Indeed, 'The hereditary peers are no longer a small, coherent social group, except for the fact that they sit in the Lords. After a few years they would find it difficult to elect representatives on personal knowledge, and would have to fall back on the advice of others, which would be likely to be political parties.' Therefore, the proposal for the hereditary peers to select their representatives would in the end degenerate into yet another creation of life peerages. For this reason the Carnarvon committee regraded the proposal as 'both unsound in principle, and impractical'.[21]

The Labour Party has, not surprisingly, always been hostile to a predominantly hereditary upper house. In its early years it called for abolition. In 1907, Labour MPs moved a resolution in the House of Commons declaring that 'the upper house, being an irresponsible part of the Legislature and of necessity representative only of interests opposed to the general well-being, is a hindrance to national progress, and ought to be abolished'. In 1918 and 1935, Labour's election manifestos called for abolition. In the years immediately after the Second World War, Labour in government turned its mind to reform rather than abolition. Indeed, by accepting the 1958 Life Peerages Act, the Labour Party has in effect kept the House of Lords in being. Had it not done so, the Lords might well have died of atrophy. The continued existence of the Lords is largely due to the eagerness of the parties of the left to accept the patronage which the creation of life peerages has made possible.

By the 1970s, however, the left in the Labour Party was gaining strength and once more urging abolition on a now unwilling front bench. In 1977, the Labour party conference supported abolition by a vote of 6,248,000 to 91,000. Nevertheless, the 1979 manifesto contented itself with a proposal to deprive the Lords of its power to veto or delay legislation. With Labour in opposition after 1979, the voice of the left again became more prominent, and in 1980 the party conference passed another motion calling for abolition. With the front bench also having swung to the left following the election of Michael Foot as leader in 1980, the party's 1983 manifesto declared that a Labour government would 'abolish the undemocratic House of Lords as quickly as possible'. Since its heavy defeat in that election, however, the Labour Party has once again abandoned abolition and concentrated on reform.

There is now a consensus, therefore, between the main political parties that Britain needs a bicameral legislature. But while there is agreement on the need for two houses, there is no agreement on how the upper house should be composed. This disagreement is in part a reflection of disagreement on the functions which an upper house ought to perform and the reasons for which it is needed.

Every majority Labour government, except that elected in October 1974, has been committed to reform of the House of Lords. It is hardly surprising, then, that the Labour Party is now, once again, putting forward proposals for reform. Labour's current perspective on reform is, however, quite different from that of the Conservatives in the 1970s. The Conservatives sought to reform the Lords because it was too weak; Labour seeks to reform it because it fears that it might prove too strong. The Conservatives sought to reform the Lords because the upper house proved unable to check Labour legislation; Labour, by contrast, after 18 years in opposition, seeks to reform the Lords because it fears that the inbuilt Conservative majority there would seek to frustrate its legislation. The Conservatives sought to strengthen the Lords so that it would be able to check an elective dictatorship; Labour seeks to weaken it to ensure that its programme meets with no hindrance. However, Labour still faces the intractable dilemma, noted above, that proposals to retain a subordinate upper house sit ill with proposals to rationalise its composition. For a House of Lords whose composition is more rationally defensible will be more inclined to use powers which the current House of Lords has allowed to fall into desuetude.

By the time of the 1992 general election, Labour, far from pledging aboli-tion of the Lords, was proposing in its manifesto to replace 'the House of Lords with a new elected second chamber'. This second chamber would be elected by proportional representation, and it would enjoy the 'power to delay, for the lifetime of a Parliament, changes to designated legislation reducing individual or constitutional rights'. This manifesto pledge was reiterated by Tony Blair at Labour's 1995 party conference, at which he promised 'a proper directly elected second chamber'.

The proposal for a directly elected second chamber has long been supported by the Liberal Democrats who, favouring as they do a federal system of government for Britain, would like to see an upper house representing the regions and nations of Britain analogous to the upper house of a federal state such as Germany. The Liberal Democrats' current proposals envisage a directly elected Senate of 225 members elected by the single transferable vote method of proportional representation (see Chapter 3) for a fixed period of six years, with one-third retiring every two years. Provision would also be made for 60 nominated members to be chosen by a committee of the Senate. In addition, MEPs would be allowed to attend and speak but not to vote. This new Senate would enjoy the power to delay all legislation other than money bills for up to two years. It would, moreover, have special powers with regard to constitutional measures: the Liberal Democrats are proposing the intro-duction of a codified constitution for Britain, and changes to that consti-tution would require a two-thirds majority in both houses of parliament.

With both of the major opposition parties apparently in agreement on the need to replace the House of Lords with a directly elected second chamber, there would seem to be the basis for a concordat between them. Labour, however, has begun to recoil from the implications of a directly elected second chamber. That is understandable. The Liberal Democrat proposal presupposes an embryonic federal Britain which does not yet exist. A federal Britain will take some time to be born, even if it were to prove at all practicable, and it would be difficult to introduce a federal upper house until legislation for devolution had been enacted. Thus a reform along Liberal Democrat lines could certainly not be introduced for some considerable time to come; and consequently it could make no contribution to resolving the problem which worries the Labour Party, that of a Conservative opposition in the Lords emasculating the legisla-tion of a Labour government elected in 1997.

Moreover, and more fundamentally, a directly elected chamber would probably prove a more powerful barrier to a government of the left than ever the House of Lords has been. The new Senate would have what the House of Lords has never enjoyed, a real democratic legitimacy, and in any clash with the Commons could claim that it represented public opinion just as effectively as the Commons. That claim would be strengthened were the mandate of the Senate to be a more recent one than that of the Commons. Suppose, for example, that there had been a directly elected Senate in existence in the 1990s, and that elections for it had been held in 1995 at a time when John Major's government was 20 per cent behind in the opinion polls. Then the Senate, with its Labour majority, could claim that it embodied the public will far more effectively than the Commons elected in 1992, whose mandate was now exhausted.

Because of the enhanced democratic legitimacy which it embodied, a directly elected Senate might well seek to acquire new powers. Indeed, were it to retain only its present limited powers, it might be difficult to persuade active and ambitious people to stand for election to it. Significantly, the European Parliament, after becoming directly elected in 1979, sought new powers for itself and was successful in obtaining them in two major amendments to the Treaty of Rome. By the Single European Act 1986 it obtained the power of co-operation, in effect a second reading on European Community legislation, while in the Maastricht Treaty of 1993 it acquired the power of co-decision, giving it a veto over some areas of Community legislation. The reformed House of Lords would probably seek to follow a similar path; but the government of the day and the House of Commons would be very unwilling to concede it extra powers, for to do so would open the way for a constitutional clash which would consume a great deal of time and energy. It is by no means easy to combine two directly elected chambers with a system of responsible government in which the government is responsible to the lower house. It is noticeable, indeed, that two of the strongest directly elected upper houses in the modern world – the American Senate and the Swiss Standerat – exist in systems based not on the principle of ministerial responsibility but on that of the separation of powers.

The difficulties of constitutional principle involved in creating a directly elected second chamber, together with the need to deal rapidly with the threat of Conservative opposition to Labour's legislative programme, have persuaded Labour to alter its policy. Labour now presents its policy as being a two-stage reform. The first stage, in the words of Tony Blair during his campaign for the Labour leadership in 1994, would be to disenfranchise hereditary peers 'within months'. This would be followed, before the second stage, by some method of elucidating consensus, perhaps through a Royal Commission. The wider reform embodied in the second stage, moreover, would probably be preceded by a referendum. Such a wider reform would, however, according to Lord Richard, Labour leader in the Lords, have to await a second term of Labour government, since 'the constitutional implications are simply too big'.[22] The cynic might suggest that the second stage would be allowed to drift further and further over the horizon, just as the preamble to the 1911 Parliament Act proposing 'a Second Chamber constituted on a popular instead of a hereditary basis' has been allowed to fall by the wayside. If that happened, the Lords would remain, in perpetuity, a repository for nominees of the party leaders.

The advantage for Labour of its two-stage scheme is that the first stage, the disenfranchisement of the hereditary peers, could, in the party's view, be carried out rapidly by means of a short bill. This would, Labour believes, assist a Labour government to secure its legislation against the peers, since the massive inbuilt Conservative majority, although not removed, would be considerably reduced.

It is sometimes suggested that the disenfranchisement of the hereditary peers would be a threat to the monarchy, since if the hereditary principle were to be discredited for one of the branches of the legislature, it could not survive as a means of choosing the head of state, the third branch of the legislature. But this argument cannot be sustained. For, although in theory the Queen is part of the legislature, in practice her power of refusing Royal Assent to bills is purely formal, last having been used in 1707. The Queen's role is quite different. It has been summed up, in Bagehot's famous phrase, as that of being consulted and encouraging and warning her ministers.[23] But she can also act as an umpire or constitutional long-stop during times of serious conflict. The functions of the head of state, further discussed in Chapter 7 below, are best undertaken by someone without any party history and so uncontaminated by political controversy. Moreover, constitutional monarchies on the continent function perfectly well without the backing of a hereditary upper house.

If Labour's proposals would be unlikely to affect the monarchy, they do, nevertheless, raise serious problems. One difficulty with the party's two-stage approach is that Labour would be asking Parliament to pass an interim bill when the outlines of the final legislation were still unclear. Parliament, and in particular the House of Lords, might well prove unwilling to pass interim legislation until it was given a sight of the final destination. In 1984, the House of Lords refused to pass the Local Government (Interim Provisions) Bill, which proposed in effect to cancel the 1985 GLC elections, substituting nominations from the London boroughs. This would have secured a Conservative majority on the GLC until the passage of the bill abolishing it at least one year later. The Lords declared themselves unwilling to pass the interim bill until they could see what was to replace the GLC. For, if the main bill abolishing the GLC did not pass Parliament, then the GLC would be permanently in the hands of nominees. The Lords therefore carried an amendment to the effect that the 1985 elections could be cancelled only after the final bill abolishing the GLC had become law. The government responded by revising its proposals so that the existing GLC was extended until abolition. The Lords, therefore, won their point, and indeed their action has been called 'probably' their 'most significant defiance of any Government over the past twenty years'.[24] It is perfectly possible that the Lords would take a similar approach to Labour's interim bill, declining to pass it until the second stage had been embodied in a published bill.

Such an approach might well meet with sympathy in the country. For the effect of disenfranchising the hereditary peers would be that the Lords would be composed totally of nominated members. It would become a house whose composition would be entirely the result of patronage – and the life peers are the product of just as arbitrary a choice as the hereditary peers. In some respects, indeed, it is more difficult to justify the life peers than the hereditary peers. For while the hereditary peers are the product of past patronage, the life peers are the product of current patronage, and the quest for a life peerage makes many people beholden towards their party leaders. Tony Benn has suggested that, for every life peerage actually created, there are 10 individuals who want one, and whose behaviour is affected accordingly. It is by no means obvious why the ability to defer to the wishes of one's party leader constitutes a better title to a place in a legislative chamber than the claims of heredity.

Labour's proposal for a purely nominated chamber would involve a quite unacceptable increase in prime ministerial patronage. In his 'Alternative Queen's Speech' in 1995, Paddy Ashdown, the Liberal

Democrat leader, declared that he 'would rather rely on the serendipitous opinion of the illegitimate progeny of past kings' mistresses than the appointees of a modern Prime Minister'. The fundamental objection to patronage is, in the words of the Labour Party's policy document of 1995, *Renewing Democracy, Rebuilding Communities*, that 'appointed bodies are not very public – far from it. Appointment is usually a private affair, secret even. The appointed do not have to tell the public who they are or what they have done. They are not exposed to public questioning or criticism before they are appointed. They do not have to get or keep the support of local people. People find it hard to lobby or influence them. They can't be held to account.' In a speech early in 1996, Tony Blair hinted at a 'better, more open and independent means of establishing membership', but so far he has given no indication of what this might be.[25] Until he does, Labour's proposals for reform of the Lords constitute a blemish upon its programme for democratising Britain. It would be unbecoming indeed if one chamber of Parliament were to be converted into the largest quango in the land.

The removal of the hereditary peers would not give Labour a majority in the House of Lords. Had the hereditary element been removed in October 1996, the party strengths in the Lords would then have been as follows:

Conservatives	143
Labour	96
Liberal Democrats	32
Cross-bench	112
Others	52

Of these life peers, just over half – 230 out of 435 – would be over 70 years of age. The Conservatives would still be the largest party and would retain an overall majority over the other parties, though not over all other groups together. Labour would have to create 48 peers to become the largest party in the Lords, and 122 to secure an overall majority. But, if a Conservative government were to be returned in the election after that, they would have a precedent for themselves creating a large number of life peers to regain their majority. The Lords would be in danger of being swamped after every general election.

But what is the point of a legislative chamber in which the government of the day enjoys an automatic majority? How can such a chamber act as a check on the government, or indeed display any independence at all? The House of Lords would become a chamber of professional politicians, of party eunuchs, and it would rapidly lose such public respect as it now enjoys. It is constitutionally quite unacceptable for the executive to arrogate to itself the right wholly to determine the party composition of one of the branches of the legislature.

V

How justified is the Labour fear that the Conservative peers would destroy the programme of a Labour government? The legislation of the Attlee governments of 1945–51 and the Wilson governments of 1964–70 suffered comparatively little from the attentions of the House of Lords. That was partly because, until 1950 and from 1966, these governments enjoyed very large majorities. But it was also because, during the early post-war years, the dominant assumptions were those of an era of consensus politics. These assumptions, however, have gradually broken down. The Heath government suffered 26 defeats in the Lords between 1970 and 1974. The Wilson and Callaghan governments between 1974 and 1979 suffered no fewer than 355 defeats in the upper house; indeed, out of a total of 427 divisions, they won only around 20 per cent. Between 1979 and 1995, the smallest number of defeats in the Lords suffered by the Conservative government in a year was six and the largest number 12. The Wilson and Callaghan governments, by contrast, suffered an average of between 70 and 80 defeats a year.

These figures, however, must be examined with some care. For the 1974–9 Labour administration, by contrast with the Attlee government until 1950 and the Wilson government from 1966, enjoyed at best a small majority of three, while for much of the time the government was in a minority in the House of Commons. Therefore, the assumption behind the Salisbury convention, that the government enjoyed the support of the country, was distinctly questionable. The Wilson majority government elected in October 1974 was in fact supported by only 39 per cent of the voting public. Moreover, the Labour Party was itself divided on many of the measures which the Lords sought to amend. This meant that the government was not always in a position to ask its backbenchers to overturn Lords' amendments.

The attitude of the Conservative majority in the Lords to a Labour government would depend, then, upon a number of factors. The first would be the political atmosphere of the country; this, after a period in which the gap between the parties was very wide, seems to be reverting to some degree of consensus. Moreover, if a Labour government were elected in 1997, there would be a strong feeling in the country that, after 18 years in opposition, it ought to be given a fair chance and not be frustrated by a non-elected chamber. The second factor would be the size of the majority which a Labour government enjoyed, and the third would be the degree of unity which Labour backbenchers showed towards the legislation of their government. It is difficult to believe that a Labour government with a solid working majority would have much to fear from a House of Lords which has come increasingly to lack confidence in the legitimacy of its legislative role. But, if the Lords did threaten Labour legislation, the party could then mobilise its plans for reform. There is a saying beloved of chess players that the threat is stronger than the execution. The best plan for Labour, surely, would be to use its reform proposals as a threat to the upper house so as to prevent the Lords emasculating Labour legislation. A Labour government has many more important things to do than wasting time 'reforming' the Lords.

If, however, the House of Lords is to survive in anything like its present form, with hereditary peers continuing to play a legislative role, it cannot remain entirely unchanged. Three reforms, in particular, are needed. The first is to impose an attendance requirement, so as to ensure that only peers attending a minimum number of sittings, and therefore clearly prepared to be part of the working chamber, are allowed to vote. The requirement might perhaps be attendance at one-third of the sittings in a session. Such a requirement would exclude the backwoodsmen – those peers, primarily Conservatives, who contribute nothing to the work of the house but who are nevertheless available *in extremis* to rescue a Conservative government.

The second necessary change is to enable more female hereditary peers to succeed to their titles and to take their place in the Lords. Until 1958, no women were admitted to membership of the house at all, but in that year the Life Peerages Act enabled them to become life peers. It was not until 1963 that female hereditary peers were admitted to membership of the upper house. But only a minority of hereditary peerages provide for women to succeed, and consequently there are only 16 women out of 767 hereditary peers. Of the 382 life peers, 67 are female. Thus, of the total membership of the Lords of 1,199, 83 – 7 per cent – are female. In March 1994, Lord Diamond proposed a bill to allow the first-born, whether male or female, to inherit. It was rejected by 74 votes to 39. The arguments used against Lord Diamond's bill cast some doubt on the claim frequently made by peers that their chamber is a unique repository of wisdom and sound judgement. The Earl of Shrewsbury, for example, was worried about those who wished to tamper with 'a system which has been with us since before the Norman Conquest'. In fact, 620 of the hereditary peerages have been created since 1832, 500 of them since 1918. Lord Mowbray and Stourton feared, however, that the eldest daughter of an ancient house 'might marry, shall we say, an American film star from Hollywood'. Even more 'appalling' would be 'if a daughter were to marry a Frenchman and the family become French'. The Earl of Strafford felt that their lordships were in danger of moving too fast![26] If the Lords wish to be taken seriously, they will have to accept the principle embodied in Lord Diamond's bill.

Finally, a way must be found to limit the patronage which the 1958 Life Peerages Act has made possible. In particular, some measure should be enacted to prevent a newly elected Prime Minister swamping the Lords with his or her own creations. This could be done through a statute limiting the number of peers who could be nominated in any one parliamentary session. Such a statute could be entrenched, by analogy with the provision in section 2 of the 1911 Parliament Act requiring the consent of both houses to extend the maximum duration of Parliament, so that it too could only be amended or repealed by both houses. It ought also to be possible for the parties to reach agreement on the relative proportion of peerages to be created each year, so as to secure a greater degree of fairness in their respective representation in the Lords. It might perhaps be possible for an inter-party committee to agree upon the precise division of the spoils. There is, after all, something of a precedent in the inter-party agreement on the proportion of party and election broadcasts to which each of the parties is entitled.

It is difficult to avoid the thought that more radical reform of the House of Lords is all too often an attempt to achieve other constitutional reforms in an indirect way. Those who seek to bring about proportional representation, for example, may believe that it could be more rapidly legitimised by being applied to the upper house rather than the lower –

although some of those who favour PR for the Lords oppose it for the Commons. Those who seek to create a federal Britain perhaps believe that they can speed up the process by constructing a second chamber that represents the nations and regions of Britain. Such a second chamber would, they hope, strengthen regional feeling in those parts of England where it is at present lacking. It is illogical, however, to seek to reform the second chamber before it is clear whether the Commons is to continue to be elected by the first past the post system, or whether Britain is to become a federal state or not. Reform of the Lords should come after these reforms have been brought about, not in advance of them. Before reforming the House of Lords, we must be clear what we want the upper house to do. Should it remain a house in which the bringing to bear of expertise is crucial, or should it become a real revising chamber or a chamber which provides constitutional protection? We cannot answer these questions until we have clarified the role of the House of Commons and answered the question of whether Britain should or should not remain a unitary state. It is for this reason that reform of the Lords is, as Ferdinand Mount has rightly argued, a 'secondary or consequential question', and not a fundamental one.[27] For this reason, a reforming government would be well advised to leave the House of Lords alone so long as it does not abuse its powers, which, on the whole, it has not done in the post-war era. For so long as that condition obtains, the House of Lords will remain too weak to do any damage to an elected government, although it will still be able to do useful work in a number of fields, especially, perhaps, in scrutinising European Union legislation.

'I am inclined to think,' John Stuart Mill wrote in *Considerations on Representative Government* (1861) 'that if all other constitutional questions are rightly decided, it is but of secondary importance whether the Parliament consists of two Chambers or only of one.'[28] For this reason the House of Lords – which Lord Beaverbrook was fond of calling the House of Make-Believe – should be allowed to survive by default so that we can retain the inestimable blessing of what has become in effect a unicameral system of government but with two chambers of Parliament.

5

The Referendum

Democracy is sometimes defined as a form of government in which the people rule. Yet in nearly all democracies – Switzerland being the main exception – the role of the people is primarily passive. It consists in endorsing or rejecting the government of the day at general elections. The people are given either no role at all or a merely minimal role in endorsing or rejecting specific items of legislation. That is perhaps particularly true of Britain, where the constitution knows nothing of the people and the central constitutional principle, the supremacy of Parliament, seems to legitimise an omnicompetent government subject to hardly any popular check.

Until the 1970s, the referendum was widely thought to be both unconstitutional and profoundly un-British. When, in 1945, Winston Churchill suggested that the continuation of the wartime coalition be put to the people, Clement Attlee, the Labour leader, replied: 'I could not consent to the introduction into our national life of a device so alien to all our traditions as the referendum, which has only too often been the instrument of Nazism and Fascism. Hitler's practices in the field of referenda and plebiscites can hardly have endeared these expedients to the British heart.' This argument, although it is still occasionally heard, is of course profoundly fallacious. Stalin, after all, rigged elections, but that is not an argument for abolishing elections. Hitler's rigged referendums offer no reason for abolishing the referendum as an instrument of democracy, only for ensuring that referendums are conducted fairly.

Almost all democracies today use the referendum. Indeed, there are only six democracies – the German Federal Republic, India, Israel, Japan, the Netherlands and the United States – which have never employed them at national level; and in the United States there have been numerous referendums at both state and local level. Most of the countries which use the referendum, unlike Britain, have codified constitutions. These constitutions generally prescribe the conditions under which referendums should take place. Britain, however, is one of three democracies – the others being New Zealand and Israel – which lacks a codified constitution.

In Britain, moreover, the central constitutional principle – perhaps the only constitutional principle – is the supremacy of Parliament. Until the 1970s it was argued that the referendum was unconstitutional because it conflicted with this principle. Parliament, it was held, being supreme, could not delegate its powers to the people. Moreover, whatever the people decided, they could always be over-ruled by Parliament. Yet, if Parliament is supreme, it can, surely, choose to exercise its supreme power by consulting the people. For, even though a clear-cut result in a referendum may impose a moral obligation upon government and Parliament, neither the government of the day nor individual MPs can ever be legally compelled to follow the result, or to embody it in legislation.

The principle of parliamentary supremacy, however, with its implication that Parliament can do what it likes, raises particular problems as to when referendums should be held and how their use is to be regulated. What, in a country without a codified constitution, is a 'constitutional' issue? Who, in a country in which Parliament is supreme, is to decide that a referendum should be held? Where there is a codified constitution, this will prescribe rules which give answers to these questions. The principle of parliamentary supremacy, however, is a discretionary one, inimical to the laying down of rules, since it implies that Parliament – or, in effect, the government of the day – can do what it likes.

In Britain, the questions of when a referendum should be held and how its use should be regulated have been answered largely tactically. On the European Community and on devolution in the 1970s, the majority of those who favoured the referendum did so with a view to defeating the policy. The same is on the whole true of those who pressed for a referendum on the Maastricht Treaty or the single currency. Most of them did so, not for the principled reason of consulting the people, but as a means of securing the rejection of a policy which they opposed. Where pressure for a referendum has triumphed, this has been less for constitutional reasons than because of political vicissitudes. In a country with a pragmatic and uncodified constitution, it is perhaps inevitable that the referendum has developed along pragmatic lines. Nevertheless, these pragmatic developments have given rise to important precedents, precedents which may now have a persuasive force that is difficult to ignore.

It follows from the fact that we do not have a codified constitution, and therefore have no distinction between constitutional and ordinary legislation, that fundamental changes can be made by very small majorities in the Commons which do not necessarily represent a majority in the country. In the 1970s, the Labour government, with the support of just 39 per cent of the voters, proposed devolution to Scotland and Wales. It was suggested, moreover, that the devolution proposals were themselves the product of pressure from an even smaller minority, the SNP, which had gained 30 per cent of the Scottish vote in the October 1974 general election. The outcome of the Welsh devolution referendum, in which devolution was rejected by a four to one majority, showed that even where changes are supported by parties with considerable support in the House of Commons, they do not necessarily represent the wishes of the people. For Welsh devolution was supported by the Labour and Liberal parties as well as Plaid Cymru, parties representing three-quarters of Welsh voters. Yet it was a policy totally unacceptable to the people of Wales.

It was for primarily tactical reasons that Britain's only nationwide referendum, on membership of the European Community, was held. When the referendum seemed to suit the interests of politicians, the 'constitutional' objections to it were ignored. They were ignored also in 1979 when it was deemed politically expedient to hold referendums on devolution in Scotland and Wales. Since then, no national referendums have been held, but the constitutional objections to referendums have been quite forgotten, and at the present time, all of the parties are committed to referendums on particular issues. That is a striking transformation in British constitutional practice.

The Conservatives are committed, with all-party support, to put any settlement in Northern Ireland to the people of Northern Ireland in a referendum. In the House of Commons on 28 February 1996, John Major declared that 'at the conclusion of the all-party negotiations – on the presumption that there is an agreement at the end of those negotiations – that agreement from the all-party negotiations with the constitutional parties, would be put to a referendum of the people of Northern Ireland. Only thereafter would it be brought to the House.'[1] The Northern Ireland Constitution Act 1973 already makes provision for a poll to be held on the border at intervals of not less than ten years, and the border poll of 1973 was held under its provisions. The Northern Ireland (Entry into Negotiations) Act 1996 adds a further general enabling provision for a referendum in relation to the outcome of the all-party negotiations. The Conservatives are also committed to a referendum on the single European currency. On 3 April 1996, John Major issued a statement saying the Cabinet had agreed that the Conservative election manifesto would include a commitment that, before joining such a currency, there would be a referendum. This would follow the passage of government legislation providing for adoption of the single currency and the normal rules of collective Cabinet responsibility would apply.

The Liberal Democrats were the only major party to advocate a referendum on the Maastricht Treaty. They now propose a referendum if the intergovernmental conference on Europe 'agrees to a new constitutional settlement within the European Union states'.[2] They further support referendums on a Northern Ireland settlement, on the electoral system and on English regional assemblies.

But it is Labour which now offers the most extensive commitment to the referendum. It proposes, in addition to a referendum on Northern Ireland once a settlement has been reached, three referendums during the first term of a Labour government. First, there will be a set of devolution referendums in Scotland and Wales in the first year of a Labour government, to precede legislation. There will also be a referendum on a strategic authority for London and on devolution in those English regions where there is a clear demand, as evidenced by the support of local authorities in the region concerned (see p. 48 above). The Scottish referendum will contain two questions, the first asking whether voters want a parliament in Edinburgh, the other whether that parliament should have tax-varying powers. Second, there will be a national referendum on electoral reform. For this referendum, the normal rules of collective Cabinet responsibility will be suspended. A Labour Cabinet will not be expected to have an agreed view on reform, and there will be an 'agreement to differ', as there was with the European Community referendum in 1975. Third, there will be a referendum on a single European currency, should a Labour government decide to join.

On this referendum, as with the devolution referendums, the normal rules of collective Cabinet responsibility will apply.

In addition to these extensive commitments by the three major parties, a Referendum Party was formed in 1995 by Sir James Goldsmith, the millionaire businessman, to seek a referendum on European unity. In November 1996, in various newspaper advertisements, the party announced that its referendum question would be:

Do you want the UK to be part of a Federal Europe? *or*
Do you want the UK to return to an association of sovereign nations that are part of a common trading market?

The Referendum Party is unique among British political parties in that it has only one aim, to secure a referendum on Europe. Once that aim has been secured, the party will disband. This commitment is explicitly written into the party's constitution.

The referendum, then, has become an accepted part of the British Constitution. It is likely to be used, not frequently, but sporadically as and when conditions seem to demand it.

II

Britain's only nationwide referendum to date was held in June 1975, on the question of whether or not Britain should remain in the European Community on the terms renegotiated by the Wilson government, which took office in March 1974. The result, on a turnout of 64 per cent, was a two to one victory for remaining in the Community, 67 per cent voting 'Yes' and 33 per cent 'No'.

The constitutional reason for holding a referendum on Europe was clear. Membership of the European Community involved a major transfer of the legislative powers of Parliament. While voters may reasonably be said to entrust their MPs as agents with legislative power, they give them no authority to transfer that power. Such authority, it might be suggested, can be obtained only through a specific mandate, a referendum. The idea that power is entrusted to the nation's representatives for specific purposes only is an important theme of liberal constitutionalism, which has its origins in Locke. 'The Legislative,' he claims in paragraph 141 of his second *Treatise of Government* (1690), 'cannot transfer the power of making laws to any other hands. For it being but a delegated power from the People, they who have it cannot pass it to others.'

The referendums that have so far been held in Britain – the European Community referendum of 1975, the Northern Ireland border poll of 1973, and the devolution referendums of 1979 – have all been concerned with whether the powers of Parliament should be transferred, either to Europe, or to Scottish or Welsh assemblies, or to the government of the Irish Republic. The referendums now proposed on a single European currency and devolution are, similarly, concerned with the transfer of the powers of Parliament, while a referendum on the electoral system would be concerned with an alteration in the method by which Parliament was chosen. Measures of this kind, if not strictly irreversible, are in practice extremely difficult to reverse. It may be argued that there is, therefore, if not a constitutional convention, a persuasive precedent, that a referendum is required before the powers of Parliament can be transferred.

However, the constitutional reason was not the only or even the main reason why Britain's first nationwide referendum was held in 1975. The Labour Party had committed itself to the possibility of a referendum on EC membership when in opposition, in 1972, for a fundamentally tactical reason: namely, as the only way of bridging the gulf between those Labour MPs who favoured continued membership and those who favoured withdrawal. The commitment to the referendum was, in James Callaghan's words, 'a rubber dinghy into which we may well all have to climb', designed to hold the party together.[3]

The European Community referendum, however, was seen by the Labour government as a unique event. The preface to the 1975 White Paper, *Referendum on UK Membership of the European Community*, declared, 'The referendum is to be held because of the *unique* nature of the issue.'[4] When the referendum was over, a Conservative backbencher asked Harold Wilson,

'Will he keep to his determination not to repeat the constitutional experiment of the referendum?'

The Prime Minister replied,

'I can certainly give the Right Honourable Member . . . the assurance he seeks.'[5]

A junior minister in the Labour government, Gerry Fowler, had emphasised the uniqueness of the European issue:

'I have made absolutely clear that in my view and that of the Government, the constitutional significance of our membership of the EEC is of a quite different order from any other issue. It is not just that it is more important; it is of a different order. There is, and there can be, no issue that is on all fours with it. That is why we say that this issue is the sole exception, and there can be no other exception to the principle that we normally operate through parliamentary democracy.'[6]

However, when, in 1972, Roy Jenkins had resigned from Labour's Shadow Cabinet in protest against the referendum commitment, he argued that a referendum would set a precedent and that there was no reason to believe that the European Community referendum would be unique.

'Who can possibly say that? Once the principle of the referendum has been introduced into British politics it will not rest with any one party to put a convenient limit to its use.'[7]

And within just eighteen months of the European Community referendum, the Labour government was forced, as a result of backbench pressure, to concede referendums on devolution to Scotland and Wales: for without such a concession, Parliament would not have passed the devolution legislation. As with the European Community referendum, the referendums on devolution were proposed to heal a split in the Labour Party; but while the European Community referendum was proposed by the government, the devolution referendums were forced on the government by dissident backbenchers.

The first devolution bill, introduced into Parliament in December 1976, linked Scotland and Wales together; it had to be withdrawn in March 1977, after a guillotine motion failed. During the parliamentary proceedings on this first bill, MPs opposed to devolution in Wales but willing to countenance it in Scotland if there were sufficient demand for it pressed for a referendum. This would enable them to defeat devolution in Wales while allowing Scottish devolution to reach the statute book. Thus the passage of the referendum amendment enabled dissident Labour backbenchers to vote for the devolution legislation while planning to speak against it in the referendum campaign. Malcolm Rifkind, at that time a supporter of devolution, declared it to be 'a unique constitutional matter that this Parliament is likely to put on the statute book a Bill in which it does not believe,'[8] while Enoch Powell, in a speech at Bexhill on 25 November 1977, called it an event without precedent in the long history of Parliament . . . that members openly and publicly declaring themselves opposed to the legislation and bringing forward in debate what seemed to them cogent reasons why it must prove disastrous, voted nevertheless for the legislation and for a guillotine, with the express intention that after the minimum of debate the Bill should be submitted to a referendum of the electorate, in which they would hope and strive to secure its rejection.

Following the abandonment of the first devolution bill, separate bills for Scotland and Wales were introduced in 1977, and these received the Royal Assent in 1978. During their parliamentary passage, however, a further amendment was passed against the government's wishes imposing a qualified majority requirement for devolution to come into effect. Not only would there have to be a majority of voters in Scotland and Wales in favour, but 40 per cent of the electorates – of those eligible to vote – in Scotland and Wales would have to support devolution if the assemblies were to come into existence. It was this provision which was to cause the defeat of devolution in Scotland.

The devolution referendums were held on 1 March 1979. In Wales, the outcome was a devastating defeat for devolution by a majority of four to one. On a turnout of 59 per cent, 80 per cent voted against the Wales Act, and only 20 per cent for it. In Scotland, there was a narrow majority for devolution, but it fell far short of the 40 per cent requirement. On a turnout of 64 per cent, 52 per cent voted 'Yes' and 48 per cent 'No'. Thus the percentage voting 'Yes' was only 33 per cent of the electorate. The Scotland and Wales Acts were, accordingly, repealed by the Conservative government which took office in May 1979.

There has been one other referendum in Britain: the Northern Ireland border poll held on 8 March 1973. In 1949, after the Irish Free State left the Commonwealth and became a republic, Parliament had passed the Ireland Act. This had declared that there would be no change in the constitutional status of Northern Ireland without the consent of the Northern Ireland parliament, Stormont, a principle first laid down in the Government of Ireland Act 1920. In 1972, however, Stormont was abolished by the British government and some alternative means of testing opinion in Northern Ireland was needed. Westminster accordingly provided, in the Northern Ireland Constitution Act 1973, for referendums in Northern Ireland at intervals of not less than ten years, and declared that there would be no change in Northern Ireland's constitutional status without the consent of the people of Northern Ireland as expressed in a referendum. The referendum thus became an intended substitute for Northern Ireland's local parliament.

However, the first border poll, in 1973, was also the only one. It was boycotted by the nationalist community, and so of those voting (the turnout was 59 per cent), 99 per cent favoured Northern Ireland remaining part of the United Kingdom, while only 1 per cent favoured Northern Ireland being joined with the Republic of Ireland outside the United Kingdom. Thus 58 per cent of the total electorate voted to remain part of the UK. Perhaps because of the nationalist boycott, however, the border poll was not repeated in 1983 or 1993.

III

It can be seen that referendums have been held on constitutional issues on which the party system did not work effectively because the government of the day was internally divided and because opinion in the country did not follow party lines. In the general election of 1970, the last before Britain's entry into the European Community in 1973, all three main parties had favoured British entry. It was thus impossible for an elector opposed to British entry to use his or her vote as an indicator of his or her opinion on the question. Edward Heath declared at a press conference on 2 June 1970, shortly before the general election, 'that you could not possibly take this country into the Common Market if the majority of the people were against it, but this is handled through the Parliamentary system'. Heath did not, however, explain how 'the Parliamentary system' would necessarily reflect public opinion when all three parties favoured entry. Admittedly, the Conservatives offered their MPs a free vote on the principle of entry, but there was nevertheless great informal pressure on Conservative MPs to support it.

In the European Community referendum of 1975, Harold Wilson agreed to suspend the convention of collective responsibility for the period of the campaign. This meant that seven dissident Cabinet ministers, including Michael Foot and Tony Benn, had full freedom to speak and campaign against Britain's continued membership outside Parliament, though not within the House of Commons itself. Tony Blair has indicated that he too would suspend collective responsibility for Labour's proposed referendum on electoral reform, though not for the referendums on devolution or a single European currency. The suspension of collective responsibility does indeed seem to follow from the logic of the referendum. For referendums are generally held when parties are divided, to allow the people to make a decision on an issue after an informed debate. If one side in that debate is denied some of its most respected supporters, because these supporters happen to be in the Cabinet, then the process of debate is being stifled, which is contrary to the basic purpose of the referendum.

The Northern Ireland border poll was an attempt to take the border issue out of Northern Ireland politics, by demonstrating that there was an overwhelming majority in favour of the maintenance of the Union. If, so it was suggested, the border question could be decided by a referendum, this would focus the minds of local politicians on the need to reach a political accommodation, and perhaps the tribal divide could be bridged.

But the fact that the party system is not working well is not the only reason for holding referendums. For there are some issues where, even when the party system is functioning effectively or when the major parties are in agreement, a referendum is necessary so that the policy in question can secure legitimacy. That, for example, is the reason why a referendum is proposed in Northern Ireland following the achievement of a political settlement there. Such a settlement would almost certainly be supported by all of the major parties in Britain, and also by at least one of the parties representing each of the two communities in Northern Ireland. Nevertheless, given the history of rejection and continuing struggle which has characterised previous attempts to reach a comprehensive settlement in Northern Ireland, a new settlement would probably not be seen as legitimate without higher-level validation or endorsement by the people as a whole.

Issues involving the transfer of the powers of Parliament, or an alteration of the method by which Parliament is elected, are rightly seen as fundamental decisions which should not be lightly made. Nor, once made, should they be lightly reversed. France provides a modern case history and a warning. The French electoral system has been changed very frequently in the twentieth century – in the post-war period alone, in 1951, 1958, 1985 and 1986. In 1985, François Mitterrand altered the method of election to the National Assembly from the two-ballot system to one of proportional representation, for what were suspected to be partisan motives, namely a desire to fragment the right. In 1986 a right-wing government under Jacques Chirac was narrowly returned in the legislative elections and promptly restored the two-ballot system. Such reversals serve only to undermine the legitimacy of the political system. Since the electoral system affects the future prospects of the political parties, the parties cannot be seen as impartial participants in the debate. There is a need for a disinterested decision to be made, a decision as to what is best for the country rather than what is best for the political parties, and that decision is best made by the electors themselves in a referendum.

A final and perhaps the most basic reason for calling a referendum on such fundamental issues is that adduced by Locke: namely, that on such issues, sovereignty ought to lie not with the parties but with the people; and that without their endorsement such fundamental changes should not be made.

IV

Britain's experience with referendums, if limited, has on the whole been fortunate. The referendum on the European Community settled the question of Britain's membership for two decades, and was perhaps the only way in which it could have been settled. 'It means,' claimed Harold Wilson, 'that 14 years of national argument are over.'[9] Tony Benn, who had advocated a 'No' vote, declared: 'I have just been in receipt of a very big message from the British people. I read it loud and clear ... By an overwhelming majority the British people have voted to stay in and I am sure that everybody would want to accept that. That has been the principle of all of us who have advocated the Referendum.'[10] However, the question was not accepted as being settled for very long. Benn's statesmanlike sentiments of 1975 did not prevent him from persuading the Labour party conference in 1980 to commit itself to withdrawal from the Community without a further referendum; and this commitment duly appeared in Labour's election manifesto in 1983.

There are further paradoxes in the European Community referendum. It was proposed almost entirely by those hostile to Britain's membership; yet the outcome proved to be a massive endorsement of Britain's European commitment. The referendum was adopted by Labour as a device to hold the party together; yet it is at least arguable that the contacts made during the referendum campaign between Labour pro-Europeans, such as Roy Jenkins and Shirley Williams, and Liberals such as David Steel were a crucial preparation for the split in the Labour Party in 1981 and the formation of the Liberal–SDP Alliance. For there were many on the pro-European right within the Labour Party who felt, during the campaign, that they had more in common with Liberals than they did with their parliamentary colleagues on the Labour left. The referendum worked not as a device to hold Labour together but as a means towards disrupting the British party system.

The outcome of the Welsh referendum served to refute the theory that a general election provides a specific mandate for a government to pursue the policies in its election manifesto. Welsh devolution had been supported by three of the four parties competing in Wales – Labour, the Liberals and Plaid Cymru, parties which had together gained 75 per cent of the vote in the October 1974 general election preceding the referendum; yet only one in five Welsh voters could be found to endorse it. That illustrates a crucial weakness in the theory of party government, one best summarised in the words of the great constitutional lawyer A. V. Dicey: 'The judge who should direct a jury that they could not properly give a verdict upon a most difficult case, unless they at the same time gave a verdict on twenty others as difficult, would not be allowed to remain a day longer upon the Bench. But the behaviour which would argue madness in a judge when asking for the verdict of a jury, is considered the wisdom or astuteness of politicians when appealing to the verdict of the country.'[11]

The outcome of the Scottish referendum was far less clear-cut, and Scottish advocates of devolution claimed that they were cheated by the 40 per cent rule. Yet the verdict of 1979 was accepted with surprisingly little resentment in Scotland. Part of the reason for this was that the case for devolution in Scotland had rested strongly on the claim that the Scottish people were clamouring for it, and that if it were not conceded the SNP would benefit, leading to demands for separation. It was this argument which convinced many MPs who were otherwise lukewarm about devolution. The 40 per cent proposal was intended to test the strength of the demand in Scotland. When the referendum result showed that Scottish opinion was fairly evenly divided on devolution, the small 'Yes' majority carried little political weight because it confounded earlier judgements of the strength of the demand in Scotland.

The devolution referendums, like the European Community referendum, were proposed by Labour largely for internal party purposes. Yet just as the European Community referendum may have prepared the way for the split in the Labour Party, so the failure of devolution in Scotland helped to cause Labour's ejection from government. For, shortly after the devolution referendums, the Labour government was defeated by one vote in a no-confidence motion in which the SNP joined with the Conservatives, and Labour was forced to go to the country in highly unfavourable circumstances.

These referendums were held at a time when the Labour government was deeply unpopular following the public sector strikes of the 'Winter of Discontent'. It may well be, therefore, that voters in Scotland and Wales used the referendums to show their disapproval of the Labour government rather than to show their disapproval of devolution. Similarly, in the European Community referendum, all three party leaderships had favoured a 'Yes' vote, the 'No' campaign seeming to be dominated by extremists such as Tony Benn, Enoch Powell and the Reverend Ian Paisley; in the circumstances, the referendum vote may have been as much a vote for moderation as it was for Europe. Both possibilities illustrate a serious problem with the use of referendums. Voters will often be unwilling to dissociate their stance on a particular measure from their attitude towards the government. So an issue-specific referendum can easily become a popular plebiscite on the fate of the government, a kind of national by-election.

Under a constitution where the calling of a referendum is discretionary, there is bound to be some problem in disentangling opposition to a particular policy from opposition to the government which has, after all, chosen to call the referendum. Where it is known that an unpopular government is committed to a particular outcome, voters may well wish to punish the government even at the cost of defeating a policy which they support. In France in 1969, President de Gaulle called a discretionary referendum on regional reform and reform of the Senate, threatening to resign if defeated. During the earlier years of the Fifth Republic, such a threat had persuaded many sceptics to vote for his proposals, since de Gaulle was seen to be indispensable in solving the Algerian problem. By 1969, however, de Gaulle was widely thought to have outstayed his welcome, and the referendum became a plebiscite on the President: a plebiscite which he lost by 56 per cent to 44 per cent. Having lost the referendum, de Gaulle resigned immediately as he had promised. Thus the referendum had become a means of toppling an unpopular political leader.

The Northern Ireland border poll was perhaps the least valuable of the referendums which have been held in Britain. It may have been of use as a propaganda exercise abroad, to demonstrate that the continued existence of the border was in accord with the principle of self-determination. But it could do little on its own to resolve the complex problems of Northern Ireland. That there was a unionist majority in Northern Ireland would be known to anyone who bothered to study the demographic distribution of the population between Protestant and Catholic in the province. Indeed, the border had been drawn in 1920 precisely to ensure that there was a solid unionist majority in that portion of Ireland which was to remain part of the United Kingdom. Therefore a referendum based on the principle of self-determination would be of little help. The problems of Northern Ireland are to be solved not by drawing new lines on a map, nor by simply reaffirming the 1920 boundary, but by developing relationships of consent both inside and outside the province. This involves producing political arrangements which are acceptable to both majority and minority community alike. The border poll made no contribution at all towards producing such political arrangements.

The referendum, moreover, has not permanently settled any of the matters upon which voters were called to express their opinions. Perhaps there is no device which can do that; for, as Disraeli once said, finality is not the language of politics. The issues of British membership of the European Union, of devolution to Scotland and Wales and of the status and government of Northern Ireland are as alive and contentious in the 1990s as they were in the 1970s when the referendums were held. Where, as in Northern Ireland, the parties concerned disagree on the definition of the issue, the referendum cannot be expected to contribute much towards a settlement. However, where, as over Europe and Scotland, there is agreement that the referendum defines the issue accurately, then a referendum can defuse the conflict, even though it cannot finally settle it. The referendum on Scottish devolution at least showed that, contrary to the suggestions of the SNP, Scotland was not straining at the leash for devolution. It therefore succeeded in isolating the extremists. No other device could have done that.

For a referendum to be able to achieve its aims, the question must be clear and precise and the alternatives posed must be achievable. To ask voters to give assent to a general proposition incapable of achievement by legislative or other practicable means is pointless. It is on these grounds that the question put forward by Sir James Goldsmith's Referendum Party can be faulted. One of the alternatives offered in that party's proposed question is that Britain should become part of a Europe which is an 'association of sovereign nations'. That, however, would involve not merely a veto on any further transfer of powers to the European Union, but a repatriation of existing European Union powers back to Britain. The other member states of the Union would almost certainly veto any such repatriation. In such circumstances, the question of whether Britain should be a member of an 'association of sovereign nations' would resolve itself into a question of whether Britain should leave the European Union if it cannot achieve its aim. Thus the question offered by the Referendum Party is profoundly misleading since it offers an unrealistic choice to the voters.

V

The referendums held so far in Britain have, then, worked comparatively successfully. Yet this may owe as much to good fortune as to the virtues of the referendum itself as a means of resolving fundamental political problems. In each case, there was much that could have gone wrong.

The 1975 referendum yielded a fairly even 'Yes' majority across the whole of the United Kingdom. Scotland and Wales voted 'Yes', ignoring the advice of their respective nationalist parties which were then hostile to membership of the Community. Voters in Northern Ireland ignored the advice of the Ulster Unionists and their most prominent spokesman, Enoch Powell, and endorsed the European Community. Had that not been the case – had Scotland, for example, voted 'No' while the rest of the country voted 'Yes' – the referendum could have given a powerful stimulus to Scottish separatism.

There was, moreover, a clear and indisputable verdict, the most important condition for a successful referendum; and the decision was in accordance with the view of the Prime Minister, Harold Wilson, the Foreign Secretary, James Callaghan, and the majority of the Cabinet. A 'No' verdict, by contrast, would have required Wilson and Callaghan to implement a policy in which they did not believe and which they thought would be ruinous for the country. Two pro-European Cabinet ministers, Roy Jenkins and Shirley Williams, had announced that they would resign from the government if there was a 'No' majority, and this could well have put the survival of the Labour government, which had a majority of only three, in doubt.

The most unfortunate result of all, perhaps, would have been a small 'No' majority on a low turnout. Would Harold Wilson have been prepared to follow a policy which he believed to be against Britain's interests if there were, for example, a 30 per cent 'No' vote and a 29 per cent 'Yes' vote? If he had, would the House of Commons have supported him? The majority of Members of Parliament were at that time strongly in favour of Britain's continued membership. 'The Government,' Edward Short, the Leader of the House, had declared before the referendum, 'will be bound by its result, but Parliament, of course, cannot be bound by it.'[12] Under a system in which Parliament is supreme, that is of course sound constitutional doctrine. Members of Parliament might well have argued that they could be morally bound only by a clear-cut verdict, and, lacking that, have insisted on Britain remaining in the Community. Whatever they decided, the referendum would have failed to resolve the problem.

In Scotland, support for devolution was, at 33 per cent, so far below the 40 per cent requirement that little serious debate in Parliament followed. The Labour government was required by the terms of the devolution legislation to lay a repeal order before Parliament. It hoped, admittedly, that it could persuade MPs to vote the repeal order down. That was impossible, given the narrow majority and the low turnout. But suppose that, given the same low turnout, the verdict had been not 33 per cent to 31 per cent, but, say, 35 per cent to 29 per cent. Would the repeal order then have been voted down? It is impossible to know, but once again it is clear that the referendum would not have settled the problem which it was instituted to resolve.

Issues of this kind could easily arise again in the referendums which are now proposed by the political parties. These raise many problems. The first problem is that of the threshold. Ought there to be a qualified majority, as in the devolution referendums, or is a simple majority always sufficient? Labour insists that a simple majority would now be sufficient for devolution. George Robertson, the Shadow Scottish Secretary, declared in a press conference in Glasgow on 27 June 1996: 'There will be no tricks. No fancy franchise. The test will be a straightforward majority of the votes cast. It is right that a democratic Parliament should be founded on a democratic vote.'

Does this mean that there are no circumstances in which it is desirable to stipulate a qualified majority? The Commission on the Conduct of Referendums, set up by the Electoral Reform Society and the Constitution Unit, declared in paragraph 94 of its report, published in 1996, that 'a simple majority of those who cast their votes carries a natural authority'. It is not clear, however, that this is so in the case of a very low turnout – as the Commission, indeed, recognised, declaring in the very same paragraph that the use of qualified majorities to approve constitutional amendments provides 'a safeguard against changing the basic laws too easily'.[13]

Suppose, for example, that there were at some time in the future to be a referendum on independence for Scotland. Many might object to Scottish independence being decided by a bare majority on a low turnout. Some would suggest, therefore, that there should be a qualified majority of 40 per cent or even 50 per cent of the electorate in favour to validate such a major change. An alternative would be to propose two referendums, one giving the government authority to prepare legislation separating Scotland from England, the second inviting the Scottish electorate to endorse this legislation.

Where it is decided to use a qualified majority, it is by no means clear that a proportion of the total registered electorate is the proper criterion to use; for the electoral register is notoriously inaccurate, as the problem of implementing the 40 per cent requirement in the Scottish devolution referendum of 1979 showed. The government deducted from the total numbers on the register those not legally entitled to vote. This included voters who reached the qualifying age after the date of the referendum and voters who had died since being registered, double-registered students and student nurses, and prisoners. The government, however, was not legally allowed to make any additional discount for those in practice unable to vote, for example, hospital patients or the seriously disabled; nor was it able to take account of the likelihood of errors in the register, assumed to be around 6 per cent. Together, these deductions would have amounted to around 14 per cent of those on the electoral register.[14] For this reason, it would be better, if a qualified majority is desired, for this to be specified in terms of a proportion of those voting rather than of the electorate, e.g. 55 per cent of those voting rather than 40 per cent of the electorate.

The effect of the qualified majority requirement in 1979, however, was not automatic rejection of devolution after fewer than 40 per cent of the voters had supported it. In such circumstances, the government was required only to lay an order repealing the act before Parliament. But of course, that repeal order could have been voted down by Parliament; and it would have been if the outcome had been, say, 39 per cent 'Yes' and 22 per cent 'No'. The 40 per cent rule thus gave Parliament the chance to reconsider the outcome. It made the referendum *advisory*. It would, however, have been possible for the 40 per cent condition to have been expressed in another way, such that the act would not come into force unless there was a 40 per cent positive vote in the referendum. That would not have given Parliament any discretion after the votes had been counted. It would have made the referendum *mandatory*. Parliament has in the past accepted an amendment proposing a mandatory referendum; this was during the passage of the Scotland and Wales Bill in February 1977. The precedent thus created was, however, never tested as the government shortly afterwards announced that the referendum would be advisory after all; and shortly after that, the bill was in any case withdrawn.[15]

Although Parliament has accepted that a mandatory referendum is possible, it seems unwise not to allow Parliament to look at the position again after the votes have been counted, to guard against absurdities. In Denmark, before 1953, a mandatory 45 per cent 'Yes' vote was required for constitutional laws to be brought into force (the new constitution of 1953 lowered this requirement to 40 per cent). In a referendum in 1939 on the abolition of the second chamber, agreed by the main political parties, 44.5 per cent of the electorate voted 'Yes', while only 3.9 per cent voted 'No'. The proposal was thus defeated; but had the Danish parliament been given the chance to think again, it would almost certainly have accepted the 'Yes' result as valid.

The devolution referendums now proposed by the Labour Party are to be held not, as in 1979, after the legislation has been passed by Parliament, but before it is introduced. In his 1996 Glasgow speech, George Robertson declared that 'as soon as Labour is returned to power, a White Paper will be published setting out the details of our plans'. There might well be a parliamentary debate, too, so that voters could acquaint themselves with the main principles of devolution on which they were being asked to vote in the referendum. A pre-legislative referendum would perform the function of inserting the people into the process of debate and enabling their views to be taken into account by Members of Parliament during the passage of the devolution legislation.

The purpose of a pre-legislative referendum is to prove to MPs that there is a strong demand for devolution so that Members of Parliament will not seek to defeat it. Blair has described this as a 'principled, tactical reason' for holding a pre-legislative referendum.[16] Alternatively, of course, if the referendums were to show that there was little support for devolution, much parliamentary time could be saved. Members of Parliament cannot, however, be bound, as the Short doctrine makes clear (see p. 135 above), by the outcome of a referendum, and so they could still defeat or, more likely, fundamentally alter the devolution legislation during its parliamentary proceedings. With devolution, as the experience of the 1970s shows, there are many complexities hidden in the detail of the legislation, and much scope for MPs to amend the proposals on which the electors would have voted. Were the final legislation to be fundamentally different from that presented in the referendum, there would perhaps be a case for a second, post-legislative referendum as well. This was the course followed in Spain, for regions seeking a high degree of autonomy, under Article 151 of the Spanish Constitution (see p. 47 above).

A post-legislative referendum allows the people to act as a check on legislation. Such a referendum is, as a matter of logic, conservative. It cannot impose on the statute book legislation which Members of Parliament do not want. All that it can do is either ratify legislation which, in the absence of the referendum, would in any case have reached the statute book; or, alternatively, prevent the implementation of legislation which Members of Parliament do want. A post-legislative referendum acts as a good second chamber is expected to act, as a check to hasty legislation or legislation which has been ill thought out. The referendum is a deterrent rather than an incentive to the legislator. It imposes, as a strong second chamber does, an extra hurdle which legislation must surmount before it reaches the statute book. That is why it has on the whole been those opposed to particular policies – whether European integration or devolution – who have been the most fervent advocates of the referendum.

There is a further complication with the proposed referendum on Scottish devolution, since Labour is intending to pose two questions, the first on the parliament itself, the second on its tax-varying powers. Suppose Scottish electors were to vote 'Yes' to the Parliament but 'No' to the tax-varying powers. Would devolution lapse or would a non-tax-varying parliament be established, a parliament without the powers enjoyed by local authorities or even by parish councils? Some voters might have voted 'Yes' to the first question on the assumption that there would also be a 'Yes' vote on the second, believing that without tax-varying powers, a devolved parliament would be a sham. Two apparently separate questions, therefore, might in reality be interdependent.

The proposed referendum on Northern Ireland raises the problem that, for it to validate a constitutional settlement, there must be a sufficient consensus. Does this mean that majorities in both communities would be required? An overall majority would be insufficient, since that might comprise a majority in the unionist community, but not in the nationalist one. Therefore, separate referendums would have to be held in each community and a majority attained in each. This would entail requiring every voter in Northern Ireland to register him- or herself as a member of one or the other community. An alternative would be to hold the referendum on a county or constituency basis. The trouble with this proposal, however, is that, were any county or constituency then to vote against the settlement, this might be seen by nationalists as constituting a case for transferring that county or constituency to the Irish Republic.

The proposed referendum on electoral reform is, like that on devolution, to precede legislation, not to follow it. Moreover, Tony Blair has said that, as with the European Community referendum of 1975, provision will be made for an 'agreement to differ' within a Labour Cabinet, so that ministers are not committed to supporting change. Indeed, Blair himself has declared himself 'not persuaded of the case for PR'.[17] A Prime Minister would, however, be taking up an odd position if he were to put a referendum to the people proposing change but ask the people to vote it down. He might well be met with the response: if you are against the proposal, why are you wasting our time by putting forward a referendum on it?

The proposed referendum on electoral reform, moreover, raises even more fundamental problems. For electoral reform involves not one but two issues. The first is whether the first past the post system should be retained. The second is what should replace it. On this second issue, electoral reformers are by no means agreed. Each of the alternatives considered in Chapter 3 has its devotees, some of them such true believers that they would prefer retention of the first past the post system to an alternative other than their own favoured option. In the past, indeed, electoral reformers have been defeated because they could not agree upon an alternative system. This happened in 1917 and 1918 after a Speaker's Conference unanimously condemned first past the post, and in 1930 when the minority Labour government was prepared to consider reform. On both occasions, reformers were divided between the alternative vote and the single transferable vote. The result was that first past the post survived by default.

A government proposing a referendum on electoral reform, then, has two alternatives. The first is to offer a single referendum. But what question should be asked? One possibility is to ask whether voters wish to retain the first past the post system. But voters might perfectly reasonably say that they cannot answer this question until they know what electoral system it is proposed should replace first past the post. Therefore it would seem more natural to offer voters a choice between the status quo and one specified alternative electoral system. That is the proposal of the Joint Consultative Committee of the Labour and Liberal Democrat parties, as reported in March 1997. The committee envisages a commission to recommend the appropriate alternative to first past the post. This would then be put to voters in a referendum containing a single question offering a straight choice between first past the post and the specified proportional alternative. The defect in this approach, however, is that the alternative put to the voters would be the one which suited the political professionals and not necessarily the one which the voters might themselves prefer.

The second possibility is a multi-option referendum. But that itself could take many forms. There could, for example, be a referendum offering the status quo and a number of alternatives. Or there could be two referendums separated by a period of time, so allowing for debate upon the possible alternatives. Or there could be a single referendum with two questions, the first asking whether voters wished to retain the first past the post system, the second asking which of a number of specified alternatives they preferred. That is the preference of the Liberal Democrats as stated in their proposed Great Reform Bill 1997, published in September 1996:

The referendum shall ask the following questions:

Question 1. Should elections to the House of Commons be by a system of proportional representation?
Answer yes or no.

Question 2. If elections are by a system of proportional representation would you prefer them to be by:
(a) the single transferable vote system? *or*
(b) the additional member system? *or*
(c) I have no preference.

The fundamental problem facing a government proposing to hold a referendum on electoral reform, then, is to decide how the alternatives should be presented to the voters. A government has to decide how many questions there should be, and whether the referendum should offer voters just a single choice or a number of alternatives. One possible model for consulting the people on electoral reform in Britain might be the two New Zealand referendums on electoral reform, held in 1992 and 1993. For New Zealand has a majoritarian political system similar to that of Britain, and of all the world's democracies is the one which approximates most closely to the Westminster model.

The issue of electoral reform in New Zealand was considered by a Royal Commission which reported in 1986 and recommended the German system of proportional representation. Both of the main parties were opposed to reform, but, following a series of political vicissitudes, the National Party government under Jim Bolger found itself committed to consulting voters on the issue.

The first New Zealand referendum, held in 1992, put two questions to the voters. The first asked whether voters favoured retention of first past the post; the second which of four specified alternatives they favoured. The alternatives in the second question were:

1 MMP: the mixed-member proportional system, the German system of proportional representation;
2 STV: the single transferable vote;
3 PV: the preferential voting system (i.e. the alternative vote);
4 SM: the supplementary member system; this would allocate one-fifth

or one-quarter of parliamentary seats to additional members in proportion to the parties' overall share of the vote.

The first two voting systems are examples of proportional representation, the latter two are not.

Voters were allowed to vote on the second question even if they answered 'No' to the first question, i.e. even if they wanted the first past the post system to remain. This left open the possibility of tactical voting by first past the post supporters, who could, in answering the second question, vote for the reform which they thought least likely to command widespread support. The government indicated that the referendum would be consultative but that, if first past the post were to be rejected, it would hold a second, binding, referendum with just one question asking voters whether they preferred first past the post to the most favoured alternative in the first referendum.

The government had advised against change, and indeed the major party leaders, together with New Zealand's business and financial leaders, favoured the status quo. But the result of the first referendum, on a turnout of 55 per cent, was a vote of only 15 per cent for first past the post and 85 per cent for change – prompting one political leader to remark that the outcome showed that PR stood for Public Revulsion against politicians.

The vote on the four options was as follows:

Mixed-member proportional	70%
Single transferable vote	17%
Preferential vote	7%
Supplementary member	6%

A second, binding, referendum was accordingly held in November 1993 at the same time as the general election, setting first past the post against the mixed-member proportional system. The outcome of this referendum, on an 83 per cent turnout, was that 46 per cent voted for retention of first past the post, with 54 per cent for the mixed-member proportional system. This system has therefore been adopted for New Zealand, and the first election under it was held in 1996.

The New Zealand referendums fulfilled their aim of eliciting public feeling on the first past the post system and the most favoured alternative to it. But, as with the referendums held in Britain, the outcome could easily have been very confused. Suppose, for example, that the vote on the four alternative electoral systems had been as follows:

Mixed-member proportional	35%
Single transferable vote	30%
Preferential vote	20%
Supplementary member	15%

Presumably, the problem of an electoral system being chosen by a minority vote could be avoided by using the preferential/alternative vote system to decide the issue, so that the second preferences of those who had supported the supplementary member system could be taken into account. It was odd that a vote to decide which of four systems other than first past the post was to be adopted should itself be carried out by the first past the post method!

But suppose the result were as follows:

Preferential vote	40%
Single transferable vote	35%
Mixed-member proportional	20%
Supplementary vote	5%

In this outcome, although the preferential vote is the most favoured system, there is a higher vote for the two proportional systems – the single transferable vote and the mixed-member proportional system – than there is for the two non-proportional systems. The original draft of the referendum bill in fact excluded the single transferable vote, which was included only after protests from reform organisations supporting this option. But its inclusion made it more likely, under first past the post voting, that a non-proportional system would triumph in the referendum.

The problem with all such multi-question or multi-option referendums, as with a referendum with a qualified majority, is that the question of what is to count as a legitimate outcome becomes controversial. With a straightforward referendum, such as the European Community referendum of 1975, with just one question and with no qualified majority, almost any outcome would be deemed legitimate in that it would be accepted by the losing side as fair. In the case of the Scottish devolution referendum, because of the 40 per cent requirement, the range of outcomes seen as illegitimate would have been wider. In the case of the multi-question and multi-option referendums, agreement on a legitimate outcome would be much more difficult to achieve. Yet it is clearly vital, if the referendum is to resolve the issue, that the range of legitimate outcomes be agreed upon by representatives of the various points of view before rather than after the referendum. If there is a dispute about whether the outcome is legitimate after the referendum has been held, its whole purpose is destroyed.

VI

The referendum as an instrument of government does two things which no other instrument can do. First, it gives every voter an equal say in deciding upon a specific issue of public policy. Second, it enables voters to decide upon such issues without reference to party interests. Often seen as an attack upon representative government, the referendum is in reality a democratic means of remedying its defects. It is incompatible not so much with parliamentary government as with an over-rigid party system which fails to articulate popular choices on certain issues. The referendum is, like the single transferable vote, an instrument to restrict the supremacy not of Parliament but of the party system. Both of these instruments seek to replace the supremacy of party with the supremacy of the elector, and both seek to achieve this aim by widening voter participation.[18] Such instruments are of particular value in a society in which political parties no longer structure the vote as effectively as they once did. In the past, voters supported political parties largely on account of their religious or class affiliation; today, in a more fluid society, with the growth of secularisation and the loosening of class ties, allegiance is bound to be more uncertain than it was. It is for this reason that political parties have declined as vehicles for mass loyalty.

It was the French political theorist Alexis de Tocqueville who pointed out that a democratic polity required a democratic social culture, and that such a culture must be a participatory one; and it was his near-contemporary Bagehot who was the first to notice that Britain's political arrangements reflected not a participatory but a deferential political culture. The role of the people in British politics was not active but, rather, passive, to give or withhold consent to government. Indeed, in the early

1960s Gabriel Almond and Sidney Verba, in their classic work, *The Civic Culture*, saw Britain as a paradigm example of a deferential political culture.[19] With the collapse of deference, however, new political instruments are needed to realise the popular demand for participation.

Public support for referendums is high. In a MORI poll in 1995, 77 per cent favoured a 'referendum system whereby certain issues are put to the people to decide by popular vote', as compared to only 19 per cent favouring a system whereby 'Parliament should decide all important issues'. There is public support for referendums not only on constitutional matters but also on non-constitutional issues such as the restoration of the death penalty. Moreover, there is a close correlation between public support for holding a referendum on a specific issue and the 'level of support for whichever option is probably seen as least likely to occur without a referendum'. Thus, support for a referendum on the death penalty has varied in MORI polls between 1991 and 1995 from 60 per cent to 80 per cent while support for capital punishment itself has been between 70 per cent and 80 per cent. Support for a referendum on a single European currency was between 60 per cent and 70 per cent in 1994–5, while opposition to the pound joining such a currency has fluctuated around 60 per cent. Support for electoral reform in a MORI 1995 State of the Nation poll was 46 per cent, precisely the same level as support in the same survey for a referendum on the subject.[20]

Although widespread support for the referendum indicates a growing gap between the political class and the people, the referendum remains a weapon in the hands of the political class; for although it allows the people to decide on certain issues, it rests with the political class whether and when it is used. Nevertheless, use of the referendum may open the way to other instruments of direct democracy which take power away from the political class. Such instruments go beyond the conventional constitutional reform agenda since they seek to increase public involvement in a very radical way.

In Switzerland and Italy, a specified percentage of voters can require the government to hold a referendum on a particular legislative proposal or, alternatively, to withdraw the proposal. In Italy this has been the means by which reforms such as legalisation of abortion and divorce, and, in 1993, reform of the electoral system, have been forced upon unwilling governments. A further step would be the 'initiative', used in Europe only in Switzerland, but also in a large number of American states. The initiative allows a percentage of registered electors to secure a referendum on any policy matter except those, such as the annual budget, that are explicitly excluded. The initiative has recently been introduced in New Zealand by means of the 1993 Citizens Initiated Referenda Act. This requires a non-binding referendum to be held on any matter if requested by a petition signed by at least 10 per cent of registered electors. So far only one referendum has been held under the provisions of this act, in December 1995 on staffing levels in the Fire Service. This resulted from a petition organised by the Firefighters Union. The question was: 'Should the number of professional firefighters employed full time in the New Zealand Fire Service be reduced below the number employed on 1 January 1995?' Turnout in the referendum, however, was only 28 per cent, and, of those voting, 88 per cent supported the position of the Firefighters Union. In Britain, there is widespread support for the initiative to be introduced alongside the referendum. In 1995, a MORI poll showed that 77 per cent of the public thought that it would in principle be a good idea 'if the British people could force the Government to hold a referendum on a particular issue by raising a petition with signatures from, say, a million people'.[21]

Referendums need not be confined to the national level. Since 1932, local authorities have been allowed to conduct referendums on the Sunday opening of cinemas; and since 1961 there have been seven-yearly referendums on the Sunday opening of public houses in the 'dry' counties of Wales. A parish council may be required to hold a referendum if six electors sign a letter to the parish clerk to call the necessary initial special meeting, or at the request of ten electors at the annual parish meeting.[22]

Local authorities, moreover, can also seek to influence national policy by holding referendums on national issues. The most significant such referendum in recent years was that held in Strathclyde in 1994 on the reorganisation of water management, the largest referendum ever conducted by any council in Britain. In Scotland, water services, instead of being privatised, were to be transferred from local authorities to water authorities with separate Customers' Councils. The members of both of these bodies would be appointed by the Secretary of State for Scotland. Strathclyde council, abolished in the Scottish local government reform which transferred responsibility for water, but at that time covering half of the population of Scotland, held a postal ballot, asking voters, 'Do you agree with the Government's proposal for the future of water and sewerage services?' The turnout was 71 per cent – 2.5 million people: a larger percentage than in either the 1975 European Community referendum or the 1979 devolution referendum. Of those participating, 97 per cent voted against the government's proposals. This referendum occurred just before the committee stage of the Local Government (Scotland) Bill which included the water proposals. The government, however, ignored the outcome of the referendum and continued with its policies unchanged.

English local authorities are empowered to hold similar referendums under section 142 of the 1972 Local Government Act. In 1992, Harlow District Council held a 'Health Trust Ballot' on whether the West Essex local hospital should become a self-governing trust. A leaflet was sent to 30,000 households, and the outcome of a postal ballot was a seven to one majority against the hospital becoming a trust. There was, however, only a 15 per cent turnout as compared with 38 per cent in the 1995 district council elections in Harlow, and it may be argued that this did not make the poll a very representative one. Perhaps a representative opinion survey would have been more useful.

Many other experiments with direct democracy are possible. Citizens' juries, for example, have been widely used in the United States. These 'juries', perhaps misnamed since their functions are purely advisory, consist of around 20 randomly selected voters and examine issues of major public interest or controversy. Their conclusions are in no way binding, although they generally attract widespread public attention. They have been found to have considerably increased the understanding of those who participate. In October 1996, the Labour Party indicated that it would introduce citizens' juries to influence large areas of public policy. The electricity, gas and water industries would be among the first to be examined by these groups, and they might also scrutinise the role of the industry regulators.[23] Local juries could also be established to consider matters of local import such as planning decisions, or policy with regard to schools. Developments in communications technology have made possible many more innovations in direct democracy.[24] These, like the initiative but unlike the referendum itself, take power away from the political class, transferring it to the people.

The future of the referendum and of other instruments of direct democracy in Britain is closely bound up with the future of the British party system. 'It is certain,' wrote Dicey as early as 1915, 'that no man, who is really satisfied with the working of our party system, will ever look with favour on an institution which aims at correcting the vices of party government.'[25] If the parties seem to represent the interests and aspirations of voters effectively, then there will be little call for further use of the referendum. If, however, as seems more likely, parties come to appear even more dissociated from public opinion than they are at present, then the referendum will be more frequently used than it has been in the past. Indeed, as we reach the end of the twentieth century, there are signs that the period in which mass parties were central to the politics of democracy may be coming to an end. In Britain, confidence in the party system was at its height in the post-war period, in the years between the 1940s and the 1960s. Since then, that confidence has steadily declined. In such circumstances, the referendum and other instruments of direct democracy, far from being regarded as unconstitutional or even unusual, are likely to become accepted as staple fixtures of the furniture of British politics in the twenty-first century.

6

The Funding of Political Parties

'Without parties,' Disraeli once said, 'parliamentary government is impossible.' A healthy democracy requires healthy parties. The methods by which parties are funded are an important determinant of the health of a country's party system. In an ideal democracy, political parties would be financed entirely from individual membership subscriptions and voluntary contributions by individual donors. But no democracy in the modern world meets this basic requirement of political health. In every democracy, individual donations are supplemented either by state aid in some form or by institutional donations, from companies and trade unions.

There are, broadly, three alternative patterns of political finance in modern democracies. The first, prevalent on the European continent, is one in which the state aids the parties. In Austria, Denmark, Finland, France, Greece, Norway, Portugal and Sweden, parties represented in the legislature are aided in proportion to votes won or seats gained. This provision is generally subject to a threshold, a minimum requirement in terms of either the percentage of the vote gained or the number of members, below which a party will not qualify for funds. A prerequisite for the success of such a pattern of political finance seems to be a high degree of consensus among the main political parties so that the taxpayer does not feel too much resentment at contributing to parties which he or she does not support. That, no doubt, is why state aid seems more appropriate in Sweden than it does in, say, France.

The second pattern is that followed in the United States and Canada, in which state aid is triggered through the decisions of individual citizens, whose donations to candidates and parties qualify for tax relief or tax credits. The state thus provides incentives for individual contributions through tax concessions for contributors. In return for this, the state exacts a quid pro quo: in order to receive these benefits, political parties in Canada and the United States are required to meet certain requirements of democratic accountability and disclosure.

The arrangements for party funding in Germany, which has a longer experience of state aid for political parties than any other democracy, display an interesting amalgam of the two patterns. State aid is provided, first, for parties and in reimbursement of election costs, and second, to all parties represented in the Bundestag to establish research institutes. Parties, however, cannot be given more money from the state than they are able to raise from their own members and supporters. There is in addition a third form of aid in that donations by individuals, although not by companies, up to around £2,400 are tax-deductible. Trade unions are not allowed to make political donations, although companies remain free to do so.

The third pattern of political finance is that with which Britain is familiar. In Britain, the state does not provide cash for the activities of the political parties outside Parliament. Instead, the two main parties – the Conservatives and Labour – rely for a considerable amount of their funding upon institutional donations, from companies and trade unions. This pattern is not, as is so often thought, typical of advanced democracies, but quite unusual. Indeed, Britain is the only country in the European Union not to give state cash aid to the parties outside Parliament.

In the past, the Labour Party was financed almost entirely by affiliated trade unions. In 1974, for example, trade unions contributed no less than 92 per cent of the party's central income. This gradually fell to around 80 per cent in the early 1980s. Since then, the proportion has fallen more rapidly, until in 1995 the trade unions contributed only 47 per cent of the party's income. (The proportion is likely to be even smaller when the accounts for 1996 and 1997 are published, since during the period of an election campaign large amounts are now raised from individual donors.) Thus, for the first time in the Labour Party's history, the trade unions are now contributing less than half of its central income. The figure of 47 per cent does not, however, include indirect trade union contribution to the financing of the party leader's office, researchers and offices for members of the Shadow Cabinet.[1] In place of trade union affiliation fees, Labour has been seeking to increase its share of income from membership subscriptions and donations. In 1995, individual membership subscriptions raised 16 per cent of central income, while commercial fund-raising, which in the 1980s provided only around 2 per cent of Labour's income, raised 18.6 per cent. Labour has thus diversified its sources of income, a trend which has been intensified under Tony Blair's leadership.[2] The trade unions' constitutional position within the Labour Party has also been weakened, as Labour has come to transform itself from a federal party based on delegate democracy to a plebiscitary party based on direct democracy.

The diversification of Labour's sources of funding and the weakening of the constitutional position of the trade unions, although they pre-dated Tony Blair's accession to the Labour leadership, nevertheless accurately mirror an important trend in 'New Labour' aimed at persuading voters that Labour is now a party of the nation, not of a particular class. The origins of the Labour Party lie in an alliance struck in 1900 between socialists and trade unionists. After a series of legal decisions at the turn of the century adverse to the interests of trade unions, many union leaders took the view that they needed a party to represent the interests of the organised working class in Parliament. Recent trends in the funding of the party have reflected a new and different conception of the role of the party. It would, however, be difficult for the party to survive financially without the trade union contribution, and consequently the threat of undue union influence remains. Tom Sawyer, the current General Secretary of the Labour Party, declared in 1992 when Deputy General Secretary of NUPE, the public service union, that, 'whilst we continue to fund the party, we will have a say. It is as crude as that. No say, no pay.'[3]

The financing of the Conservative Party is quite different from that of Labour. In the year ending 1 March 1996, of a total Conservative income of £21,419 million, £18,822 million came from 'donations'. The remainder came from the constituencies and income from the sale of publications and services. Of the total of donations, three-quarters is accounted for by 'personal donations'.[4] The bulk of the rest presumably derives from companies. If this is so, then companies now fund a smaller proportion of Conservative Party income than in the past; an estimate in 1981 put the proportion of the party's total central income derived from company donations at between 55 per cent and 60 per cent.[5]

Although it is not as crucial as once it was, nevertheless the prominent role played by companies and trade unions in the provision of money to the two main political parties is a peculiar feature of political finance in

Britain. Here, perhaps more than in any other democracy, 'there exists a constant tension between the interests of the organised groups in possession of the bulk of technical, material and monetary resources needed by the parties and the principle of "one man, one vote" which underlines democratic systems'.[6] In no other modern democracy do institutional donors play so marked a role.

II

It is institutional finance which enables Britain to avoid state aid to the party organisations. Without monies given by companies and trade unions, the two major parties would find that they had insufficient funds to carry out their activities.

The fundamental argument against state aid is that political parties are voluntary organisations. Citizens choose whom to vote for, and whether or not to join a party or to give it financial support. Citizens are not required to take part in the political process; the vote, for example, is not compulsory. There can, therefore, be no argument for requiring individuals to contribute, through taxation, to parties with whose views they may be in disagreement. This argument, however, is deeply flawed. First, it assumes that private finance is necessarily voluntary finance. This is not so. Institutional finance is private finance. It is not, however, necessarily *voluntary* finance. Companies generally contribute to political parties without obtaining, or even seeking, the approval of their shareholders. In a report in 1991, Pensions Investment Research Consultants questioned various companies on their policy with regard to political contributions. Of 35 companies which made contributions, only three had consulted their shareholders.[7] Trade unions, through the arrangements for the political levy, rely upon the inertia of their members in making contributions to Labour Party funds. Second, the argument ignores the extent to which the state already aids political parties and candidates. The argument cannot, therefore, be one about whether the state should aid political parties – it already does; it has to be one about the extent and scope of such aid.

A trade union wishing to make payments for political purposes must do so from a separate political fund. Any trade union wishing to contribute to a political party must, under the provisions of the 1992 Trade Union and Labour Relations (Consolidation) Act, hold a ballot every ten years on whether its members wish to establish such a fund. Around 38 per cent of political fund spending goes to the Labour Party. The rest is spent on lobbying activities or on general political advertising, much of which, of course, helps the Labour Party.[8] Any trade unionist who does not wish to make political contributions can 'contract out' of contributing to the political fund. In 1994, 47 unions maintained political funds to which 5,079,654 members contributed, while 983,715 contracted out, and in general around one-fifth of trade unionists normally contract out. Since, however, around 53 per cent of trade unionists vote for parties other than Labour, there seems good reason to believe that many non-Labour trade unionists contribute to the political fund out of either inertia or ignorance of the purposes for which it is used.

Even if the contracting-out system worked entirely satisfactorily, it would not follow that the contributions of trade unionists to the political fund could be correctly described as voluntary. This point was made by a constitutional lawyer, W. M. Geldart, advocating the system of contracting out in 1910: 'To allow a conscience clause for the dissentient unionist is not the same thing in principle as to make the payment a purely voluntary one. Vaccination was not made optional when relief was given to the conscientious objector. Some evidence of conscientious objection must be given before the plea can be allowed.'[9]

The state, it can be argued, enlists through legislation the forces of apathy on behalf of the Labour Party. The argument for this at the beginning of the century was that the forces of organised labour needed special protection if they were to be able to compete with other interests. Nevertheless, trade unions are the only organisations whose political contributions are so tightly regulated by law. Other organisations are allowed to donate money for political purposes without seeking the approval of their members. The reason for this was that, until 1984, industrial relations were governed by the closed shop. This meant that employees had to join a union in order to obtain employment. It would be iniquitous to require someone to contribute to a political party as an automatic obligation on obtaining employment.

Parallel to the non-Labour trade union member who may be inadvertently contributing to the Labour Party, there is the non-Conservative shareholder or pension fund member whose company makes contributions to the Conservative Party. It is easier for companies to make political contributions than it is for trade unions. A company wishing to make a political contribution over the sum of £200 faces only one statutory requirement. Under the 1985 Companies Act, all such contributions must be disclosed in the directors' report; but it can take up to two years for these reports to be lodged in Companies House. Political parties are not themselves required to declare either the size or the source of company donations, and so anyone seeking to discover the total picture of company donations to the Conservative Party would have to investigate every company report in Companies House, a task that is hardly feasible. In practice, therefore, researchers have to content themselves with trawling through a sample of major companies and reporting their findings.

Companies, unlike trade unions, are not required to hold a shareholders' ballot to establish a separate political fund, nor is there any provision enabling dissenting shareholders to 'contract out'. Indeed, company shareholders, unlike trade unionists, have no rights in law if they disagree with the political contribution being made by their company. Shareholders can, it is true, raise the question of political contributions at their company's annual general meeting; this process has been likened to 'a right to slide the stable door across after the animal has galloped into the Conservative Party's coffers'.[10] In effect, their only way of withholding contributions is to sell their shares, thereby making what ought to be a commercial judgement on political grounds. Of course, even this option is not available if they happen to belong to a pension fund which purchases shares of companies making political contributions.

In the past, allegations have been made that chairmen of companies which make large contributions to the Conservative Party are more likely to receive honours than the chairmen of companies which do not so contribute.[11] Before someone can be nominated for a peerage, the government Chief Whip has to sign a certificate stating whether he or she has donated more than £20,000 to the government party. If the answer is 'Yes', this does not debar the candidate, but it must be made known to the Political Honours Scrutiny Committee, which consists of three Privy Counsellors meeting in private. Lord Shackleton, a former member of this committee, has claimed nevertheless that 'it is highly likely that these secret donations are bypassing the scrutiny system and that honours are effectively being bought'.[12]

No concrete basis has ever been found for the allegations that contributions to the Conservative Party help secure honours. It would be a contravention of the Honours (Prevention of Abuses) Act 1925 for an individual or company to give money as an inducement to obtain an honour. This act was passed to prevent any repetition of the sale of honours which occurred in Lloyd George's government from 1916 to 1922, under the auspices of his agent, Maundy Gregory, called by Lord Birkenhead 'the Cheerful Giver'. No one has ever been convicted under this legislation, however, and no one is ever likely to be. For 'unless someone makes the mistake of putting an offer in writing, it is impossible to establish any causal connection between a cheque written by an individual to a political party and a knighthood conferred by the Queen five years later'.[13]

It remains the case, however, that while only around 6 per cent of companies make donations to the Conservative Party, 50 per cent of knighthoods and peerages have gone to directors of companies which have made such donations. Such a correlation cannot statistically be a matter of chance. 'The chances that the 6 per cent who make donations just happen to have been awarded 50 per cent of the honours by coincidence and without any causative link are infinitesimal.'[14] Thus, individual trafficking in honours seems to have been replaced by a system of bulk purchase. Conservatives object to the political levy by means of which members of affiliated trade unions contribute to Labour unless they take the trouble to opt out; yet is the system by which company contributors to the Conservative Party are rewarded with honours anything more than a rich man's political levy?

Moreover, it may be believed that corporate contributions will yield greater access to government ministers than is possible for those who do not contribute. In the words of the Canadian Royal Commission on Corporate Contributions in 1978: 'Corporate contributions may lead to some sense of obligation and conflict of interest, as well as suspicion, even though the companies involved . . . neither ask for nor expect any quid pro quo.'[15] In a system of political finance in which companies did not make corporate contributions to party funds, by contrast, no one would be able to question the genuine merit of company directors who receive honours, nor the probity of businessmen and women who gain access to senior ministers.

Party leaders no doubt cannot be blamed for using the honours system as a method of eliciting contributions. It is perhaps an inevitable consequence of a structure of party funding dependent upon company finance. In any well-run democracy, it is right that companies and trade unions should enjoy a certain degree of influence in the political process. The danger in Britain, however, is that they might enjoy more influence and access than they are entitled to owing to the political contributions they make. Moreover, a system of party finance which depends upon the willingness of companies and trade unions to contribute imposes an unfair handicap upon those parties which are unable to, or do not wish to, solicit such contributions. In Britain, it is the Liberal Democrats, who obtain no trade union money and infinitesimal company contributions, who suffer from such a handicap. In a democracy, surely, all significant political parties ought to have a roughly equal chance of putting their case to the electorate. They should not have to face an additional and extraneous hurdle in the form of the pattern of party finance, which rewards parties who can attract one particular source of finance and penalises parties which cannot.

As regards their activities outside Parliament, then, the two main parties are privately but not necessarily voluntarily funded. The British pattern of political finance flouts the principle that political contributions should be made only as a result of the positive decisions of individuals.

The issue of state aid, then, is not one of voluntariness versus compulsion, but one of corporate versus public funding. A basic argument for public funding is that too high a proportion of the money funding British parties is tarnished in that it comes from sources which serve sectional interests. The pattern of party finance tends to emphasise the roles of the two main parties – Conservatives and Labour – as parties representing particular interests, when the interests themselves are of declining importance in this country. If a scheme of public finance had the effect of reducing the importance of institutional donations while also encouraging the parties to seek new members and new donors, that would indeed be a gain of great importance to the democratic health of the country.

III

In 1937 the Ministers of the Crown Act recognised the position of Leader of the Opposition and assigned a salary to the post, recognising the principle that an effective opposition is just as important to the health of democracy as an effective government. One MP, opposed to the proposal, correctly saw that it established a principle which could be extended. 'Once you concede the payment to an Opposition, you automatically concede that an Opposition provides certain functions in this House, not merely as an Opposition, but as servant of the country and of the Crown, and that, therefore, every part of its machinery ought to be paid.'[16]

Today, the state subsidises the political process in a number of different ways. Public meeting rooms are provided free to candidates at election time and their election addresses are delivered free by the Post Office. Gifts to political parties are exempt from inheritance tax and bequests of up to £1,000 are exempt from capital transfer tax. More important, perhaps, is the fact that parties cannot advertise or buy time on radio or television. Broadcasters are required to carry party political broadcasts, and, during the election period, party election broadcasts. The annual value of party political broadcasts has been estimated by the Conservatives at £3 million for each party, while the Institute for Public Policy Research has valued party election broadcasts at £10 million per party.[17] The prohibition on advertising by political parties in the broadcast media assists less well-resourced parties, since it prevents a richer party from purchasing extra media time for itself. In the United States, where there are no subsidised party or election broadcasts, 85 per cent of campaign finance is spent on advertising, the vast bulk of it the purchase of television time to obtain recognition. In Britain, by contrast, one authority has suggested that adding an estimate of the value of subsidies in kind to the parties' election spending reduces the gap between the Conservatives, Labour and the Liberal Democrats from a ratio of 9:4:1 to one of 25:20:17.[18]

Since 1975, funds have been made available to the opposition parties to help them in carrying out their parliamentary tasks. These funds are often labelled 'Short money' after Edward Short, Leader of the House of Commons at the time. The amount of 'Short money' paid to opposition parties is calculated on a formula related to the support which the parties gained at the previous general election. Since April 1994, there have been annual upratings linked to the retail price index. For 1996/7, financial assistance was provided as follows:

Labour Party	£1,530,190.51
Liberal Democrats	£316,480.54
Ulster Unionists	£46,357.18
SNP	£36,782.68
SDLP	£23,134.12
Plaid Cymru	£22,040.36
Democratic Unionists	£15,954.37

Britain, therefore, as Professor Martin Harrison has pointed out, 'already has a system of state aid to political parties – though in a typically British fashion it has evolved ad hoc and without being acknowledged for what it is'.[19]

The provision of state aid for the research and campaigning activities of the party organisations, therefore, is merely an extension of a principle which has already been recognised. However, the 'Short money' may be spent only on the parties' parliamentary work; it is held that some major issue of principle is involved in not providing money to the parties for their extra-parliamentary work. The basis of this supposed principle is, however, not clear, for monies provided for the parties within Parliament release monies to be spent outside Parliament. The 'Short money' presumably replaces funds which would otherwise have to be raised from outside donors. Thus, to provide state aid to the parties outside Parliament would not be to introduce a new principle, but to extend an existing one. For, as George Buchanan said in 1937 when the Ministers of the Crown Act was being introduced, the opposition, like the government, are servants 'of the country and of the Crown'. The provision of public funds to assist the parties in carrying out essential democratic tasks is therefore as much a matter of the public interest today as was the payment to the Leader of the Opposition in 1937.

When the 'Short money' was being instituted, Edward Short declared that, without such funds, it would become 'increasingly difficult for Opposition parties to keep up with those who are backed by the vast resources of Government, either in research or in administration'.[20] Yet the research needed to enable opposition parties to function effectively cannot be undertaken solely within the parliamentary arena, by research assistants to frontbench spokespersons; the bulk of research and policy-making activity must be undertaken outside Parliament, in the headquarters of the political parties. There are good grounds for believing that opposition parties lack sufficient funds to produce serious and well-thought-out policy proposals, to conduct proper analysis. The really serious work on manifesto commitments tends to be undertaken by civil servants in anticipation of a new government. This often uncovers important factors which have been neglected by the working parties and committees producing the manifesto. This lack of preparation creates problems for an incoming government and for civil servants who have to put manifesto commitments, which are often inadequately thought out, into effect. The problem arises because opposition parties, in the absence of sophisticated policy-making machinery, find it easier to indulge in adversarial and destructive criticism than to engage in constructive policy-making.

The Conservatives, with their superior financial resources, are better equipped to develop policies than the other parties. But when the party was in opposition between 1974 and 1979, much of the preparatory work for government was carried out not by the Conservative Research Department but by sympathetic think-tanks such as the Centre for Policy Studies and the Institute of Economic Affairs. However, the existence of friendly think-tanks is not an adequate substitute for a professional 'counter civil service' in the political parties themselves. Sometimes think-tanks leave their policy recommendations at precisely the point from which the political parties need to have them developed, stopping at general analysis and recommendation without producing specific, detailed proposals which can stand up to Civil Service and parliamentary scrutiny. The think-tanks can only complement, rather than substitute for, the analysis which is needed.

The research organisations of the political parties are unable to employ sufficient staff to act as a real counterweight to the Civil Service when their party is in opposition. Frequently a large policy area such as housing or education is left in the hands of one person, who has to advise shadow ministers and local councillors and service party committees, as well as attempting to develop policy and keep abreast of relevant publications and research in the field. Even the Conservatives, despite being the wealthiest party, suffer from this problem. During the 1970s, when the Conservatives were last in opposition, Professor Esmond Wright, a former Conservative MP, wrote that 'the thirty or so people in the Conservative Research Department – however competent – cannot hope to take on the civil service team; and they have to service shadow committees as well as shadow Ministers. I recall how inadequate I felt on the opposition benches in 1967–70 in attempting to tackle government Ministers, with their answer books carefully written and annotated by teams of bureaucrats.'[21] Conditions for the parties are far more stringent financially today than they were 20 years ago, and, should the Conservatives find themselves in opposition again, they might well find themselves unable to employ 'the thirty or so people' in the Conservative Research Department in the 1970s. Parties in opposition generally have to rely on their recent experience of office, a few faithful party advisers, academics who will offer part-time unpaid advice, and special interest groups affected by impending government legislation. The difficulties which opposition parties face in developing policies for government constitute a real weakness in our democratic machinery. It means that oppositions come to power with inadequately developed policies, and that the Civil Service alone is in a position to provide a practical assessment of the costs and gains associated with particular policy proposals.

In 1992, a Westminster Foundation for Democracy was set up to advise the new democracies of Africa and Central and Eastern Europe on democratic practices and procedures. It provides funds from its grant-in-aid to the political parties so that they can fund projects in the new democracies. Much of this funding is used to assist with party building and education. It is ironic that funds are provided for this purpose in the new democracies but not in Britain.

State aid to the parties in Britain would enable them to establish genuine research organisations, perhaps based on the model of the German 'Stiftungen' or party foundations. Each of the parties represented in the Bundestag has one of these foundations, named after a prominent figure of the party concerned. The CDU foundation, for example, is known as the Konrad Adenauer Stiftung, while that of the SDP is known as the Friedrich Ebert Stiftung, after the first President of the Weimar Republic. These party foundations employ large staffs whose function it is to develop policies for the parties. Many would argue that this is one of the reasons why policy-making in Germany is more sophisticated than it is in Britain. The comparatively small amount of state aid needed to establish party foundations of this kind would be a small price to pay for helping to improve the quality of the policies which opposition parties were able to develop.

Were Britain to follow Germany's example and provide money for the establishment of foundations attached to the political parties, not only would it make for a more sophisticated politics, it might also give greater meaning to party membership. At present, party members seem to have no real function, beyond that of ritual activities such as canvassing. That is perhaps the reason why able young people find themselves more drawn to single-issue groups which seem to provide the political discussion and debate not offered by the parties. Party foundations could do a great deal to attract young people into the political system and so counter the apathy and alienation from politics prevalent among the young.

IV

The case for state aid is three-fold. First, it would reduce the proportion of institutional support to the two main parties; second, it would enable the research and policy-making activities of the parties to be properly financed. But third, properly used, as will be shown below, it could be a device to increase participation.

It has already been shown that state aid to the parties would be an extension of a principle already accepted, and not the introduction of a new principle into British political life. Much of the hostility to state aid derives from the feeling that the taxpayer ought not to be asked to subsidise parties with which he or she may disagree. If the parties themselves cannot raise sufficient funds, it may be suggested, that is no reason for the state to help them. After all, the right to donate money to the party of one's choice must also include the right to stop donating money if one so chooses. If a party is in financial difficulties, therefore, it would be the reverse of democratic for the state to shore it up through public funds. State aid, indeed, could give an artificial lease of life to parties which were losing popular support. On this view, those who support state aid are in danger of becoming a 'Society for the Preservation of Old Parties'.[22] It ought not, then, to be the role of the state to assist parties solely because they may happen to be in financial difficulties. In such circumstances parties, like other organisations and indeed individuals, must seek either to reduce expenditure or to raise more income. Furthermore, state aid, it is suggested, far from encouraging political participation, might well discourage it by making the parties over-reliant upon public funds and more, rather than less, remote from their members.

These objections could be overcome if state aid were made conditional upon some index of party activity, such as party membership. The US and Canadian patterns of party finance are based, as we have seen, on the principle that state funding to political parties and candidates should be dependent upon some visible index of public support. The tax system is used to benefit donations to parties and candidates. State aid is not unconditional but has to be 'triggered' by the decisions of individuals to contribute. It is thus conditional upon popular endorsement of particular parties and candidates. This gives the parties an incentive to seek supporters. There seems, however, no reason why the benefits of a scheme whose aim is to relate aid to an index of political activity should be restricted to income-tax payers. Wage-earners below the tax threshold, as well as students, pensioners, the unemployed and the disabled, have an equal right to support the candidate or party of their choice without being discriminated against because they do not happen to pay income tax. Nevertheless, the principle of the US and Canadian schemes, that aid to political parties should not be unconditional but should be triggered by the decisions of individuals, can easily be adapted to British conditions.

One method of doing this would be to tailor state aid to party membership subscriptions and donations. It would be possible for the state to contribute, for example, a matching payment of £10 to each party for each £10 raised in membership subscriptions or donations, subject to a maximum. With the unit set at £10 for each person, the state would be matching only small donations and not substantial gifts by wealthy individuals. The maximum amount of money spent on the scheme might be calculated so that, in order to achieve its maximum, each party would have to secure membership subscriptions from, say, 1 in 12 of those who had voted for it in the previous general election.[23] There would also be a threshold requirement for a party to qualify for such aid. This threshold might be as proposed in the report by the Committee of Inquiry on Financial Aid to Political Parties, the Houghton Committee.[24] This stipulated that, for a party to qualify as eligible, it must, at the previous general election, have either:

(a) secured 12.5 per cent of the vote in at least six constituencies, or
(b) had at least two of its candidates returned as Members of Parliament, or
(c) had one of its candidates returned as a Member of Parliament and received as a party a total of not less than 150,000 votes.

Conditions (b) and (c) were the criteria used to decide whether a party qualified for financial aid to opposition parties under the 'Short money' scheme. Condition (a) offers an indication that a political party is capable of commanding genuine public support, even if it has not actually won a seat in the Commons.

The proposal can be illustrated with an actual example, confined, for the sake of simplicity, to the Conservative, Labour, Liberal Democrat and nationalist parties, and making the assumption that only these parties qualify for aid. The Northern Ireland parties are excluded.

In the 1992 general election, roughly 14 million people voted Conservative, 11.5 million people voted Labour, 6 million people voted Liberal Democrat and 800,000 voted for the nationalist parties, SNP and Plaid Cymru. On this basis, if 1 in 12 of those who voted for these parties were prepared to contribute £10 each to the party for which they voted, the sums raised would be as follows:

Conservatives	£11,666,666
Labour	£9,583,333
Liberal Democrats	£5,000,000
Nationalists	£666,666
TOTAL	£26,916,665

The maximum amount spent on matching funds, then, might reasonably be put at £27 million per year. Of course, the parties would not only receive the matching funds; they would also receive the subscriptions and donations. So, if around 1 voter in 12 were willing to contribute, the scheme would generate in total £54 million for the political parties. The scheme would provide aid only to parties which succeeded in persuading individuals to contribute. No money could be disbursed by the state except by the wish of individual contributors. This kind of scheme, therefore, avoids the danger of some schemes of state subsidy to parties, of shoring up parties which the public does not wish to support.

A scheme of this kind would have the virtue of encouraging the parties to broaden their appeal by seeking a large number of small donations rather than relying, as at present, upon large and institutional donations. The greater the number of individual donors, the less reliance the parties would need to place upon institutional donations and large donations from wealthy individuals. Thus, such a scheme would help to redress the imbalance under the British pattern of political finance towards the individual donor. According to one authority, since the Election Expenses Act 1974 in Canada, which provided for a scheme of tax credits analogous to that proposed here, 'the number of individuals contributing to parties (or candidates) has increased fivefold'.[25] The percentage contributing, however, is still low, at under 2 per cent.

The Canadian legislation has also succeeded in lessening the importance of institutional donations, although the two major Canadian parties, the Conservatives and the Liberals, do still rely heavily on such donations.

Until 1974, however, the Conservatives were financed almost entirely by a small number of large companies, while by 1993 companies provided only 47 per cent of the Conservative Party's income and 41 per cent of the Liberal Party's income. The New Democratic Party, which used to rely for the predominant part of its finance on the trade unions, was by 1993 raising only 15 per cent of its income from the unions.[26]

The scheme proposed above might reverse the decline in party membership in Britain. The Conservatives, whose membership peaked at around 2,800,000 in 1953, found that by 1994 it had fallen to around 750,000. Even when Margaret Thatcher became leader in 1975, the party had one and a half million members; so the Conservatives have lost one in two of their members since that time despite winning four general elections.[27] Labour reached a peak of just over one million members in 1952; its membership at the end of 1996 was just over 400,000, following membership drives under John Smith and Tony Blair which raised it from its previous low of around 250,000. Liberal Democratic membership is probably around 150,000. Thus, total party membership is probably not much higher than 1,300,000. That is smaller than the total membership of the Royal Society for the Protection of Birds.

A scheme of the kind put forward here would allow both constituency parties and the national headquarters of parties to benefit. The constituency parties would benefit from the membership subscriptions, while national headquarters would benefit from the matching payments. Thus a further danger of some schemes of state subsidy is avoided by ensuring that the balance between constituency parties and headquarters does not tilt towards the centre. The autonomy of constituency parties, an important feature of the British political system, would be preserved.

V

Reform of party funding on the lines suggested here could also be used as leverage to secure necessary reforms in party funding. A scheme of state aid such as that proposed ought to lead to an alteration in the legal status of the political parties. For it would be wrong to provide aid from public funds to the parties outside Parliament without requiring a much greater degree of public accountability from them. There must be a clear specification of what is to count as a political party and of the conditions under which payments are to be made.

At present, political parties in Britain, although mentioned in various acts and statutory instruments, do not exist as legal entities, and they possess no legal personality. In law, they are not distinguished from clubs and associations. Their activities are regulated not by statutory rules, but by internal rules, conventions and inter-party agreements. Parties are not even recognised in electoral law, which sees a parliamentary general election as a series of separate contests between individual candidates in each constituency. The Labour and Liberal Democratic parties have the legal status of unincorporated associations, the components of the party being separate entities, but legally bound together by contract. The Conservative Party, however, exists from the legal point of view only as three separate elements: the parliamentary party; Conservative Central Office, the party organisation, which controls party funds; and the National Union, representing the membership. These parts are not linked together contractually.[28]

The view prevalent in Britain in the past has been that the less the law has to do with political parties, the better. When it was proposed in 1968 that the Representation of the People Act establish a Registrar of Political Descriptions which would keep a list of 'registered political descriptions' – a proposal deleted before the bill reached the statute book – the eminent psephologist David Butler, among others, objected, on the grounds that 'by making the ownership of a party label a justiciable matter, the law is quite unnecessarily brought into politics'.[29] One consequence of the lack of any such register, however, is that while a candidate is entitled under the Representation of the People Act to have put on the ballot paper beside his or her name a political description not exceeding six words, 'there seems to be no requirement that the description should be accurate and no remedy if it is misleading'.[30] The issue arose in the Glasgow Hillhead by-election of 1982 when Roy Jenkins, the SDP candidate and eventual winner of the by-election, whose middle name is Harris, was unable to obtain redress against a candidate who had changed his name to Roy Harold Jenkins, and claimed to represent an alternative Social Democrat party. In the 1994 elections to the European Parliament, a candidate for the Devon and Plymouth East constituency calling himself a 'Literal Democrat' gained over 10,000 votes. The Liberal Democrats failed to overtake the Conservatives in this seat by just 700 votes. It is highly likely that natural voter confusion cost the Liberal Democrats a seat. Yet they could obtain no redress.

Reservations about the role of the law in politics were also responsible for the 'Short money' scheme being introduced in 1975 by parliamentary resolution rather than by statute. This left some ambiguity surrounding the question of who should receive the grant within each party, and in 1979 there was a dispute between the National Executive Committee of the Labour Party and the Parliamentary Labour Party as to which body had the right to receive the money. In the event, the money was paid to the Parliamentary Labour Party. Had the funding been placed on a statutory basis, the details of its distribution would have been more clearly established.

The law prescribes certain minimal constitutional requirements for such bodies as charities, trade unions, building societies, limited companies – indeed, every body in which the public has a legitimate interest. Yet it treats political parties as if they were private clubs. 'It is,' argued the Liberal Democrat peer Lord Holme, 'an extraordinary anomaly that a party can organise itself to become the Government of this country, and is yet not subject to the basic reporting requirements to which every club, association and company is subject. I do not think that the voters, the people of this country, understand why it is that political parties are somehow special and should not have to present accounts which declare in full where they received their money and how they spent it.'[31] Were the parties to accept public money, it would be a reasonable quid pro quo that they be required in return to account for the way in which the money had been used and to publish accounts in standardised form. Such accounts ought to be required to show the proportion of funds provided by individual and institutional donors, and the respective proportions of income derived from fund-raising, from foreign donations, from large individual donations and from membership subscriptions.

Constituency parties should not be exempt from the general rule that receipt of public funds should be conditional on financial accountability. Precisely because the activities of the constituency parties have political consequences, they should no longer be seen as purely private bodies like golf clubs, but rather as bodies with important public functions. It would, of course, be impracticable for the Comptroller and Auditor General to enter into a direct relationship with every constituency party. But there is no reason why constituency accounts should not be professionally audited so that the local party associations are required to conduct their activities in a properly business-like manner. Moreover, the parties should be required to consolidate donations made to the constituency parties. Otherwise companies or large donors could avoid disclosure or controls at the centre by spreading the money around at constituency level.

The issue of the funding of political parties leads inexorably on to that of disclosure. The argument against disclosure is that individuals and institutions have the right in a free society to donate to political parties of their choice, as to other bodies, without these donations being publicly known. In the case of large donations, however, the right to privacy may reasonably be held to be outweighed by the public interest in allaying suspicion that the reason for the donation was to purchase access or influence. For, in the words of Justice Brandeis, sunlight is the best disinfectant. In a free society, it may be wrong to prevent people from giving large sums to political parties. But, if donations above a certain amount are declared, the voter will be in a position to make a judgement as to the probity of the donor. The Labour Party now makes it a practice to decline donations from those who are not British nationals or voters or institutions based in the United Kingdom. It also voluntarily makes public all donations over £5,000. It does not, however, reveal the size of such donations, which could be either £5,001 or £10 million. The Conservatives do not accept money from foreign governments or rulers, but they do accept money from individuals living abroad.

Were political parties to be legally registered and to have a legal status, it would be possible to update the law on election expenditure, which is seriously out of date. The law in this area is still based on the Corrupt Practices Act 1883, which first limited the amount that individual candidates could spend. There are no limitations, however, upon the amounts which the parties can spend nationally. In the nineteenth century, a general election was seen largely as a contest between individual candidates, and spending by party headquarters was comparatively negligible. In 1880, for example, total central spending on the election by the Conservative and Liberal parties seems to have amounted to just £50,000.[32] The law restricting the expenditure of individual candidates therefore controlled virtually all election spending. Today, however, it controls but a small proportion of it, and the law on election expenses achieves only the illusion of control.

The law ignores two vital features differentiating contemporary election campaigns from campaigns in the nineteenth century: the nationalisation of politics, and the fact that campaign activity is not restricted to the immediate pre-election period. The law still treats a general election campaign as a series of individual constituency contests, so that a poster proclaiming 'Vote Smith, Conservative', falls under the election law, while a poster exhorting 'Vote Conservative' does not. This is clearly anomalous. The purpose of restrictions at constituency level is, after all, to ensure fairness between competing candidates. In the modern world, however, the fortunes of the candidates depend primarily upon the fortunes of their national parties. Thus, if it is thought desirable to promote fairness between candidates, it must surely be right also to promote fairness between parties.

Moreover, contributors and taxpayers have a right to be protected from financial abuse through extravagance on the part of the parties. The control of political expenditure following upon the introduction of the tax credit scheme in Canada has brought a much greater concentration upon record-keeping, financial planning and financial control. The national secretary of the New Democratic Party in Canada, Robin Sears, declared that the Canadian legislation had 'forced a sense of fiscal responsibility on all of us – which was not common among political parties before'.[33]

Constituency election expenditure is controlled through the requirement that each party appoint a registered agent, who can alone authorise election expenditure for that party in that constituency. A ceiling is imposed upon how much expenditure can be authorised, and any expenditure incurred without the agent's authorisation is illegal. This principle could be adapted at national level, as has been done in Canada under the Election Expenses Act 1974 and the Canada Elections Act 1985. Under this legislation, each party must, at national level, appoint a national agent, and the only legal party expenditure is that authorised by the agent. Party expenditure is subject to a ceiling, which is dependent on the number of constituencies being contested by the party and the number of electors in these constituencies.

One problem with this and other forms of control of party funding is that it is easy to evade the provisions. If, for example, there were to be a national ceiling on party expenditure, a party might channel the funds to a related but non-party organisation. The Conservatives might, for example, set up an organisation called 'Free Enterprise plc', which would spend money on its behalf, while Labour might establish an organisation called 'Community Spirit plc' to do the same. Even if they did not do that, independent organisations could of their own volition spend money which affected the fortunes of the political parties. An organisation supporting grant-maintained schools, for example, could publish advertisements warning voters against a party which did not support such schools. This would, in effect, be propaganda for the Conservative Party. Another organisation might advertise in favour of the minimum wage, which would, in effect, be propaganda for Labour. Therefore, expenditure by non-party organisations – and, indeed, individuals – would have to be embraced by the legislation, such that it could only be authorised by a party agent, and would count towards the party's total election expenditure. That might, however, be seen as a restriction of freedom of speech and debate. It would mean that only party professionals could take part in the political debate in so far as that involved the spending of money. But this is already the case with constituency campaigning. A private individual cannot put up a notice in his or her garden, saying, for example, 'Vote for the candidate who favours grant-maintained schools', unless that expenditure has been authorised by a party agent and is included in its total of election expenses. In Canada, this principle has been taken to its logical conclusion, and no independent expenditures designed to influence the electoral battle are allowed. In the United States, the approach has been different. The Supreme Court held in the leading case of *Buckley* v. *Valeo* 424 U.S. 1 (1976) that expenditure limits violated the First Amendment, protecting freedom of speech. However, the Court declared, those who accept public subsidies may legitimately be required to abide by expenditure and contribution limits which would otherwise not be constitutionally applied to them. These rules then become conditions attached to the voluntary acceptance of public funds. Thus, presidential candidates who accept public financing for their campaigns are required as a quid pro quo to accept expenditure limits.[34] Such an approach could perhaps be adopted in Britain. It would be likely that all parties, including the Conservatives, would accept public funding. Even Ronald Reagan did not allow his hostility to the state to prevent him from accepting public funding for his presidential campaigns of 1980 and 1984.

VI

Finally, and perhaps most importantly of all these considerations, state aid to the political parties could be used as leverage to help secure a fairer and more rational pattern of institutional finance. There would be no reason to maintain the tight regulation of trade union affiliation fees without imposing comparable regulations on company donations. It would be perfectly possible to require companies wishing to make political donations to establish a separate political fund, following a postal vote by the shareholders, and for that postal ballot to be repeated every ten years. Political donations would then be deducted from shareholders' dividends. Collective shareholders such as pension funds should, however, always be required to contract out of such contributions. So should individuals without a United Kingdom address. Individual shareholders should be given the option to contract out; or, alternatively, individual shareholders should be required to contract in, with contracting out in the trade unions then also reverting to contracting in.

Until recently, party funding in Britain could be presented as a success story. The extent of corruption – although there is some – is negligible compared with most other democracies, and, despite the absence of statutory restrictions on the amounts that parties can spend at national level during election campaigns, costs are not excessive by international standards. Whatever theoretical anomalies could be found, the arrangements seemed to be working reasonably effectively in sustaining a two-party system in which the financial gap between the major parties, although real, was not such as to impose an insuperable handicap upon the financially weaker party, Labour.

Party funding now needs reform, however, because the preconditions for the effective working of the traditional arrangements no longer exist. The decline of class feeling has made the conception of a natural tie between the organised working class and the Labour Party quite anachronistic, as the leader of the Labour Party, Tony Blair, has himself admitted. 'Nobody,' he declared in September 1995, 'seriously believes in this day and age that the business of the Labour Party is to be the political arm of the trade union movement.'[35] Trends towards a multi-party political system have caused many to question the fairness of arrangements which offer such great advantages to parties which can command institutional finance for themselves. It could indeed be argued that the pattern of party finance, like the electoral system, has entrenched a two-party system against which the electorate has been reacting for nearly 25 years, since the general election of February 1974, when the two major parties gained only 75 per cent of the vote. Since then, Labour and the Conservatives have not once been able to secure as much as 80 per cent of the vote between them. It is for this reason, fundamentally, that reform of political funding is needed, to make the arrangements for party funding more congruent with the state of electoral feeling.

The scheme proposed in this chapter would allow state aid to the political parties to be used, not to ossify the party system or bureaucratise it, but to improve the internal health of the parties. Aid, tied to an index of political activity such as membership subscriptions and individual contributions, would certainly not protect the parties from the consequences of falling membership or from an inability to attract support. Far from discouraging participation in politics, it would encourage the parties to search for new members and new sources of support. It would stimulate, not inhibit, that voluntary activity which is so important to a healthy polity. In this way the public funding of political parties would make its contribution to the strengthening of our system of democracy.

7

The Monarchy

The twentieth-century monarchy has not, until recently, been in the forefront of the constitutional reform debate. In Victorian times there was a debate, often a very robust one, on the role of the monarchy, and in the 1860s leading radicals did not hesitate to voice republican sentiments. From the 1870s until the 1990s, however, attacks on the monarchy were almost taboo. Indeed, for much of the twentieth century, the monarchy attracted to itself a degree of adulation and a mystique which are difficult to explain in rational terms. As recently as 1956, four years after the present Queen's accession, an opinion poll showed that 35 per cent of the population believed she had been chosen by God.[1] The phrase 'the magic of monarchy' occurred frequently in discussions of monarchy, the implication being that it was an institution whose inspiration was fundamentally irrational. Today, for the first time in well over a hundred years, the monarchy in Britain finds itself on the defensive. Republicanism, no longer a taboo subject, is publicly advocated and there are now media debates on the future of the monarchy, something unthinkable even ten years ago.

There are two constitutional issues involved in the debate on the monarchy. The first is whether Britain should remain a monarchy or become a republic. The second is whether the sovereign's current constitutional role should be retained, or whether it ought to be fundamentally altered, by, for example, transferring the sovereign's remaining constitutional prerogatives to the Speaker of the House of Commons.

But why is it that perceptions of monarchy have changed so rapidly? Obviously the personal difficulties of members of the Royal Family and the intrusion of the media into their private lives have affected popular attitudes. But that is only a small part of the explanation. More fundamental has been the rapidity of changes in social attitudes. Deference is no longer, as it was until perhaps the 1960s, a powerful force in society, and the past is no longer seen as a source of authority or legitimacy. Instead, social attitudes are based upon a pervasive utilitarianism. An institution can no longer be defended simply by virtue of the fact that it has existed for a long time. It must also be shown that it fulfils some practical and useful purpose.

In the years since the Second World War, the other symbols with which the monarchy was associated – in particular the Church of England and the Commonwealth – have declined in importance. They no longer play the same role in social life that they did when the Queen was crowned. After the coronation service in 1953, the Archbishop of Canterbury was to claim that the nation had been near to God on that occasion. When, in February 1947, on her twenty-first birthday, Princess Elizabeth, as the Queen then was, dedicated herself to the service of Britain and the Commonwealth for the rest of her life, she spoke of 'our great imperial family to which we all belong'. 'Without the Crown', thundered the Coronation Supplement of the *Westminster Bank Review*, 'there can obviously be no Britain and no Commonwealth. Without Britain and the Commonwealth, there can be no tolerable future.'[2] Such high-flown sentiments undoubtedly encapsulated the spirit of the age, a mood of optimism that, with the end of austerity, Britain was embarking upon a new Elizabethan era of power and greatness. But it could not last; with assumptions about the role of the church and Britain's relationship to the rest of the Commonwealth having changed so radically since the immediate post-war period, and with Britain's decline as a world power, it was perhaps inevitable that the mystique of monarchy would come to be undermined as well.

All these trends were emphasised during the long premiership of Margaret Thatcher between 1979 and 1990. For 'Thatcherism' aimed to modernise British society by reforming its traditional institutions – the Civil Service, the BBC, the Church of England, the universities – so that they reflected a more market-orientated and competitive ethos. This programme of reform did not include the monarchy, for Margaret Thatcher was herself a fervent monarchist. But nevertheless, the ethos which she represented could not leave the monarchy unaffected. The sceptical and reforming spirit which Margaret Thatcher inculcated led some to ask why the monarchy, alone among British institutions, was to remain exempt from critical questioning. Indeed, a rather peculiar anti-monarchical alliance developed between the traditional left-wing hostility to inherited privilege and a Thatcherite insistence that traditional institutions be required to justify themselves.

Today, then, the monarchy needs to be defended in rational and practical terms rather than by appealing to its mystical significance, the approach which was prevalent until recently. It is not difficult to construct such a rational defence. Indeed, the case for constitutional monarchy is as powerful today as it has ever been; and its preservation is in the interest of constitutional reformers as much as of constitutional conservatives.

The fundamental argument for constitutional monarchy is that it yields a head of state who has no political history and will therefore be free of party ties. In a republic, there can never be a guarantee that the president will not be a party politician, opposed perhaps by half of the nation. That is, of course, particularly likely to be the case in a republic such as France or the United States where the president is head of government as well as head of state. Bill Clinton, for example, is deeply resented by a large proportion of the population of the United States, who do not see him as representing them or personifying their aspirations at all. The same is true of Jacques Chirac in France.

Even where the president is a largely symbolic head of state with no executive role, as in Germany and Italy, he or she is still likely to be a former party politician whose motives may always be suspect to some citizens. In Britain, the names of various respected non-party celebrities are often canvassed as possible presidents. But in practice, the choice of president, whether it is made by direct popular election or through some indirect method of election, perhaps by the House of Commons, would inevitably be dominated by party politicians. For no independent candidate, unless he or she were a multi-millionaire, would be able to finance or organise the campaign needed to secure election. The most likely president would be a retired party politician such as Neil Kinnock or Lord Howe. Thus, under a republic, in Bagehot's words, the head of state

would inevitably be a party man. The most dignified post in the state must be an object of contest to the great sections into which every active political community is divided. These parties mix in everything and meddle in everything; and they neither would nor could permit the most honoured and conspicuous of all stations to be filled, except at their pleasure. They know too, that the grand elector, the great chooser of ministries, might be, at a sharp crisis, either 'a good friend or a bad enemy. The strongest party would select someone who would be on their side when he had to take a side, who would incline to them when he did incline, who should be a constant auxiliary to them and a constant impediment to their adversaries. It is absurd to choose by contested party election an impartial chooser of ministers.[3]

These words remain as true today as they were when Bagehot wrote them in the 1860s.

Mary Robinson, president of the Irish Republic, is often put forward as a counter-example. The President of the Irish Republic is directly elected, and the election is dominated by party politics. Mary Robinson was the candidate of the Irish Labour Party, but she has nevertheless managed to project herself as a representative of the whole Irish nation and is accepted as such by the vast majority of Irish people. The example of Mary Robinson, however, shows not how easy, but how difficult it is for a president to represent the whole of the nation. For, between 1937 when the Irish Constitution was enacted, and 1990, when Mary Robinson assumed office, every President of Ireland was chosen from the dominant Fianna Fail party, representing one side in the Irish civil war which racked the country in the 1920s. Indeed, between 1959 and 1973 the President of Ireland was Eamon de Valera, the former Prime Minister and leader of the anti-Treaty forces in the civil war. He was a particularly controversial figure and could not be expected to represent the descendants of the pro-Treaty forces in the civil war, some of whom were present in the Irish parliament during de Valera's presidency.

In 1976, there was a striking illustration of how an elected president can find himself at the mercy of the government of the day. The Irish President, Cearball O'Dalaigh, in the proper exercise of his constitutional functions, decided to refer a government bill to the Supreme Court. In a public speech, the Minister of Defence called the President 'a thundering disgrace'. The President demanded an apology from the Prime Minister. When he did not receive one, he resigned. He was in effect driven from office by a government of the opposite political colour. That could not happen with a constitutional monarch.[4]

The sovereign, moreover, has the advantage of permanence and of continuous political experience, which is not open to any other candidate for the role of head of state. By 1997 the Queen had been on the throne for forty-five years. She enjoys a longer political experience than anyone else active in public life, and nine Prime Ministers have served under her. 'In the course of a long reign,' Bagehot remarks, 'a sagacious king would acquire an experience with which few ministers could contend.'[5] 'I am not a clever man,' George V once said, 'but if I had not picked up something from all the brains I've met, I'd be an idiot.'[6] In a presidency, by contrast, each incumbent would have to master the processes of government anew every few years.

In modern times, the sovereign fulfils two complementary roles. The first is a constitutional one, as head of state. The second is a symbolic one, as head of the nation. Both roles are best undertaken by someone free of all party ties. During the 1995 commemorations of VE Day and VJ Day, the Queen was seen fulfilling her symbolic role. She was able to represent the nation to itself in a way which would have been more difficult for any former party politician, however well respected. It is, indeed, this function of representing the nation to itself at critical periods of its history which defines the symbolic role of head of the nation. A president with a political history will always find it harder to perform this function in a way which allows the whole nation to identify with him or her as its personification.

I I

The sovereign's constitutional functions flow from her role as head of state. In form, the sovereign is head of the executive and, as the Crown, can in theory perform a wide range of functions under prerogative powers. 'It is wonderful,' wrote Bagehot in *The English Constitution*, 'how much the sovereign can do. . . . she could disband the army . . . she could make a peace by the sacrifice of Cornwall or begin a war for the conquest of Brittany. She could make every citizen in the United Kingdom, male or female, a peer; she could make every parish in the United Kingdom a "university"; she could dismiss most of the Civil Servants; she could pardon all offenders.'[7]

These prerogative powers, however, are now exercised almost entirely upon the advice of the Queen's ministers. For, although the sovereign is formally the head of the executive, the vast bulk of her prerogative powers are now exercised not by her personally but either by her on the advice of ministers or by ministers themselves. The Queen retains only two major personal prerogatives. These are the right to appoint a Prime Minister and the right to agree to or to refuse a dissolution of Parliament. Her Christmas message to the Commonwealth is also undertaken on her own prerogative, without advice.

The sovereign, however, very rarely has any discretion over the use of these prerogatives. A general election under the first past the post system normally yields a clear majority government, and the leader of the winning party will then automatically be appointed Prime Minister. There have been only three hung parliaments since the end of the First World War in 1918 – after the general elections of 1923, 1929 and February 1974. A Prime Minister leading a majority government can normally rely upon securing a dissolution at a time of his or her choice, for in these circumstances there will be no alternative leader able to command a parliamentary majority. The sovereign has not refused a dissolution of Parliament since before the Great Reform Act of 1832, although there have been such refusals by governor-generals acting as the Queen's representative in Commonwealth countries.

Until 1965, the power to appoint a Prime Minister was a genuine prerogative of the sovereign when the Conservatives were in power. For, unlike Labour or the Liberals, the Conservatives had no machinery for electing their leader so that, upon the death or resignation of a Conservative Prime Minister, the sovereign had to appoint a successor following consultations with senior party figures. In 1963, however, there was considerable controversy over the selection of Lord Home as the successor to Harold Macmillan as Prime Minister, and by 1965 the Conservatives had adopted an electoral procedure of their own to choose their leader and, when in office, Prime Minister-designate. This procedure has been used on three occasions when the Conservatives have been in office: in 1989 when Anthony Meyer challenged Margaret Thatcher, in 1990 when Michael Heseltine challenged Margaret Thatcher, and in 1995 when John Major resigned as party leader and was challenged by John Redwood. On each occasion, it worked perfectly smoothly and the sovereign was in no way involved.

For the foreseeable future, the sovereign is likely to be called upon to exercise her personal prerogatives in only three situations: first, when there is a hung parliament; second, in emergency conditions, such as occurred in 1916 after the resignation of Asquith, when Lloyd George was asked to form a government, or in 1931 when an emergency National Government was formed to deal with the slump; and third, in the pathological circumstance of an improper request for a dissolution. Even in such situations, however, the sovereign cannot exercise her powers as she pleases. She must endeavour to act in a non-partisan manner even though the results of her actions may have the consequence of disadvantaging one or more of the political parties; and she must act in such a way as to ensure that the Queen's Government can be carried on, i.e. that a government is formed which can survive for more than a short period and is capable of offering her effective advice.

Were Britain to adopt one of the systems of proportional representation outlined in Chapter 3, then the sovereign might be required to exercise her personal prerogatives more frequently. For, under proportional representation, there would not be a majority single-party government unless one party succeeded in gaining 50 per cent of the vote, something that no government has achieved in Britain since 1935.[8] An election would be far more likely to yield an inconclusive result, and there might be some real exercise of discretion open to the sovereign on whom she should call to the Palace to appoint as Prime Minister. Moreover, a coalition or minority government which takes office after an election may or may not retain the support of a majority in Parliament for its full term. In these circumstances, the granting of a dissolution would no longer be automatic, for there might well be alternative governmental combinations possible in the existing House of Commons. Thus proportional representation could well lead to a greater role for the sovereign, as it does in the continental constitutional monarchies – Belgium, Denmark, Luxembourg, the Netherlands, Norway, Spain and Sweden – all of which have legislatures elected by PR.

With the likelihood of a hung parliament being greater in the 1990s than it was in the 1950s, and with the possibility of a switch to proportional representation which would make hung parliaments the norm, interest in the way in which the Queen would seek to resolve such a situation has been increasing. The responsibility does, in the last resort, lie with her alone, rather than with the so-called 'golden triangle' of the

Cabinet Secretary, the Principal Private Secretary to the Prime Minister and the Queen's own Private Secretary.[9] Those three officials have different responsibilities. The Cabinet Secretary and the Prime Minister's Principal Private Secretary are responsible to the incumbent Prime Minister; the Queen's Private Secretary is responsible to the sovereign, and is indeed her principal constitutional adviser. However, the decisions to be made are the Queen's alone. She would not be able to shuffle off the responsibility of a controversial decision by blaming her Private Secretary, whose advice remains entirely private.

In the government formation process, the sovereign, and most governor-generals in Commonwealth countries, have generally been guided in recent times by two principles. The first is that the problems of government formation ought to be resolved as far as possible by the politicians themselves, and that the sovereign or governor-general should intervene only as a last resort. 'Probably in most cases,' Bagehot declares, 'the greatest wisdom of a constitutional king would show itself in well-considered inaction. . . . The responsibility of Parliament should be felt by Parliament. So long as Parliament thinks it is the sovereign's business to find a government it will be sure not to find a government itself.'[10] This comment was echoed in a speech in May 1996 by Sir Michael Hardie Boys, the Governor-General of New Zealand, whose task it was to preside in that year over New Zealand's first general election held under proportional representation. Sir Michael declared that 'because the head of state must be, and must be seen to be, politically neutral, removed, aloof from politics, it is the responsibility of politicians to protect her and her representative from the need to make what is, or may be seen to be, a political decision. . . . My job in all this is to ascertain the will of Parliament, that is, to find out where the support of the House lies and make an appointment accordingly. It is for the politicians themselves to provide the necessary information.' Sir Michael correctly sums up the role of the governor-general in the government formation process, which is that not of an arbitrator but of a facilitator. The sovereign's position is broadly similar, although she enjoys greater authority than a newly chosen governor-general.

The question is often asked: whom would the Queen call to the Palace in the event of a hung parliament? This, however, is a profoundly misleading question. The question of who would form a government in each of the three hung parliaments in Britain since 1918 – those after the general elections of 1923, 1929 and February 1974 – was resolved through the actions of the party leaders, and no intervention by the sovereign was necessary. In the case of a future hung parliament, it is likely that the key decisions will once more be made by the politicians, and the Queen's responsibility will be limited to registering them.

After an inconclusive general election result, the first decision lies with the Prime Minister. He must decide whether he should resign immediately, as Stanley Baldwin did in 1929, seek an agreement with another party or parties, as Edward Heath sought unsuccessfully to do in 1974, or wait to meet Parliament as Baldwin did after the 1923 general election. Once the Prime Minister has resigned, the Queen would normally appoint the leader of the largest party – or if the Prime Minister was, as with Baldwin after the 1923 general election, himself the leader of the largest party, the leader of the second largest party – as Prime Minister.

With an uncertain parliamentary situation, it could take some time for a new government to be formed after an election, especially if it were necessary to draw up a formal coalition agreement between two or more parties. Were that to happen, the resigning Prime Minister might well be asked to continue in office with his government acting in a caretaker capacity. His resignation would then actually take effect only when it became clear who should succeed him. The State Opening of Parliament, the date of which requires the agreement of the Queen, could be postponed were the incumbent Prime Minister to advise her to issue a proclamation to this effect under the Proclamation of Prorogation Act 1867, under which the summoning of the new Parliament can be deferred by not less than 14 days. Once a new Prime Minister is appointed, he will test his support in the Commons. If defeated, he would probably be able to secure a dissolution unless another MP, normally a party leader, could demonstrate, through public agreement with other parties, that he could command and sustain a House of Commons majority.

In the past, the sovereign had the option of calling a conference of party leaders, as occurred in 1916 and 1931. Such an option is probably not now available, given the media attention that it would probably provoke. Sir Michael Hardie Boys did not call such a conference in New Zealand after the 1996 general election, even though it took eight weeks for a government to be formed. Even if such a conference were to be called, the sovereign would still content herself with registering the decisions of the party leaders, rather than seeking to impose a solution upon them. Thus, under modern conditions, the sovereign would normally expect to play a passive role if a general election yielded a hung parliament.

The second principle on which the sovereign acts is that, in the words of Lord Esher, a confidant of Edward VII, in 1910, 'the principle' of the prerogative 'is entirely dependent upon the circumstances in which the prerogative is used'.[11] For the sovereign may be called upon to do what is best in a specific situation whose precise contours cannot be predicted. The sovereign, therefore, although always guided by past precedents, cannot be bound by them. Her options cannot be determined in advance, nor can they be laid down in the form of a set of rules. There is a tension between this principle and the basic rule of constitutional monarchy, that the sovereign must remain politically neutral. For the greater the discretion the sovereign enjoys, the greater the possibility that she will use her discretion in a manner which is contrary to the interests of one of the parties in the state. This is, however, more a theoretical conflict than a practical one, for the reason perhaps that constitutional crises requiring the intervention of the sovereign have been rare in British twentieth-century politics.

Many of the conventions of the British Constitution may in reality be conventions of the two-party system. The fundamental reason why there has been so little intervention on the part of the sovereign during the twentieth century may be the fact that Britain has retained a two-party system for much of the period. This, of course, is contingent and might well change with the advent of proportional representation.

The possibility of a more frequent use of the personal prerogatives has persuaded some to argue that the principles on which the Queen would operate in the event of a hung parliament ought to be published so that they may become publicly known. Such principles might perhaps be drawn up by a committee of Privy Counsellors. What Peter Hennessy has christened the 'good chap' theory, according to which the politicians can be relied upon to act with discretion and not to embarrass the sovereign, is no longer sufficient. In Hennessy's words, 'the rubric surrounding the "reserve powers" of the monarch belongs not to the Queen, the Prime Minister and the "golden triangle", but to all those who legitimately aspire to capture the state by open and democratic means. These particular constitutional power-lines really should be brought to the surface for all to see and inspect. Ours, after all, is the era of transparency and regulation.'[12]

The British monarchy differs from those on the European continent in that we alone have no codified constitution. It might be thought, therefore, that the proposal to make public the principles on which the sovereign would use her discretion in the case of a hung parliament would do no more than bring the British monarchy into line with the monarchies of the continent. In fact, however, the constitutions of continental monarchies make hardly any reference to what the sovereign should do in the case of a hung parliament. For example, Article 14 of the Danish Constitution declares merely that the sovereign appoints and dismisses the Prime Minister and all other ministers. It does not discuss the principles on which the sovereign should act when making her choice. Similarly, Article 96 of the Belgian Constitution declares simply that 'The King appoints and dismisses his Ministers', while Article 43 of the Dutch Constitution declares that 'The Prime Minister and the other ministers shall be appointed and dismissed by Royal Decree'. Constitutions say nothing about the conventions by which the sovereign acts. Uncertainty about what the sovereign will do is just as great, if not greater, in Denmark, Belgium and the Netherlands as it is in Britain. From the point of view of the government formation process, therefore, the significance of a codified constitution is entirely emblematic; and even if Britain were to adopt a codified constitution, this would in no way clarify the way in which the sovereign would exercise her discretion.

There is a fundamental reason why it is not possible in a constitution, or indeed in any other agreed document, to lay down the principles guiding the sovereign's choice. It is that the principles themselves will be matters of contention among the party leaders because they affect the conditions under which they acquire political power. Moreover, hung parliaments or other situations giving rise to a need for the intervention of the sovereign often blow up out of a clear sky. Such was the case, for example, with the hung parliament of 1974. No one, therefore, can predict the precise contours of the situation in which the sovereign will have to act.

The basic conventions of the constitution governing the actions of the sovereign can be found in any textbook of constitutional law. The trouble is, however, that they are of little use in a real constitutional crisis; for when such a crisis arises, it will generally do so because there is a conflict of conventions, and the problem will be that it is not clear which set of conventions is the relevant one. This is particularly the case at the present time, when we may be living in a period of transition between a two-party system and a multi-party one, for the conventions applicable to a two-party system may well cease to apply in a multi-party system. For example, the near-automatic entitlement to a dissolution will be much less applicable in a multi-party situation when there will be the possibility of an alternative government being formed from the existing Parliament. Nor will it always be obvious who should be appointed Prime Minister in a multi-party Parliament.

The conflict between the conventions appropriate under a two-party system and a multi-party system is not merely a theoretical one. It is political, affecting as it does the fortunes of the main parties. The Conservatives, no doubt, would wish to insist that the conventions appropriate to a two-party system should continue to hold, since they are the only party unequivocally committed to the first past the post mode of election which sustains the two-party system. The Liberal Democrats, by contrast, would wish to argue that the conventions appropriate to a multi-party system should begin to operate now. They might argue, for example, that no Prime Minister should be appointed after a general election resulting in a hung parliament unless he or she could be proven to enjoy the support of a majority in the House of Commons. In the past, by contrast (in 1924, 1929 and 1974), hung parliaments have yielded minority governments. But the Liberal Democrats might argue that these conventions related to a period that has gone, and that we are now in a state of transition to a multi-party system in which new conventions are needed. This argument, whatever its merits, also of course contains a good deal of party political self-interest. For if a candidate for the premiership were required to demonstrate majority support, he or she would almost certainly have to negotiate with the Liberal Democrats. Thus what may seem at first sight a purely constitutional argument is also an argument about political power.

Constitutional conflicts of this deep-seated kind cannot, therefore, be resolved by any published statement of principles, and indeed the right way to resolve such conflicts cannot be determined in advance of the actual situation. Such constitutional conflicts are of course possible in all political systems, whether monarchies or republics. The difference is that in a monarchy they can be resolved in the last resort by a figure who has no party history and is not beholden to any of the political forces in the country. The umpire, never having been one of the players in the game, will not have acquired obligations to any of the players. Thus the move to a regime of proportional representation, if it occurs, would in no way undermine the value of a constitutional monarchy.

III

Some advocates of proportional representation, however, fearful of the extra responsibility which this might give the sovereign, would seek to deprive her of her personal prerogatives. All of her actions would then be taken on advice.

How might the formation of a government and the dissolution of Parliament be carried out, if not through the prerogative of the sovereign? There are three possible methods. The first, adopted in Sweden, transfers the powers of the sovereign to the parliamentary Speaker. This proposal, championed by Tony Benn before he became a republican, is favoured by the Liberal Democrats.[13] The second method has been proposed by the left-wing think-tank, the Institute for Public Policy Research, in its proposed constitution for Britain.[14] It advocates that the powers of the sovereign be transferred to Parliament. The third method is the so-called 'constructive vote of no confidence' used in Germany to ensure that the Chancellor can be removed by a vote of confidence only if an alternative Chancellor is available. All three of these methods, however, suffer from fundamental flaws. They will be considered in turn.

In Sweden, the new constitution of 1974 deprived the sovereign of any role at all in the process of government formation or dissolution. Instead, it is the Speaker who appoints the Prime Minister by convening the party representatives for consultation and then submitting the name of a potential premier to the single-chamber Parliament, the Riksdag. Dissolution is determined solely by a parliamentary vote, and the sovereign plays no part in that process either.

It was the Social Democrats who pressed for the provisions in the Swedish constitution eliminating the sovereign from the process of government formation and dissolution. Their aim was to ensure that a left-wing government in Sweden would not suffer from the supposed prejudices of the king. The proposals were a compromise with those Social Democrats who favoured the abolition of the monarchy entirely.

The trouble is, however, that the Speaker in Sweden, being a party man, is far more likely to misuse his power than the sovereign. The sovereign, as a non-party figure, has a far stronger interest in impartiality than the Speaker. The danger in Sweden, which has by no means been entirely avoided, is that the parties choose for the Speakership not a respected politician who remains above the political struggle, as in Britain, but a skilful political operator who can be relied upon to offer advantage to his party in the battle over the appointment of the Prime Minister. In Britain, were this solution to be adopted, and the Speakership to be given these powers, a Conservative majority might not have allowed the election of Betty Boothroyd, a Labour MP, as it did in 1992. Instead, it might have chosen a less worthy figure who could be relied upon to defend the interests of the Conservative Party in a tight corner. This would be a real accretion of power to the governing party and its advocacy sits ill with the general position of the constitutional reform movement, one of whose main aims is to limit the powers of government and place them under constitutional control. The Swedish solution threatens to politicise the Speakership, something that would radically alter our parliamentary system. This 'solution', therefore, would cause more problems than the 'problem' which it seeks to cure.

The Institute for Public Policy Research (IPPR) in its draft constitution proposes that the House of Commons itself decide who should be appointed as Prime Minister and when Parliament should be dissolved. The proposal is that the Prime Minister be elected from the House of Commons by its members, and that the Commons sit for a fixed four-year term. It could be dissolved earlier only if a vote of no confidence in the Prime Minister were passed and the Commons were unable, within 20 days, to elect a new one; or, alternatively, if a vote of no confidence in the government were passed.

The proposal on dissolution avoids the inflexibility associated with a fixed term where there is no provision for an early dissolution at all. Fixed-term parliaments are favoured by some advocates of proportional representation since they deprive the Prime Minister of the possibility of a tactical dissolution, such as Harold Wilson secured seven months after the formation of his minority government in March 1974. He was able to choose a favourable moment for his party and was returned in the general election of October 1974 with a narrow overall majority. A fixed-term parliament, by contrast, forces the Prime Minister of the day to negotiate with other parties and this, some believe, would encourage compromise in politics. In Western Europe, however, there are only two legislatures with fixed terms. One is Switzerland; but the Swiss is not a system in which the executive depends for its existence upon the confidence of the legislature. The only system in which the executive does so depend upon the confidence of the legislature and where there is a fixed-term parliament is Norway.

The dangers of fixed-term parliaments, however, greatly outweigh the advantages. If dissolution is impossible, the result, far from being constructive compromise, could easily be stagnation and weak government. For it is by no means the case that in every parliamentary situation a viable government can be formed capable of securing the confidence of parliament. Deadlock is a perfectly possible alternative, and the only way of overcoming it may be through an appeal to the people. So it is that, in the words of the French parliamentarian, Waldeck-Rousseau, 'the ability to dissolve . . . is not a menace to universal suffrage, but its safeguard. It is the essential counterbalance to excessive parliamentarism, and for this reason it affirms the democratic character of our institutions.'[15]

The purpose of the IPPR's proposals, as with those who propose fixed-term parliaments, is to make the formation and dissolution of government automatic so that no element of discretion enters into the process at all. There is, however, no modern democracy where some discretion by the head of state or equivalent is not needed when a general election fails to produce a clear winner. And in fact the IPPR's proposals do not secure the automaticity of government formation and dissolution. The IPPR constitution does not provide for the situation, after a general election, when the Commons cannot elect a Prime Minister since no candidate has the support of a majority of MPs. That was the situation after the February 1974 general election when, under our system, the Queen was able to appoint Harold Wilson Prime Minister of a minority Labour government. Under the IPPR's proposed constitution, however, it seems that the device of appointing a minority Prime Minister might not be available. The only possibility then would be an immediate second general election. A second election, however, might simply have reproduced the deadlock. Suppose, moreover – a possibility which cannot be excluded – that a multi-party House of Commons refused to endorse any Prime Minister and yet also refused a dissolution. Alternatively, a multi-party House of Commons might endorse a Prime Minister but refuse to him or her the right of dissolution. Either situation would lead to a constitutional deadlock.[16]

The IPPR constitution does indeed take away from the sovereign the power to refuse a dissolution. But a Prime Minister who wanted a dissolution could often secure one by engineering a vote of no confidence in his or her government and asking his or her own MPs to support it. That is precisely what Willy Brandt did in Germany, where an analogous convention applies, to secure a dissolution in 1972; Helmut Kohl was to use the same device in 1983. On both occasions, the German Chancellor, seeking to dissolve the Bundestag at a favourable moment, asked his supporters to ensure that a vote of no confidence was passed. Under the current British system, by contrast, the Queen's right to refuse a dissolution could be brought into play if a Prime Minister sought to abuse the rights of Parliament by, for example, seeking to dissolve a newly elected House of Commons. So it is that under the IPPR's constitution a very real protection against an abuse of the rights of Parliament by the governing party would be lost. Thus the IPPR constitution fails to provide for the possibility of minority government and fails to prevent the possibility of an abuse of the provisions for dissolving Parliament.

One final alternative method of depriving the sovereign of her personal prerogative would be the constructive vote of no confidence. This instrument is employed in the Basic Law of the Federal Republic of Germany, the German constitution, Article 67 of which declares that:

(1) The Bundestag can express its lack of confidence in the Federal Chancellor only by electing a successor with the majority of its members and by requesting the Federal President to dismiss the Federal Chancellor. The Federal President shall comply with the request and appoint the person elected.
(2) Forty-eight hours shall elapse between the motion and the election.

The purpose of this Article is to prevent a government being brought down by a coalition of incompatibles, a merely negative and destructive majority, as occurred in the Weimar Republic between 1919 and 1933 when governments were brought down by an unnatural combination of Nazis and Communists. The constructive vote of no confidence means that an opposition which overthrows a government must be able and willing to take over the responsibility of government itself. This device has been used only once in the Federal Republic, in 1982, when it was used to replace Helmut Schmidt as Chancellor with Helmut Kohl.

The constructive vote of no confidence, however, only achieves its aim at the cost of allowing a weak minority government, which has lost the support of parliament, to hobble on without a dissolution. For if there is a coherent majority against the government, it can dismiss the government without need for the constructive vote of no confidence. If there is a coalition of incompatibles, the constructive vote of no confidence prevents it from bringing the government down. Yet the government, *ex hypothesi*, is a minority one which has lost the confidence of the legislature. The proper solution in such circumstances is a dissolution; but the constructive vote of no confidence allows this weak minority government to continue in office. 'By making the overthrow of cabinets difficult, it [the constructive vote of no confidence] threatens to encourage lame-duck chancellors.'[17] It is difficult, therefore, to see what this device has to offer to Britain under a regime of proportional representation.

Many of those who favour the Swedish method of forming a government, the IPPR constitution or the constructive vote of no confidence would like to see a 'modernised' monarchy on the Scandinavian or Benelux model. With the exception of Sweden, however, the Scandinavian monarchies have preferred to retain the sovereign as umpire rather than handing over the sovereign's prerogatives to the teams on the field. The Belgian and Dutch sovereigns, indeed, have far greater political influence and are accustomed to play a far more active role in the government formation process than would be appropriate in Britain. Proposals to deprive the Queen of her prerogatives would take Britain away from the Scandinavian or Benelux model of monarchy, not towards it.

IV

This does not mean, however, that the monarchy should remain immune from change. In the summer of 1996 it was revealed that a 'Way Ahead' group comprising the Queen, the Duke of Edinburgh, the Prince of Wales and other members of the Royal Family, together with advisers such as the Queen's Private Secretary, were considering a series of reforms to the monarchy. These would in no way affect the fundamental constitutional role of the sovereign; but they would help to modernise the monarchy. The subjects discussed were said to include reform of the law of succession to enable females to succeed to the throne on the same basis as males, and repeal of the clause in the 1701 Act of Settlement which prohibits any Catholic or any person married to a Catholic from succeeding to the throne.

At present, succession in the Royal Family, like succession to the peerage, is governed by the eleventh-century rule of primogeniture. Under this rule males inherit before females. Thus, were the Prince of Wales and his children to die, the succession would revert to Andrew, the Duke of York, and then to his children, and after that to Prince Edward, rather than to Anne, the Princess Royal, even though Anne is older than the Duke of York or Prince Edward. In these days of equal opportunities, it seems absurd to retain a rule of this kind and the case for change, therefore, must be very strong. It would be particularly appropriate to make the change at the present time since moving the Princess Royal from eighth in line, after the Duke of York and his two children and after Prince Edward, to fourth in line, after Prince Harry, the second son of the Prince of Wales, would be unlikely to be of any practical effect.

The prohibition against Catholics in the 1701 Act of Settlement means that any member of the Royal Family who marries a Catholic, such as Prince Michael of Kent who did so in 1978, automatically excludes himself or herself from succession to the throne. This prohibition is a product of the religious wars of the seventeenth century, when it was feared that Catholics might be disloyal citizens who would subvert the constitution in the interests of the Pope. Such fears have long since disappeared, and this provision must be deeply offensive to Catholics not only in Britain but also in those Commonwealth monarchies with large Catholic populations such as Canada and Australia. Moreover, repeal of the prohibition would not break the link in England between the Church of England, which is an established church, and the state. For the sovereign would still be required, under the Act of Settlement, to be in communion with the Church of England, of which he or she remains Supreme Governor. There is, however, no statutory requirement that the sovereign actually be a member of the Church of England; indeed, in the eighteenth century, two sovereigns – George I and George II – were German Lutherans. There is, all the same, a presumption that the sovereign is a member of the Church of England, since the coronation at which he or she is crowned and anointed is a Church of England ceremony.

Even here, however, reform may be desirable. The Prince of Wales has asked how, when he becomes sovereign and hence Supreme Governor of the Church of England, he can meaningfully represent the multi-cultural and multi-denominational society that Britain has now become. The Prince has declared that he would like those belonging to other denominations and faiths than the Church of England to be able to participate at his coronation. For the sovereign represents the whole nation. If the coronation is intended as a religious affirmation of the sovereign's commitment to the whole nation, why should one particular denomination be singled out? It is for this reason that the Prince has said that he would prefer to be thought of as 'Defender of Faith' rather than as 'Defender of the Faith'.

These reforms would of course require legislation. They are not therefore a matter for the Queen and the Royal Family alone, but would inevitably involve the Prime Minister and government of the day. Moreover, most of the reforms would also involve the other 15 Commonwealth monarchies – Canada, Australia, New Zealand and Jamaica, etc. This would not be the case in respect of any alteration in the relationship between the monarchy and the church, for the Church of England is the established church only in England. It is not the established church in Scotland, Wales or Northern Ireland, nor in any of the other Commonwealth monarchies. The rules of succession, however, do apply to all of the Commonwealth monarchies. It would be absurd to have a different rule of succession in, for example, Canada from that in Britain. Therefore, by convention, no country can unilaterally alter the rule of succession, either to abolish primogeniture or to allow Catholics to succeed. The same reform would have to be passed in all 16 Commonwealth monarchies according to their own particular constitutional provisions. In the case of Canada, this would involve passage not merely in the federal parliament but also in the ten provincial parliaments. In the case of Australia, a referendum would be required, and to be passed, the measure would have to be approved by a double majority – a majority of the voters and a majority of the states. The process of altering the rules of succession, therefore, is a highly complex one and might well re-ignite republican sentiment in Australia and Canada.

A further issue apparently discussed by the 'Way Ahead' group was the royal finances. There is considerable misunderstanding about the financing of the Royal Family. Since 1993, admittedly, Buckingham Palace has prepared and distributed a booklet on the royal finances clarifying the constitutional and financial arrangements. A second edition of this booklet was published in 1995. Most of the facts relating to the royal finances are, therefore, publicly available. Nevertheless, the arrangements are complex and anything that could be done to simplify them would be greatly in the interests of the monarchy.

One frequent source of misunderstanding relates to estimates of the Queen's wealth. Many such estimates include in this category the Royal Palaces, such as Buckingham Palace, St James's Palace and Windsor Castle, of which members of the Royal Family are life tenants, art treasures from the Royal Collection and the Crown Jewels. These, however, are owned by the Queen as sovereign and not as an individual. They are therefore inalienable; they cannot be disposed of by the Queen but must be passed on to her successors. They belong to the Queen just as little as 10 Downing St belongs to the Prime Minister or the White House belongs to President Clinton. The Queen's private wealth remains, as with any other individual, a private matter. However, the Lord Chamberlain declared in 1993 that estimates of £100 million and upwards were 'grossly exaggerated'.[18]

The fundamental constitutional principle that has determined the financing of the monarchy since the seventeenth century is that it should be funded by Parliament. Accordingly, the sovereign's public expenditure is financed primarily from two sources. The first is the Civil List, currently £7.9 million per annum. This now covers the official expenses only of the Queen herself, the Queen Mother and the Duke of Edinburgh. Official expenses for all other members of the Royal Family have, since 1993, been reimbursed by the Queen. Such reimbursements amount annually to around £1.5 million. Around 70 per cent of the expenditure of the Civil List is incurred on the salaries of those working directly for the Queen in her role as head of state.

The second source of finance for the sovereign's public expenditure is government departments; sums from this source in 1994/5 amounted to around £24 million. In addition, Parliament votes annual grants-in-aid to the Department of National Heritage for the upkeep of Royal Palaces and various other buildings used by the Royal Family. In 1996, these amounted to around £20 million. Much of this expenditure, for example that on the upkeep of the Royal Palaces, the Royal Collection and the Crown Jewels, would of course still be necessary were Britain to become a republic. The payments to the Duke of Edinburgh and the Queen

Mother may be compared with the provision made in, for example, the United States and Germany for ex-presidents and their wives and also widows of ex-presidents, all of whom receive pensions from public funds. Compared with such provisions, payments to two members of the Royal Family who, although beyond the age of retirement, still fulfil numerous public engagements, do not seem excessive.

The total annual cost of the monarchy under these various headings amounts to around £52 million – less than £1 per year for every person in the country. This may be compared, for example, with the expenditure of the Driver and Vehicle Licensing Agency, which in 1995/6 amounted to £173 million, over three times the cost of the monarchy.[19] Moreover, the monarchy raises far more each year for charity than it receives in Civil List payments.[20]

The categories mentioned above, however, do not exhaust the sources of the Queen's official expenditure. Expenditure which, historically, is not charged to the Civil List is financed from the Privy Purse, which also finances that part of the Queen's private expenditure as sovereign not financed from her own personal income. The Privy Purse is financed from the Duchy of Lancaster, and in 1996 raised £5.3 million. It is the responsibility of the Chancellor of the Duchy of Lancaster, normally a Cabinet minister. Since 1993, the Queen has agreed voluntarily to pay tax on the Privy Purse and on her personal income, with the exception that she is exempt from inheritance tax in relation to bequests left to her successor. Since 1981, the Prince of Wales has paid 25 per cent of his income from the Duchy of Cornwall to the government. He has also, from the same date, been paying income tax on a voluntary basis on revenues which he receives from the Duchy of Cornwall, and both he and the Princess of Wales have always paid tax, including income tax, in all other respects. Other members of the Royal Family are taxed on the same basis as ordinary taxpayers.

The above highly simplified account of the royal finances shows both the comparatively small cost of the monarchy and also the complexity of the financial arrangements, a result in part of the archaic categories in which they are expressed. There is a strong case for simplifying the arrangements and making them more transparent so that they can be more easily understood by the general public. It would in particular be helpful if annual accounts could be presented in standardised form show-ing the total cost of the monarchy. Since this is, as argued above, much

smaller than is generally imagined, the effect would be likely to be beneficial rather than harmful to the monarchical cause.

V

It may seem paradoxical that, in a book which looks benignly on so many
constitutional reforms, the monarchy should be seen as the one major
institution not in need of radical change. For there are many who now
regard the monarchy, based as it is on the rule of hereditary succession,
as a prime obstacle to the modernisation of Britain. On this view, the
monarchy sustains an archaic structure of society and militates against
the principles of openness and accountability which ought to animate a
modern democracy. 'The monarchy,' Roy Hattersley has declared,

> points Great Britain in quite the wrong direction. First of all, it points
> Great Britain towards the past. The monarchy is a relic of the great
> days of empire, the great days of British domination of world power
> and world politics.... It encourages people to think that Britain's
> greatness lies in the past rather than in the possible future. The second
> objection is that it is an institution which glorifies the deferential
> society, the hierarchical society. It announces by its existence that some
> people, as a result of blood and birth, are superior to others.[21]

On this view, the problems of the monarchy arise because it is an institution which is no longer in harmony with society. As traditional class
relations have broken down and Britain has become a more assertive
society, the monarchy comes to be seen as an embarrassing anachronism.
It is an institution from another age fundamentally unsuited to the twentieth century, legitimising a form of society which has long outlived its
usefulness.

Roy Hattersley has argued for 'a people's monarchy' such as operates
in Scandinavian countries. This would involve scaling down the Royal
Family so 'that the size of the family itself, those people who are regarded
as "royal", has to be diminished'.[22] However, as we have seen, the official
expenses of members of the Royal Family are not a burden on public
funds except in the case of the Queen, the Queen Mother and the Duke
of Edinburgh; the taxpayer contributes nothing towards the official
expenses of the so-called 'minor royals'. Moreover, the total cost of the

monarchy cannot be regarded as excessive. The 'Way Ahead' group, if press reports are to be believed, has been considering 'streamlining' the Royal Family so that only the Queen, the Duke of Edinburgh and their children undertake official functions. That, however, would be a pity, for the Queen and her immediate family could not possibly fulfil all of the various engagements which they are asked to undertake. Many of these are of merely local importance – the opening of a new County Hall, for example, or patronage of a local charity. They are therefore given little attention in the national press, but they are noticed in local newspapers. The attendance of even a 'minor' royal at such an event offers a boost to local morale and helps to sustain community spirit, the revival of which politicians of all parties have been trying to achieve.

One cannot help feeling that there is something profoundly insular in the views of those who believe that the monarchy is a barrier to change. For a brief inspection of other political systems shows that there is no necessary connection at all between backwardness and monarchy. On the continent, Denmark, Norway and Sweden did not find the creation of an egalitarian social democratic society incompatible with the continued existence of the monarchy. In Japan, the creation of an efficient advanced industrial society has proved perfectly compatible with the retention of a monarchy of a highly traditional kind. Nor is there any reason to believe that the monarchical Netherlands is any less modern than republican France, or that monarchical Spain is somehow less modern than republican Portugal. There is thus no reason why, if so minded, the British people should not, under a constitutional monarchy, take the Scandinavian path to social democracy. If radicalism has failed in Britain, it is the electorate who are to be blamed, for not voting radical governments into power, and not the Queen.

Admittedly, the Scandinavian monarchy operates in a very different atmosphere from the monarchy in Britain; an atmosphere best summed up in the phrase 'the bicycling monarchy'. Roy Hattersley has said that 'frankly, I prefer monarchs on bicycles than monarchs in seventeenth-century gilded coaches'.[23] Many of those who argue for a 'Scandinavian monarchy', however, fail to appreciate that, as noted above, in Denmark and Norway the sovereign enjoys more political influence than in Britain, not less. Moreover, as for the idea of a more informal monarchy, it is often the very same people who favour the Scandinavian 'bicycling monarchy' who also complain that Norway and Sweden are rather dull countries, somewhat lacking in glamour. The fact is that the style of monarchy is bound to vary in different countries since it depends so much on popular attitudes. Were the British people so minded as to seek a more utilitarian style of monarchy, that could be achieved without any change in the sovereign's constitutional position. Government, however, is of its nature rather dull. It would perhaps be a mistake to make it even duller.

The position of the monarchy has come into question not only as a result of the dissolution of traditional class relationships but also because of the decline of community feeling and what now seems to have been the temporary abandonment of consensus politics in the 1980s. For the monarchy is in a sense the symbol of the nation as a community. It represents the basic factors unifying the nation rather than the party political issues dividing it. Lord Charteris, a former Private Secretary to the Queen, has speculated in the following terms. 'You might say that the Queen prefers a sort of consensus politics rather than a polarised one, and I suspect this is true, although I can't really speak from know-ledge here. . . . I suspect – and I think it's only natural – that politics which are very polarised are very uncomfortable to the Sovereign. I think that must be so.'[24] There is bound to be some tension, then, between the monarchy, which is a symbol of continuity as well as community, and a truly radical government, whether of the right or of the left. Yet radical Prime Ministers, such as Gladstone, Asquith, Attlee, Wilson and Thatcher – Lloyd George being the only conspicuous exception – have been fervent monarchists. They all appreciated that the legitimacy which the monarchy confers is of as much value to a government which seeks to undermine the consensus as it is to a government which sustains it.

The project of constitutional reform, supported by many on the left, involves altering many of the familiar landmarks of the British Consti-tution. That could easily have a disorientating effect on the ordinary citizen who perhaps takes our constitutional arrangements too much for granted. In such circumstances, might it not become more rather than less important that there be a symbol of continuity beyond the realm of party politics in the form of a constitutional monarch? A government committed to constitutional reform might have need of the monarchy even more than a government committed to the status quo.

As a symbol of continuity, the monarchy may also be of value in helping the British people to retain and at the same time redefine their national identity *vis-à-vis* the European Union. It is sometimes suggested that the EU poses a threat to the monarchy. Of course, to the extent that British governments may choose to transfer sovereignty to the Union, the Queen's formal powers and influence will come to be exercised over a narrower sphere. Since, for example, powers over agriculture have been largely transferred to the European Union, that is no longer a matter on which British governments still advise the Queen. But the development of the European Union in no way affects the Queen's constitutional position. In February 1993, Lord Tebbit asked in the House of Lords whether the Maastricht Treaty would alter the constitutional position of the Queen. The reply given by the Foreign Office minister Lady Chalker was that 'the treaty in no way alters the Monarch's constitutional position in the United Kingdom. Nor does it impose specific duties on any individuals. Her Majesty would be entitled to exercise the rights set out in Articles 8a to 8e of the Maastricht Treaty. But in this, she would act on the advice of Ministers.'[25] For example, the Queen enjoys, under the Maastricht Treaty, the right to vote for elections to the European Parliament. She is only able to exercise this right, however, with the advice of her ministers, who would undoubtedly advise her not do so.

Whatever the arguments for or against European Union, they ought not to involve the monarchy. To argue that the integration of Europe threatens the monarchy would be implausible, given that, of the 15 member states of the Union, seven – Belgium, Denmark, Luxembourg, the Netherlands, Spain, Sweden and the United Kingdom – are monarchies. There is little evidence that the European Union has threatened the position of monarchy on the continent, or that the continental monarchies have ceased to provide a focus for the national identity of their peoples. Within a developing European Union, even perhaps in a federal Europe, should one ever come about, the monarchy would still be able to function as a focus of national loyalty within the broader unity.

The monarchy, admittedly, has always been at its strongest during periods of national self-confidence – during the wars with Napoleonic France, the years of imperial grandeur at the end of Queen Victoria's reign and the years of the Second World War. During the post-war period, by contrast, Britain has been a nation whose self-confidence has been in decline. 'We are a people,' Lord Hailsham declared in the 1960s, 'that has lost its way.'[26] That is perhaps even more true in the 1990s. And when things go wrong, it is easy to blame the symbol of our nationhood rather than our defective institutions. We blame the mirror rather than what is reflected in it. Perhaps, indeed, the current obsession with monarchy distracts our attention from what is really wrong with our constitution as well as from our very real social and economic problems.

Constitutional monarchy, as the one fixed point in a changing age, is a form of government which yields legitimacy by settling beyond argument the crucial question of who is to be the head of state, and placing the position of head of state beyond the reach of the political parties. To undermine the constitutional position of the sovereign would have the effect, therefore, not of increasing openness and accountability, but of providing yet another arena for party conflict. For the position of head of state would become one which the parties would claim as their own. Constitutional reformers, however, are hardly minded to increase the power of the political parties. On the contrary, many of them seek to circumscribe the role of the parties by opening up their activities to public control. From that perspective, the continued existence of the monarchy is of as much value to constitutional reformers as it is to constitutional conservatives.

8

Beyond Constitutional Reform

Most of the constitutional reforms described in this book would have the effect of redistributing power among the political parties and widening the range of those involved in decision-making. Proportional representation would probably lead to coalition government. Devolution would lead to the participation of more politicians from Scotland, Wales and the English regions in the government of their nations and regions. Reform of the House of Lords would have the effect of bringing a new group of professional politicians into the second chamber. Power would indeed be redistributed; but politicians and political professionals would remain the dominant figures. Such greater involvement of the public as occurred would be primarily, though not wholly, confined to choosing from this wider range of political professionals. These professionals are, almost by definition, unrepresentative of the wider population. The trouble with socialism, Oscar Wilde once said, is that it takes up too many evenings. That is even more true today, not only of socialists, but also of politicians who support New Labour, the Liberal Democrats or the Conservatives. Politics today is, for most of those engaged in it, a full-time activity. It is a career rather than a public duty.

For this reason, the constitutional reform agenda is probably insufficient fully to satisfy popular aspirations. It is unlikely of itself to overcome the considerable popular disenchantment with politics, a disenchantment which is especially marked among young voters, and manifested in the low electoral turnout of those between 18 and 25.[1] There is, however, a dual dynamic to constitutional reform. Its effect need not be confined to redistributing power among the political professionals. It could also point the way towards a much more important redistribution of power, a redistribution of power between the politicians and the people.

Democracy in Britain today is predicated upon the passivity of the vast majority of the country's citizens. The role of the people is limited to that of consenting or withholding its consent to the government of the day at periodic intervals. The British Constitution has become a system for selecting, maintaining and dismissing a governing elite, the leaders of the ruling party. For government in Britain today is fundamentally party government; and any analysis of the value and consequences of constitutional reform must therefore begin with an estimate of how it would affect the dominance of party in the British system of government.

The referendum and electoral reform each have the potential to open up party government to popular control. The referendum would ensure that major constitutional changes could not be made without popular approval. It is, however, not a weapon for regular use, but rather one to be resorted to on very rare occasions. It is unlikely that it would be employed regularly or for non-constitutional legislation. However, were the referendum to come to be employed more frequently, this might well lead to a demand for the initiative, by means of which a specified proportion of the registered electorate could require the government to call a referendum on a particular issue. That would be a fundamental change, taking this weapon of direct democracy out of the hands of the political class and giving it to the people.

For the referendum is an instrument which can repair a government's sins of commission. It prevents unpopular measures from reaching the statute book. Its function is an essentially negative one; it is a check on government. It could do nothing to repair a government's sins of omission, its failure to put on the statute book measures which the public favour. The referendum, although it yields a popular veto, thus remains a weapon in the hands of the political class. For it is the politicians, not the people, who determine when it comes into play. Thus the referendum, although a weapon of great value, would not be of great help in redistributing power away from the political parties to the people. It points the way, however, to the introduction of other instruments of direct democracy, such as the initiative, citizens' juries, people's parliaments and other innovations which technological advance makes possible.

Electoral reform is the fundamental constitutional change which, if properly implemented, would have the capacity to open up the political system. At one level, the main effect of electoral reform would be to put the coping-stone on the Westminster model of government. That model implies that government operates through the potential alternation of opposing political parties; but underlying the model is the premiss that the government of the day represents the majority of the voters. In Britain, however, the government represents, not the majority, but the largest minority. The electoral system produces a government which the majority do not want. Under proportional representation, by contrast, a majority in the Commons would genuinely reflect a majority in the country. The premiss underlying the Westminster model, that alternating majorities in Parliament represent majorities in the country, would then be realised.

But electoral reform could have a second effect. It could serve to increase popular participation in politics. Whether it does so or not depends on the precise system which is adopted. Debate on electoral systems is sometimes dismissed as a merely technical matter and therefore a waste of time. No greater mistake could be made. For different electoral systems have quite different political consequences. 'Proportional representation' is not the name of a single electoral system, but a generic term for a wide variety of systems whose effects vary considerably. Some varieties of proportional representation would open up the party system, so yielding greater power to the voter; others would render the grip of party even tighter than it is at present.

The key question is whether a particular system allows the voter to choose the candidate of his or her party, or whether this choice is determined for the voter by means of a rigid party list. What is required is a system of personal proportional representation, by means of which a voter can choose between individual candidates. The single transferable vote is the best-known such system of personal proportional representation, but there are also list systems which provide for such choice. These systems offer a range of candidates among whom the voter is able to choose. Where public opinion seeks it, such systems favour the fair representation of women, of ethnic minorities, and of different points of view, e.g. Europhile or Eurosceptic, within parties.

The primary motivation behind the electoral reform movement is to secure the fair representation of parties. But, properly implemented, electoral reform could also secure greater popular participation in politics. It is at this point that one moves beyond the contours of the constitutional reform to consider its wider implications. For, in the last resort, the constitutional reform movement looks towards a political system in which

the people, not Parliament, are the source of legitimacy. In Northern
Ireland, which has long been a laboratory for constitutional change, it
has been accepted by political leaders of all parties for some years that
the orthodoxies of the British Constitution, locating sovereignty at Westminster, are unsuitable. In Northern Ireland it is the people, not the
politicians, who are the source of constitutional legitimacy. Following
the abolition of Stormont in 1972, the Northern Ireland Constitution
Act 1973 provided that Northern Ireland will not cease to remain a part
of the United Kingdom without the consent of its people. The border
poll of 1973 was held to test the claim that the people of Northern
Ireland sought to remain within the United Kingdom. The Claim of
Right prepared by the Campaign for a Scottish Assembly similarly finds
sovereignty to lie with the Scottish people, not with Parliament. Proponents of a Bill of Rights believe that citizens are endowed with rights,
and that any incursion into these rights by government needs some special
justification. Supporters of freedom of information legislation believe that
information belongs with the people, not with government, so that the
onus should be, not on the people to prove why they need information,
but on government to defend its unwillingness to provide it.

Thus the constitutional reform movement points beyond a political
system in which the role of the people is to consent, to one in which
their role is to participate. It points towards a system in which the people
have become stakeholders rather than merely subjects. In the 1980s,
Margaret Thatcher opened up the economic system to popular participation through her labour market reforms, and through policies which
encouraged the ownership of property, shares and other forms of wealth.
John Major sought to open up the public services through such policies
as the Citizen's Charter. Both Prime Ministers sought in this way to
disperse power and to allow for greater participation by citizens in the
decisions which affected their lives. What neither of them achieved or
even sought to do, however, was to open up the political system itself. Yet
it is, in the last resort, impossible to bifurcate human beings, impossible to
create active economic citizens or active consumers of public services
without also creating a demand for active political citizenship.

It is, John Stuart Mill believed, 'the discussion and management of
collective interests' which is 'the great school of public spirit'.[2] We need,
then, to go beyond the orthodoxies of the constitutional reform agenda
if we are to create a new relationship between the people and the poli-

ticians. For the aim of constitutional reformers must be to replace government by the political professionals with government by the people. Only then will there have been a real transfer of power from government to the governed, a transfer from the rulers to the people.

Notes

CHAPTER 1: INTRODUCTION

1 Peter Hennessy, *The Hidden Wiring: Unearthing the British Constitution* (Gollancz, 1995), pp. 207, 184, 183.
2 *Delivering Constitutional Reform* (Constitution Unit, 1996), p. 1.
3 *The Economist*, 14–20 September 1996, p. 3.

CHAPTER 2: DEVOLUTION

1 Cited in *Scotland's Parliament: Fundamentals for a New Scotland Act* (Constitution Unit, 1996), p. 15.
2 *House of Commons Debates*, 29 November 1995, vol. 267, col. 1234.
3 For some of the difficulties of executive devolution, see Vernon Bogdanor, *Politics and the Constitution: Essays on British Government* (Dartmouth, 1996), pp. 200–4.
4 The distinction between the mace and the maze is derived from Richard Rose, *Understanding the United Kingdom: The Territorial Dimension to Government* (Longman, 1982).
5 Stein Rokkan and Derek Urwin, 'Introduction: Centres and Peripheries in Western Europe', in Rokkan and Urwin (eds), *The Politics of Territorial Identity: Studies in European Regionalism* (Sage, 1982), p. 11.
6 'Tacit understandings' is a phrase of Sidney Low's. See his *The Governance of England* (T. Fisher Unwin, 1904), p. 12.
7 Iain McLean, 'The Representation of Scotland and Wales in the House of Commons', *Political Quarterly*, vol. 66 (1995), p. 266.
8 This electoral system is discussed in more detail in Chapter 3.
9 *House of Commons Debates*, 6 May 1965, vol. 711, col. 1561.
10 Ibid., col. 1562.
11 See Vernon Bogdanor, *Devolution* (Oxford University Press, 1979), ch. 2.
12 H. C. G. Matthew, *The Gladstone Diaries*, vol. XI, (Clarendon Press, 1990), p. 542, entry for 28 April 1886.
13 BBC TV, *On the Record*, 16 February 1992.

14 Professor William Miller in a letter to *The Scotsman*, 23 January 1995, cited in *Scotland's Parliament*, p. 109.

15 Speech at Swansea, 4 June 1887, in A. W. Hutton and H. J. Cohen (eds), *The Speeches and Public Addresses of the Right Hon. W. E. Gladstone MP* (Methuen, 1894), vol. IX, p. 226.

16 G. Stoker and D. King (eds), *Rethinking Local Democracy* (Macmillan, 1995), p. 16.

17 *A Choice for England: A Consultation Paper on Labour's Plans for English Regional Government* (Labour Party, 1995), p. 6.

18 *House of Commons Debates*, 4 November 1993, vol. 231, col. 524.

19 *A Choice for England*, p. 7.

20 *A New Voice for England's Regions: Labour's Proposals for English Regional Government* (Labour Party, September 1996).

21 Royal Commission on the Constitution, *Minutes of Evidence*, Cmnd 5460 (1973), vol. 1, para. 14.

22 Lord Salisbury to Revd M. MacColl, 12 April 1889, in G. W. E. Russell (ed.), *Malcolm MacColl: Memoirs and Correspondence* (Smith, Elder, 1914), p. 137.

23 *The Times*, 21 July 1995.

CHAPTER 3: ELECTORAL REFORM

1 See also John Curtice, 'The British Electoral System: Fixture without Foundation', in Dennis Kavanagh (ed.), *Electoral Politics* (Clarendon Press, 1992), pp. 188–206.

2 John Curtice and Michael Steed, 'The Results Analysed', app. 2 in David Butler and Dennis Kavanagh, *The British General Election of 1992* (Macmillan, 1992), pp. 353, 342.

3 Ibid., pp. 332, 336.

4 This paragraph is based on ibid., pp. 350–1.

5 Robert Waller and Byron Criddle, *The Almanac of British Politics* (Routledge, 1996), p. xxii; Curtice and Steed, 'The Results Analysed,' p. 351.

6 *Guardian*, 7 April 1992.

7 The story is told in Henry Ashby Turner Jr, *Hitler's Thirty Days to Power: January 1933* (Bloomsbury, 1996).

8 The figures for 1974–87 are taken, with slight modifications, from R. M. Punnett, 'The Alternative Vote Re-visited', *Electoral Studies*, 1991, p. 284. The figures for 1992 were calculated by the author.

9 Peter Mandelson and Roger Liddle, *The Blair Revolution: Can Labour Deliver?* (Faber, 1996), p. 208.

10 Enid Lakeman, *How Democracies Vote*, 4th edn (Faber, 1974), p. 77.

11 *Report of the Working Party on Electoral Systems* (Labour Party, 1993), p. 5.

12 See also Eckhard Jesse, 'Split Voting in the Federal Republic of Germany: An Analysis of the Federal Elections from 1953 to 1987', *Electoral Studies*, 1987, pp. 109–24.

13 *Report of the Commission on Electoral Reform* (Hansard Society, 1976), para. 93.

14 *New Statesman*, 5 July 1996, p. 15.

15 The debate can be found in *House of Commons Debates*, 25 January 1977, vol. 924, cols. 1222–1404. See also 'Scottish Snakes and Welsh Ladders', *The Economist*, 22 January 1977.

16 See e.g. D. R. Woodall, 'Computer Counting in STV Elections', *Represen-tation*, Winter 1982–3.

17 Michael Gallagher and Michael Laver (eds), *How Ireland Voted, 1992* (Folens/PSAI Press, 1993), pp. 67–8.

18 Ibid., p. 69.

19 Ibid, pp. 105, 106.

CHAPTER 4: REFORM OF THE HOUSE OF LORDS

1 D. Leonard and R. Natkiel, *World Atlas of Elections: Voting Patterns in Thirty-nine Democracies* (Hodder & Stoughton, 1987).

2 Law lords are life peers created under the Appellate Jurisdiction Act 1876.

3 Walter Bagehot, *The English Constitution*, 2nd edn [1872], ed. Norman St John-Stevas (*The Economist*, 1974), p. 287.

4 Between 1911 and 1949, only three bills – the Government of Ireland Bill of 1914 providing for Home Rule for Ireland, the Established Church (Wales) Bill, disestablishing the Welsh Church, and the Parliament Bill of 1949 itself – were enacted without the Lords' consent.

5 *House of Lords Debates*, 20 October 1994, vol. 558, col. 360.

6 *House of Lords Debates*, 17 June 1968, vol. 293, col. 342.

7 *House of Lords Debates*, 20 October 1994, vol. 558, col. 361.

8 Quoted in Janet P. Morgan, *The House of Lords and the Labour Government 1964–1970* (Clarendon Press, 1975), p. 156.

9 Ibid., p. 4.

10 *The Reform of the Second Chamber*, Cd 9038 (HMSO, 1918).

11 Donald Shell and David Beamish, *The House of Lords at Work: A Study Based on the 1988–1989 Session* (Clarendon Press, 1993), pp. 185–6.

12 Morgan, *The House of Lords*, p. 166.

13 Lord Windlesham, *Politics in Practice* (Cape, 1975), pp. 142, 137.

14 *House of Lords Debates*, 3 December 1957, vol. 206, col. 615.

15 G. H. L. LeMay, *The Victorian Constitution* (Duckworth, 1979), p. 214.

16 *Report of the Inter-Party Conference on the Parliament Bill*, Cmd 7380 (HMSO, 1948).

17 The abortive attempt to secure House of Lords reform in the 1960s is dis-cussed in Morgan, *The House of Lords*.

18 Lord Hailsham, *The Dilemma of Democracy* (Collins, 1978).

19 *The House of Lords, Report of the Conservative Review Committee* (Conserva-tive Central Office, 1978), para. 24 (emphasis in original).

20 See e.g. Robert Skidelsky, 'Reform, not Revolution in the Lords', *The Times*, 3 July 1996.

21 The Earl of Carnarvon and others, *Second Chamber: Some Remarks on Reforming the House of Lords* (privately published, 1995), para. 167.

22 *Reform of the House of Lords* (Constitution Unit, 1996), para. 82.

23 Bagehot, *English Constitution*, p. 253: 'the right to be consulted, the right to encourage, the right to warn'.

24 Earl of Carnarvon et al., *Second Chamber*, para. 140.

25 Cited in *Reform of the House of Lords*, para. 82.

26 *House of Lords Debates*, 7 March 1994, vol. 552, cols 1286, 1321, 1304, 1305, 1317.

27 Ferdinand Mount, *The British Constitution Now* (Heinemann, 1992), p. 188.

28 John Stuart Mill, *Considerations on Representative Government* (1861), Everyman edn (1972), p. 324.

Chapter 5: The Referendum

1 *House of Commons Debates*, vol. 272, col. 901, 28 February 1996.

2 *Meeting the European Challenge* (Liberal Democrats, 1996), p. 10.

3 Quoted in Michael Hatfield, *The House the Left Built* (Gollancz, 1973), p. 70.

4 *Referendum on UK Membership of the European Community*, Cmnd 5925 (HMSO, 1979), p. 2 (emphasis added).

5 *House of Commons Debates*, 9 June 1975, vol. 893, col. 37.

6 *House of Commons Debates*, 22 November 1974, vol. 881, cols. 1742–3.

7 *The Times*, 11 April 1972.

8 *House of Commons Debates*, 15 February 1978, vol. 944, col. 595.

9 Quoted in Philip Goodhart, *Full-Hearted Consent* (Davis-Poynter, 1976), p. 181.

10 Quoted in David Butler and Uwe Kitzinger, *The 1975 Referendum* (Macmillan, 1976), p. 273.

11 A. V. Dicey, 'The Referendum', *National Review*, March 1894, p. 66.

12 *House of Commons Debates*, 11 March 1975, vol. 888, col. 293.

13 The author was a member of this Commission.

14 See Vernon Bogdanor, *Politics and the Constitution: Essays on British Government* (Dartmouth, 1996), pp. 232–3.

15 *House of Commons Debates*, 15 February 1977, vol. 925, col. 382.

16 Interview with Tony Blair, *New Statesman*, 5 July 1996, p. 15.

17 Ibid.

18 For the history of the referendum and the single transferable vote in Britain, see Vernon Bogdanor, *The People and the Party System* (Cambridge University Press, 1981).

19 Gabriel Almond and Sidney Verba, *The Civic Culture* (Princeton University Press, 1963), p. 361. See also the same authors on the decline of deference in *The Civic Culture Revisited* (Little, Brown, 1980), pp. 133–4, 156–8.

20 Written evidence by MORI to Commission on the Conduct of Referendums, 1996, pp. 1, 5.

21 *Report of the Commission on the Conduct of Referendums* (Constitution Unit, 1996), p. 78.

22 Tony Byrne, *Local Government in Britain*, 6th edn (Penguin, 1994), p. 457n.

23 *The Times*, 24 October 1996.

24 For a stimulating consideration of some of these methods, see 'Lean Democracy', *Demos Quarterly*, 1994, no. 3.

25 A. V. Dicey, 'Introduction', in *Introduction to the Study of the Law of the Constitution*, 8th edn (Macmillan, 1915), p. c.

Chapter 6: The Funding of Political Parties

1 See the comments of Paul Blagbrough, Labour's head of finance, in 'Unions Use "Hidden" Funds to Pay Labour', *Sunday Times*, 20 October 1996.

2 Philip Bassett, 'New Labour and the Ties that Bind', *The Times*, 30 September 1996. This article provides a great deal of up-to-date information on the financial relationship between 'New Labour' and the trade unions.

3 Quoted in Keith Alderman and Neil Carter, 'The Labour Party and the Unions', *Parliamentary Affairs*, 1994, p. 336.

4 Conservative Party, Annual Report and Accounts, 31 March 1996, p. 8.

5 *Paying for Politics* (Hansard Society, 1981). The author was Secretary of this Commission.

6 K. Z. Paltiel, 'Campaign Finance: Contrasting Practices and Reforms', in David Butler, Howard R. Penniman and Austin Ranney (eds), *Democracy at the Polls* (American Enterprise Institute, 1982), p. 171.

7 See Vernon Bogdanor, 'State Aid and the Reform of Political Finance in the UK', *Financial Times*, 27 November 1991, which cites the PIRC report.

8 Bassett, 'New Labour and the Ties that Bind'.

9 W. M. Geldart, *The Osborne Judgement and After*, Manchester Guardian, 1910, p. 43.

10 Peter Archer MP, *House of Commons Debates*, 3 March 1980, vol. 980, col. 103.

11 See e.g. John Walker, *The Queen has been Pleased* (Secker & Warburg, 1987).

12 *House of Lords Debates*, 17 June 1995, vol. 564, col. 1359.

13 Martin Linton, *Money and Votes* (Institute for Public Policy Research, 1993), p. 73.

14 Ibid., pp. 75–7.

15 Cited in Keith Ewing, *The Funding of Political Parties in Britain* (Cambridge University Press, 1987), p. 41.

16 George Buchanan MP, *House of Commons Debates*, 29 April 1937, vol. 3232, cols. 614–15.

17 House of Commons Home Affairs Committee, *Funding of Political Parties, Second Report*, HC 301 (1993–4), para. 11.

18 Linton, *Money and Votes*, p. 15.

19 Written Evidence to Home Affairs Committee, *Funding of Political Parties*, HC 726 (1992–3), p. 169.

20 *House of Commons Debates*, 20 March 1975, vol. 888, col. 1871.

21 Esmond Wright, 'Public Funds for Political Parties', *The Parliamentarian*, 1976, p. 82.

22 Bernard Crick, 'Paying for the Political Parties: A Review', *Political Quarterly*, vol. 46 (1975), p. 413.

23 This is a variant of the scheme proposed in 1981 by the Hansard Society's Commission on the financing of political parties in its report, *Paying for Politics*.

24 *Report of the Committee of Inquiry on Financial Aid to Political Parties*, Cmnd. 6601 (HMSO, 1976).

25 Professor Peter Aucoin, Written Evidence to Home Affairs Committee, *Funding of Political Parties*, HC 726 (1992–3), p. 144.

26 Linton, *Money and Votes*, p. 50.

27 Michael Pinto-Duschinsky, 'Tory Chiefs in Danger of Losing their Troops', *The Times*, 10 October 1994.

28 *Conservative and Unionist Central Office* v. *Burrell* [1980] 3 All ER 42; *Conservative and Unionist Central Office* v. *Burrell* [1982] 2 All ER 1.

29 Letter to *The Times*, 27 November 1968.

30 H. W. Wollaston (ed.), *Parker's Conduct of Parliamentary Elections* (Charles Knight, 1970), p. 134.

31 *House of Lords Debates*, 17 June 1995, vol. 564, col. 1376.

32 Trevor Lloyd, *The General Election of 1880* (Oxford University Press, 1968), p. 76.

33 *Globe and Mail* (Toronto), 29 November 1980.

34 David Adamany, 'Financing Political Parties in the United States', in Vernon Bogdanor (ed.), *Parties and Democracy in Britain and America* (Praeger, 1984), p. 156.

35 David Farnham, 'New Labour, New Unions and the New Labour Market', *Parliamentary Affairs*, 1996, p. 588.

CHAPTER 7: THE MONARCHY

1 Jonathan Dimbleby, *The Prince of Wales: A Biography* (Little, Brown, 1994), p. 9.

2 Cited in Ben Pimlott, *The Queen: A Biography of Elizabeth II* (Harper-Collins, 1996), p. 203.

3 Walter Bagehot, *The English Constitution*, 2nd edn [1872], ed. Norman St John-Stevas (*The Economist*, 1974), p. 252.

4 This episode is described in Vernon Bogdanor (ed.), *Coalition Government in Western Europe* (Heinemann, 1983), pp. 255, 267.

5 Bagehot, *The English Constitution*, p. 253.

6 Cited in Kenneth Rose, *King George V* (Weidenfeld & Nicolson, 1983), p. 109.

7 Bagehot, *The English Constitution*, pp. 243, 182.

8 In practice, under most PR systems, the figure would be a little lower than 50 per cent.

9 Peter Hennessy, *The Hidden Wiring: Unearthing the British Constitution* (Gollancz, 1995), pp. 66–7 and elsewhere in ch. 2 of that book.

10 Bagehot, *The English Constitution*, pp. 250–1.

11 Lord Esher to Lord Knollys, 9 January 1910, Royal Archives (RA) K2552 (1), cited in Vernon Bogdanor, *The Monarchy and the Constitution* (Oxford University Press, 1995), p. 75.

12 See Hennessy, *The Hidden Wiring*, p. 67. See also his Johnian lecture of 1997, 'Principles Codified: Her Majesty's Puzzle: Politics, The Monarchy and the Constitution'.

13 Tony Benn, 'Power and the People', *New Socialist*, September–October 1982, pp. 9–15.

14 *The Constitution of the United Kingdom* (Institute of Public Policy Research, 1991).

15 Cited in B. S. Markesinis, *The Theory and Practice of Dissolution of Parliament* (Cambridge University Press, 1972), p. 234.

16 Norman Gash, 'Power in Suspense', *Times Literary Supplement*, 3 June 1983.

17 Peter Pulzer, 'Responsible Government in the German Political System', in Herbert Doring and Gordon Smith (eds), *Party Government and Political Culture in Western Germany* (Macmillan, 1982), p. 24.

18 Buckingham Palace, *Royal Finances*, 2nd edn (1995), p. 17.

19 *Next Steps Review 1996* (HMSO, 1997), p. 56.

20 Frank Prochaska, *Royal Bounty: The Rise of the Welfare Monarchy* (Yale University Press, 1995).

21 These remarks were made in a BBC Radio Four *Analysis* programme, 'Monarchs to Measure', broadcast on 27 May 1993.

22 Ibid.

23 Ibid.

24 Hennessy, *The Hidden Wiring*, p. 70.

25 House of Lords, *Written Answers*, 10 February 1993, vol. 542, col. 43.

26 Cited in Keith Middlemas, *Power, Competition and the State*, vol. II (Macmillan, 1990), p. 263.

CHAPTER 8: BEYOND CONSTITUTIONAL REFORM

1 These paragraphs are based on Andrew Adonis and Geoff Mulgan, 'Back to Greece: The Scope for Direct Democracy', *Demos Quarterly*, 1994, no. 3, pp. 2–9.
2 Cited in David Marquand, 'Preceptoral Politics, Yeoman Democracy and the Enabling State', *Government and Opposition*, 1988, p. 273.

Index